Anarchist Perspectives in Peace and War 1900-1918

None can judge with certainty who is right and who is wrong, who is nearest to the truth, or which is the best way to achieve the greatest good for each and everyone. Freedom coupled with experience, is the only way of discovering the truth and what is best …
Errico Malatesta[1]

'What is to be done' is the demand which with greater or lesser impetus tortures the spirit of people struggling for an ideal, and which resurfaces of its own accord in moments of crisis, whenever a setback, a disappointment promotes the re-examination of tactics adopted and for the critique of particular errors; seeking more effective means …
Errico Malatesta[2]

'Revolution, one that is truly liberating, cannot be the particular work of one school, or of one party, but the work of the masses, of the widest masses possible.'
Errico Malatesta[3]

While libertarian communist theory is certainly indispensable, it is largely engendered from below upwards, through actual experience of popular struggle. And this 'theory', if it is not to remain as an abstraction, must, to avoid risks of wandering away, be proved, constantly enlivened, nourished and corrected by the experience of those in whose name it is expressed and for whom it is destined: the workers.
Daniel Guérin[4]

Anarchist Perspectives in Peace and War 1900-1918

A W ZURBRUGG

ANARRES EDITIONS

First published in 2018
by Anarres Editions, an imprint of
The Merlin Press
Central Books Building
Freshwater Road
London
RM8 1RX

www.merlinpress.co.uk

© A.W. Zurbrugg, 2018

ISBN 978-0-85036-741-6

The moral right of the author has been asserted

A CIP record of this book is available from the British Library

Printed in the UK by Imprint Digital, Exeter

Contents

Chronology		v
Introduction		1

Part 1 – Peace

1	The international scene 1900-1907	11
2	Latin America before 1907	20
3	Italy before 1907	27
4	France and the CGT	33
5	The Amsterdam Congress of 1907	44
6	Spain	65
7	Argentina after 1907	69
8	The Industrial Workers of the World	71
9	Germany	75
10	Syndicalism and anarchism in France after 1907	87
11	Syndicalism and anarchism in Italy after 1907	103
12	International endeavours and perspectives	112
13	Syndicalism in 1913-14	140

Part 2 – War

14	August 1914	157
15	Opposition to the war	170

Organisations, terms, abbreviations	182
Notes	185
Index	203

Chronology

1864: Foundation of the International Workers' Association (IWA).

1871: **France** – Paris Commune.

1870-3: Most IWA federations reject the leadership of Marx and the General Council, and meet in congress in Geneva in 1873.

1876: Death of Bakunin.

1877: Last IWA congress, in Verviers (Belgium).

1889: Anarchist conference in Paris.

1890: **Germany** – repeal of anti-Socialist laws; unions conditionally legalised.

1891: An international congress meets in Brussels, anarchists are excluded. **Germany** – exclusion from the SPD of youth opposition, part of which evolves towards anarchism, influenced by Gustav Landauer.

1893: Zurich, international congress insists on the priority of political (parliamentary) action, dissident socialists and anarchists are excluded. (Some fifty met independently.)

1895: **Cuba** – beginning of third war of independence. **France** – formation of the CGT. Fernand Pelloutier is elected the secretary of the national federation of *bourses du travail*.

1896: A 'Universal' Workers' Congress meets in London: it excludes delegates of unions and other organisations rejecting the priority of parliamentary politics.

1897: **Germany** – first congress of the localist or FVdG unions (FVdG is founded in 1901). **Spain** – Prime Minister del Castillo assassinated.

1898: An international anti-anarchist conference in Rome, prepares the way for cross-border police co-operation and Interpol. **Italy** – army uses artillery to bombard Milan, some hundreds are killed.

1899: **France** – socialist Alexandre Millerand becomes a minister in the cabinet of Waldeck-Rousseau alongside General de Galliffet, the butcher of the Paris Commune. **Italy** – Malatesta escapes from isolation on the isle of Lampedusa and eventually makes his way to Paterson, New Jersey.

1900: As a congress of the Second International takes place in Paris, an alternate libertarian international revolutionary workers' congress is prohibited from meeting by the French government. **Italy** – King Umberto I assassinated by an anarchist, in revenge for the army massacre in Milan two years earlier.

1901: Argentina – formation of the Argentinean Workers' Federation later renamed FORA. **USA** – Czolgosz, an anarchist sympathiser, kills President McKinley.

1902: Argentina – New law to facilitate the deportation of foreign labour activists; general strike. **France** – fusion of the *Bourses du Travaille* federation into the CGT. Formation of an Anti-militarist league.

1903: Germany – Renaming of the Free Revolutionary Workers' organisation as the Anarchist Federation.

1904: German troops conduct genocide in South West Africa. **Argentina** – general strike in Buenos Aires. **Italy** – general strike, protests against killing of miners in Sardinia.

1905: Argentina – fifth FORA congress adopts libertarian communism as its aim. **Chile** – 'Red Week' in Santiago. **Russia** – defeated in war against Japan, revolution, soviets formed; **Uruguay** – foundation of the FORU. **USA** – foundation of the IWW.

1906: France – CGT, 'Charter of Amiens', defeat of strikes for eight-hour day. IWW spreads to **Australia** and **Canada**. **Italy** – CGL formed. **Spain** – Matteo Moral throws bomb at royal procession in Madrid, royals escape but several passers-by killed.

1907: Amsterdam Congress brings together anarchists and radical socialists. INSTUC Congress refuses the CGT's proposal to discuss militarism. **Brazil** – strike movement, 132 foreign workers deported. **Chile**. Army massacres 2000 miners in Iquique. **Italy** – Anarchist congress in Rome; direct action congress in Parma. **Spain** – 'Solidaridad Obrera' libertarian syndicalist federation formed.

1908: Argentina – general strike against deportation laws. **Bolivia** – Local Workers' Federation founded. **France** – Villeneuve-Saint-Georges – strikers shot, two killed, arrest of CGT activists. **Germany** – SPD members of the FVdG ordered to re-join majority union movement or suffer expulsion; FVdG membership halved. Landauer founds the Socialist Federation. **Italy** – Syndicalist tendency emerges in the CGL and Socialist Party. **Mexico** – anarchists support peasant risings.

1909: Recession, international anarchist congress cancelled. **Argentina** – May, police kill eight demonstrators; 70,000 persons protest in the capital (1% of Argentina's entire population.) Many arrests follow; the police chief in question was assassinated six months later by a Russian anarchist, Simón Radowitzky. The FORA is dissolved in subsequent state repression. **Spain** – Barcelona, tragic week: confrontations and reprisals, execution of Francisco Ferrer, worldwide protests.

1910-11: Japan annexes Korea. **France** – foundation of a Revolutionary Communist Federation, (later renamed the Anarchist-Communist Federation). **Libya** invasion by Italy, opposed by anarchists, who highlight massacres by colonial troops; general strike. **Mexico** – Zapata publishes the Plan of Ayala. Liberal Party adopts an anarchist manifesto, ephemeral Socialist Republic of Lower California. **Spain** – formation of the CNT. **Sweden** – Foundation of the SAC. **Uruguay** – first general strike. **USA** – law passed to prohibit anarchist immigrants.

1912: Balkans wars (to 1913). **Italy** – formation of the USI. **Peru** – Anarchists promote general strike in Lima; Regional Labour Federation founded. **Spain** – an anarchist, Manuel Pardiñas, assassinates Prime Minister José Canalejas. **UK** – mass campaign and demonstrations help prevent deportation of Malatesta.

1913: International syndicalist meeting in London. The ISNTUC conference in Zurich renamed International Federation of Trade Unions. **France** – July, protests against the extension of military service to three years; August, national anarchist congress. **Greece** – King George killed by Alexandros Schinas. **Italy** – Syndicalist meeting in Milan. General strike in Turin. **UK** – August, Dublin lockout and strike begins.

1914: August: First World War begins; affiliates of Socialist International support the war effort; London International Anarchist Congress, scheduled to begin on 29 August, cancelled. **Argentina** – a radical syndicalist network joins the FORA. **Bohemia**: Czech Anarchist Congress. **Italy** – June: 'Red Week' centred around Ancona, many workers injured in clashes, USI calls a general strike. Malatesta returns to London. **UK** – February, defeat of Dublin strike.

1915: International anti-war manifesto. Anti-war conference in El Ferrol, with libertarians from Spain, Portugal and Brazil; an ephemeral IWA created. **Argentina** – 9th FORA congress adopts political neutrality. Anarchists separate to maintain FORA-V, (FORA of the 5th congress, committed to libertarian communism). **Italy** – joins First World War as an ally of France and Britain; general strike in Turin. The USI anti-war tendency around

Armando Borghi defeats pro-war group. **USA** – execution of Joe Hill.
1916: Kropotkin and others write pro-war 'declaration of the sixteen'. Malatesta publishes a critique and refutation. **Portugal** – joins war against Germany. **Spain** – CNT-UGT call joint general strike. **USA/Mexico** – Flores Magón condemned to 20 years' imprisonment for opposing war.

1917: **Brazil** – joins war; General strike in Rio de Janeiro, and São Paulo. **France** – some 60,000 soldiers mutiny. **Italy** – bloody suppression of revolt in Turin. **Russia** – February: revolution, fall of the Tsar; October: second revolution, Bolsheviks take power. **Peru** – Massacre in Huacho of women protestors demanding eight-hour day. **Ukraine**: Anarchist and Makhnovist movements organise. **Uruguay** – eight-hour day law. **USA** – joins First World War, 'Palmer' raids on IWW offices, repression of radicals and leftists.

1918: March, Treaty of Brest-Litovsk; November, end of First World War. **Brazil** – Popular committees organise against high prices, anarcho-syndicalist insurrection in Río de Janeiro. **Germany** – (October-November) Fall of the Kaiser, creation of a republican state. **Italy** – spread of factory commissions. **Russia** – Constituent assembly dispersed, black guards disarmed, anarchists repressed, Confederation of Anarcho-Syndicalists organises; civil war commences. **Spain** – Joint CNT-UGT call for a general strike. **Ukraine** – fought over and occupied by Germany and Austria, Nabat organisation formed. **USA** – Mass imprisonment of IWW leaders.

1919: Treaty of Versailles, foundation of the Third International. **Argentina** – Bloody or 'Tragic' Week, some 1,300 killed, 55,000 arrests; the libertarian FORA seeks to declare a general strike; anarchists arrested, their papers and offices closed. **Brazil** – strike wave for 8-hour day. **Bulgaria** – foundation of anarchist-communist federation. **Canada** – general strike in Winnipeg. **Chile** – IWW centre formed. **Germany** – January: Spartacist and radicals defeated in Berlin; March onwards: a council republic is formed in Bavaria; other dissident centres suppressed piecemeal, with thousands of radicals and revolutionaries imprisoned or assassinated (including Landauer, Liebknecht and Luxemburg); April: Anarchist-Communist Federation formed. FAUD formed. **Hungary** – short lived left republic. **Italy** – Mussolini organises fascist squads. January, Milan: USI conference rejects calls for Constituent Assembly and calls for workers' unity and revolution. March-April: factory occupations. Factory councils and *Ordine nuovo* germinate, influenced by maximalist socialists (Gramsci) and anarchists (Garino). April: fascists burn offices of *Avanti,* revolutionary committee proposed. Florence: Anarchist-Communist Union congress; July: USI committee arrested. October: assembly of factory councils. December: return of Malatesta; USI congress.

Mexico – death of Emilio Zapata. **Peru** – Anarcho-syndicalist led strike wins an 8-hour day. **Portugal** – formation of the CGT. **Russia** – September: anarchists and Left SRs bomb Moscow Communist Party HQ; 12 killed, 45 wounded, other anarchists disavow this action. **Spain** – Mass 'Canadiense' strike in Barcelona: some 4,000 workers imprisoned. Decree for 8-hour day. The CNT, some 800,000 strong, holds congress in Madrid, adopts libertarian communism as its goal and affiliates to the Comintern. Wave of assassinations. **Ukraine** – Nabat congress, Trotsky publishers order #1824, outlawing libertarians; Makhnovist army defeats Denikin. **USA** – Seattle general strike; deportation of radicals and anarchists, including Emma Goldman; J. Edgar Hoover begins career.

A list of organisations and abbreviations can be found at the end of this volume. A list of persons and a bibliography will be included in a later volume.

Introduction

This book – the first in a series of four – brings together a sketch of anarchist organisation and perspectives in the twentieth century. It focuses on the perspectives of organisations, activity and reflection, and looks at how anarchists attempted to move closer to achieving social change. The focus here is on organisation and policy rather than anarchist ideas in general, or abstract or utopian anarchism.[5] Libertarians were proposing changes which, because of their roots in labour and social life, they could already glimpse and work for, if only in a limited fashion. Their thinking was not unlike that of the Bakunin who wrote: 'If there is something dreamy and mystical in imagining that the International should contain – in germ, and in some way – the whole future organisation of human society, then we should have to humbly confess that we were mystics and dreamers. But, dear friends let us firstly console ourselves we are absolutely not alone in sharing this belief.'[6]

Anarchism developed in the era of the Paris Commune of 1871 and of conflicts in the First International. Bakunin and his co-thinkers briefly glimpsed examples of 'mass democracy', i.e. decision-making in popular and participatory assemblies in contrast with 'committee democracy' where delegates made decisions for other working people. They worked in and through workplace organisations, stressing both everyday concerns and ultimate ambitions; they also worked to develop ideas-based organisations. Anarchists worked to replace the state with networks of workplace organisations and communes, in line with the resolution of the Basel congress of the International Workers' Association of 1869: 'Federations [of workplace unions] should be responsible for the collection of information relative to their particular industries, for shaping common measures that should be taken, for regulating strikes and for working to ensure their success until the time comes for wage labour to be replaced by a Federation of Free Producers.'[7] Revolutionary socialists and anarchists sought to destroy the state – not just because contemporary states were run by and for the bourgeois and other upper classes, but also because the state form – its hierarchical relations and its remote and alien structures – suited the bourgeoisie and was seen as incompatible with egalitarian, participatory and socialist relations. Working people, they believed, could not use bourgeois, hierarchical organisational forms to build socialism.

> Strikes, riots, rebellion, everywhere in Europe, and in various forms the blood-soaked intervention of the authorities – in Trieste, Barcelona and Turin – the measures may vary but the result is the same, except that from country to country one must count the numbers of the dead either in single numbers, dozens, or hundreds. On 25 February in Bucharest, two thousand workers attempted to take hold of Parliament. After having thrown a few stones at the defenders of order they were dispersed by a cavalry charge; there were two hundred arrests but no deaths ....[8]

This lead article, from March 1902, suggested that authoritarian regimes in much of Europe and Russia were living on borrowed time. There were high hopes for radical change. There were anarchist leaders in the national structures of the French general labour confederation (the CGT). A large part of the Argentinean labour movement would adopt libertarian principles in 1905. Half a million workers went on strike in Germany. An insurrection mobilised a million Russian workers. 1905 saw the foundation of the Industrial Workers of the World (IWW). A revolution began in Mexico in 1910. Hopes were excited and new organisational forms rippled through labour movements. Reformist socialism had great strength, especially in Germany, but it was contested by a range of radical tendencies. Syndicalism, industrial unionism and anarchism all seemed to be making progress.

Anarchists and syndicalists were centre stage in the history of labour movements in much of 'Latin' Europe and in most of Latin America in the first two decades of the twentieth century. Syndicalists and libertarians sought to develop solidarity and workers' power, rejecting both cautious and conservative trade-unionism and the prevalent strategy of socialist parties. Criticising the chauvinism that engulfed the Second International and its most powerful section, German Social-Democracy, they campaigned for class solidarity across frontiers and for the subversion of the discipline that bound soldiers to imperialist states.

Libertarians investigated democratic, modern and scientific ideas and challenged obscurantist, religious and authoritarian conventions. They sought to focus and organise the strength of working people whose voices could not be registered in parliamentary politics, working at a time when many working people had no right to vote. These movements sometimes challenged patriarchal gender relations. Progressive women – Emma

Goldman among them – were seeking means of birth control and exploring new and more equitable ways of living.[9]

What were the ideas inspiring such movements?

'Anarchy and socialism', wrote the veteran Italian anarchist, Errico Malatesta, 'are not sciences, they are propositions, projects, that anarchists and socialists want to put into practice, and which therefore need formulating in considered programmes.'[10] Malatesta very often qualified his statements with 'according to me', he sought to persuade, drawing on many years of experience. He rejected the priority of electoral politics in favour of the politics of direct action. He, and James Guillaume, another veteran of the First International, contributed both to the continuity and the evolution of libertarian theory and practice.

Malatesta believed that different names might encapsulate similar ideas. He wrote in February 1920: 'There are those among the anarchists [some] who like to call themselves communists, or collectivists, or individualists, or what have you. Often it is a question of different interpretations of words which obscure and hide a fundamental identity of objectives; sometimes it is only a question of theories, hypotheses with which each person explains and justifies in different ways identical practical conclusions.'[11]

Malatesta was not over-concerned if organisations were destroyed. If some popular confidence remained, that confidence and solidarity would foster the regeneration of organisation, so that a setback that destroyed one structure might be remedied by the solidarity that remained.

Malatesta also acknowledged that names evolved and changed – such changes might reflect the distinctions that tendencies sought to make between themselves and those they criticised and opposed. Bakunin for example – for the most part – called himself a revolutionary socialist, rather than an anarchist in an era in which other bourgeois socialists sought to take over the state – a bourgeois state. He believed bourgeois socialists would betray socialism.

Name changes might reflect new circumstances and new perspectives – for example, after the revolutions in Russia organisations designated themselves as 'anarchist-communist', stressing the communism they thought was now being constructed; later as Russia's communism was seen to be a sham, and came to be equated with Bolshevism, anarchists dropped the 'communist' tag. The comments that Bakunin made on state-managed collectivism presciently foresaw the dangers inherent in a party-led, hierarchical state, and so the content of 'anarchism' drew on his thinking, but the names and organisations changed over time as they focused on new strategies.

Anarchism, then, was not a fixed and eternally valid set of opinions, but rather a set of critical thinkers and thought, evolving as ideas and struggles interacted, refashioned and refocused over the course of time, inevitably, arguing, disputing and rethinking priorities and directions.

Sometimes differences could not be reduced to questions of semantics. Anarchism and syndicalism encompassed a wide range of priorities. Some definitions of movements and theories obscured evolving complexities and divergences. A 'syndicalist' might look like a trade-unionist, but might be something else, or something more – a radical who prioritised direct action, in a federalist organisation, with a dual structure which linked a local union to both a national industrial federation and to a local union council (in a city or a region). He or she might also be organising educational and cultural activities in the community. All such activities might look forwards towards radical change, eschewing a limited or reformist perspective that was constrained by the priority of working through a state legislature, primarily, or solely, for bettering conditions within capitalism.

In North America, an 'Industrial Unionist', (a term associated with the IWW), might advocate one big industrial union and be fiercely opposed to everyday (business) unionism, as practised by the American Federation of Labor. He or she might be working in the IWW which stressed the need for centralised industrial organisation to counter the employers' cartels that regulated industries. In Britain, a form of 'industrial unionism' was practised by the National Union of Railwaymen. This big union aspired to represent all workers in the rail industry, but it was linked to the Trades Union Congress (TUC) and not to a new, radical or independent union centre. British IWW sympathisers who advocated 'industrial unionism' were sympathetic to big industrial unions, but only a few of them were determined to work for a new radical union network as an alternative outside and beyond the TUC.

There were times when the use of particular terms indicated new paths and organisations. After 1918 German radicals fought for new-unions-of-a-sort: '*Unionen*' – on the model of the IWW. These '*Unionen*' were an alternative to the politics and structural forms of the older, hierarchical, centralised trade unions, the *Gewerkschaften*. The movement to leave the latter (supported by, among others, Rosa Luxemburg) made sense in the context of the burgeoning of a *Unionen* alternative. But when a discussion on working in unions, or leaving them, does not distinguish between *Unionen* and *Gerwekschaften*, the meaning of a decision to 'leave the unions' may be lost. Inadequate translation may conceal or distort choices.[12]

Anarchisms and syndicalisms have often been poorly and loosely defined by Anglophone writers, and are often lumped together pell-mell. Many did share some preferences. But some libertarians embraced collectivism, others communism and others individualism – lumping them all together, and failing to examine what they had in common, and what differentiated one stream from another among them is not so helpful.

Anarchists' opinion of syndicalism varied and evolved depending on contexts and on their perspectives for their future organisation in a new society. For example, among those syndicalists who had an anarchist agenda, there were some who placed a great emphasis on that anarchist agenda and came to call themselves anarcho-syndicalists, while others, who still called themselves anarchists, were more careful and cautious in their workplace politics.

Some anarchists came to view any attempt to clarify a political strategy as a form of coercion, and rejected socialism, 'politics' and 'party'. Others were happy to write that they worked for an Anarchist 'party'. Naturally, for these libertarians, their socialism was libertarian socialism, and their party was not an electioneering-political party with a hierarchical internal structure. Malatesta came to define party in terms of those who would struggle and share the same cause.[13] Of 'politics', he noted that this was a word that worked, for some, like a red rag to a bull; however, he wrote:

> As I see it, it is not 'anarchist politics', a politics that would be destructive of the authority and the state, which would retain within itself some danger for our ideas. Rather, it is the *disdain* shown towards politics which retains the danger of leaving aside the struggle against the government and which has already generated ill effects, such as: weakening the revolutionary sprit and giving birth to that workplace organisation, that would theoretically gut the state and that in reality, at a later time, calmly leaves it be, with the result that, when the fascists came, workers let themselves be beaten up without reacting.[14]

What is sketched here is not so much one definition of 'anarchism', but rather a set of experiences and conflicts among convivial movements and allies. Experience, dynamics, and potential allies all changed over time. Conviviality was something ephemeral rather than fixed. Perhaps, an example will bring this out: when Bakunin talks of the Paris Commune he recognises that rebel Jacobin republicans played a key part; they supported, lived and died for the revolution. He notes that at the back of their minds they still had lingering statist prejudices – for which Bakunin had no sympathy – but, he writes, this mattered little. People do not change ideas as quickly as they change their clothing, and old ideas may be mixed up with new ones. These rebel Jacobins fought for the Commune. Anyone who would live and die for the revolution was not to be reproached.[15]

Such a definition of revolutionary politics captures well some of the complexities of revolutionary movements. In 1871, libertarians and anarchists had a place alongside rebel republicans. Revolutionary socialist politics, a.k.a 'anarchism',* was not the result of some a priori theory, although no doubt revolutionaries were certainly influenced by several past theories; rather 'anarchism' evolved and was defined in practice by the choices women and men made to join this or that workplace movement, or protest, stressing certain choices and perspectives. It was not one immutable doctrine, it was a set of mixed and agitated conversations, encounters, debates, reflections and synthesis, coming together at one moment and evolving. Out of these conversations there emerged strands of federalist and decentralised socialism.

One of the problems in any discussion of anarchism relates to the relationship between the several forms of anarchism and syndicalism. In the texts below much of the focus is on forms of (radical and revolutionary) syndicalism. Some writers stress that even the best forms of syndicalism are really not up to much, and do not engage with the plenitude of human liberation.[16] Such a comment is no doubt both somewhat correct and somewhat unhelpful.

In 1936, for example, one would find both anarchists and syndicalists making decisions to work with the Popular Front government. It was maybe a doubtful choice, a turn down a street that was not leading towards the destination desired but, whatever it was, it was not a turn made by imperfect syndicalists alone, but one made by many sorts of libertarians, and under duress. Utopian socialism may work in a vacuum, but libertarian organisations do not; they had to choose how to act within circumstances and their constraints.

Libertarian movements and ideologies can perhaps be viewed then as a set of historical conversations where experiences were judged by past ideas, encountered, re-assessed and reconceptualised. If such a 'definition' is accepted, libertarianism is – among other things – *work in progress.* So, this sketch is sympathetic to the views of the *Federação Anarquista do Rio de Janeiro* when they make the point that:

---

* Properly speaking 'Anarchism' was not theorised in 1871, it emerged as a particular twist on revolutionary socialist politics some seven or eight year later, as the last bastions of the International Workers' Association was disrupted and disorganised in and after 1877.

... ideology is not a set of abstract values and ideas, dissociated from practice with a purely reflective character, but rather a system of concepts that exist in the way in which it is conceived together with practice and returns to it. Thus, ideology requires voluntary and conscious action with the objective of imprinting the desire for social transformation on society.[17]

The focus here is mainly on urban societies[18] in Western Europe and to a lesser extent on Latin America. Such a focus should not be taken as implying that Western European anarchism was necessarily at the centre of all things. (Eurocentric perspectives are challenged by Steven Hirsch and Lucien van der Walt,[19] in *Anarchism and Syndicalism in the Colonial and Postcolonial World*.[20])

This survey focuses on the varied strategies, programmes and policies adopted by anarchist-communists, and by anarchist and radical syndicalists in various contexts. A brief sketch of one hundred years of a world-wide radical movement necessarily focuses on a few high points. There is some distortion of perspective here – below the peaks of the passing icebergs there were layers of activity sustaining those peaks. More might have been said. Many libertarians worked in broad-based bodies, such as workplace organisations and may have had a limited *influence* within them. Libertarians also worked in ideas-based organisations – in these they sought to make policy on a broader range of issues, sharing capacities and responsibility.

Policy-makers in the more influential revolutionary syndicalist and anarchist organisations worked to shape political developments; they worked to promote their ability to take initiatives and to build counter-power. Isolated libertarian sympathisers in mixed organisations may have had a diffuse or cultural impact, but isolation tended to limit their capacity to understand, respond and shape policy for their own agenda. Other strands of the anarchist movement, for example mutualists and individualists, receive scant attention here.

Some, perhaps many, libertarians were not particularly sensitive to contradictions between insiders and outsiders, between more vulnerable or precarious workers and those with steadier positions, and between men and women, between majority and minority communities and between settlers, migrants and indigenous peoples. Even within movements that sought revolutionary change, the poorest and the powerless were more easily disregarded. And they have left fewer records. As consciences were pricked, more rebels emerged into the limelight and the scope of 'history' widened. In this view, history is never neutral, and is never solely based on 'objective facts'. Histories are selected and interpreted; they are affected by the poverty and 'space' of the governed, and the interests of often privileged record keepers, writers and editors.[21] This sketch seeks to understand the development of ideas respecting their chronological and geographical context.

Some themes recurred. For example, libertarians who supported some sort of specific libertarian organisation were often compelled to consider how specific and mass organisations might relate to each other? Libertarians might also discuss how they might relate to other political forces and their convergent or divergent strategies? Libertarians might seek how to remedy deficiencies where 'their own' labour movements lacked the support of the second sex, or failed to defend all ethnicities. They might reflect on how a left agenda that focused on state ownership could be shifted to encompass the socialisation of management ... and so on. Of course, current issues arose in conjunction with events: war, revolution, fascism, cold war, and so on; but there were also recurrent questions as to libertarians' strategy and perspectives.

This first volume surveys developments in the period before the First World War. Subsequent volumes consider developments in the 1920s and 1930s – crucially in Spain. The fourth volume concludes the series with a survey of developments after 1945.

I am indebted to Adrian Howe of Merlin Press for his ongoing support and good humour. I would like to thank David Berry, Carl Levy and Lucien van der Walt, for reading early drafts of parts of these texts, and Axel Barenboim for help with reports on the 5th IWA congress. This sketch draws on, and is indebted to, these writers and the work of many other historians who have striven to re-examine libertarian histories. It is hoped that it may be useful and thought-provoking – but not the last word on this subject.

Part One – Peace

I
THE INTERNATIONAL SCENE, 1900-1907

Libertarians and anarchists have a tradition of working across frontiers and building international solidarity, a tradition dating back to the 1860s. The International Workers' Association or First International organised from 1864 and petered out after its last congress, held in Verviers in 1877.[22]

The defeat of the Paris Commune in 1871 and subsequent repression began a depressing period in labour history. It was an era in which Europe was increasingly threatened by militarism and nationalism.

Bakunin had highlighted the difference between modernity and progress. Taking pride in a nation's progress slipped easily into an endorsement of imperialism, into the view that modern civilised lands – and their people – were naturally better than uncivilised backwards lands and peoples.[23]

Progressive and revolutionary movements struggled to challenge patriotic, racist and nationalist sentiments. Parts of the labour movement in northern Europe, influenced by German Social-Democracy, shuffled towards an accommodation with capitalism. In German, Italy, Russia and Spain strong states regularly attacked feminist, labour and libertarian movements. In other states with a more democratic façade – Britain, France and Switzerland – there was perhaps a little more space to organise. But nowhere did women and migrants have rights equal to those of male citizens.

In 1892, Errico Malatesta, in concert with Kropotkin, Charles Malato and Louise Michel, had advised anarchists:

> To enter more and more into the unions and to show our brothers, proletarians, [by deeds] that in fact anarchists do not have the intention of joining in the movement in obeisance to feelings of vanity, of for personal interest, but rather to struggle with and for them, in the interest of common liberation. There, where a union is lacking, anarchists should create them and where they already exist, they should mix in with its members. If entry into certain unions has not been made possible, others should be created alongside those already in being.[24]

Where there was little space for public political action, diverse forms of illegal organisation developed. Rudolf Rocker wrote that clandestine organisations had their limitations. Small secret bodies were perhaps a trap for young romantics and could not promote social revolution. They might intimidate certain supporters of the system, but: 'acts of individuals can never serve as the foundation for a social movement and, in no way are they capable of transforming the social system. ... Social transformation can only be carried through by mass movements.'[25] Such perspectives were written to support the development of the syndicalism which grew up as an alternative to the tactics and practices of individualist anarchism in western Europe.

Many syndicalists and anarchists rejected individual action, and the so-called 'propaganda of the deed'.[26] Errico Malatesta argued:

> Anarchists who rebel against every sort of oppression and struggle for the complete freedom of all ought thus to shrink instinctively from all acts of violence which cease to be mere resistance to oppression and become oppressive in their turn ... also are liable to fall into the abyss of brutal force. The excitement caused by some recent explosions and the admiration for the courage with which the bomb-throwers faced death, suffices to cause many anarchists to forget their programme, and to enter on a path *which is the most absolute negation of all anarchist ideas and sentiments.*

In the early 1890s, Rudolf Rocker, a long-lived German activist, had concluded from French experience: 'what is distinctive in anarchism, as compared with every other tendency, is the thinking that one cannot force people through violence to be free.'[27] People needed a belief in their rights, strength and determination, and collective cohesion, to be ready to take things into their own hands. Malatesta was looking to change consciousness on a wider scale: 'The brilliant acts of a few individuals may help in this work, but cannot replace it, and in reality, they are only useful if they are the result of a collective movement of spirit of the masses ... being accomplished under such circumstances that the masses understand them, sympathise with, and profit by them ...'[28]

Malatesta took the view that planning and co-ordination were needed in any revolt. In August 1899, he wrote that preparations were needed – things could not be improvised in a moment. Groups needed to work together and co-ordinate action so that cities did not become isolated, and picked off by the army, as Milan had been in 1898 when a labour conflict escalated into an uprising. Against the force of the Italian monarchy some form of coalition was needed.[29] In an article published at the end of the year, Malatesta also went on to suggest that change would not come at the drop of a hat – but gradually – as social conditions matured.[30]

Different perspectives prevailed in Russia where there was little space for labour organisation within the law. Here Anarchist Communists endorsed more violent action; they continued in this line after the defeat of the revolutions of 1905-6. Anarcho-Syndicalism gained some ground, but was condemned as being too gradual and legalistic by Anarchist-Communists. Emerging libertarian syndicalists, who looked to the French CGT for a model, commanded little respect from partisans of armed resistance, who thought that syndicalism was inappropriate in Russian conditions. There were ongoing divisions between Anarchist-Communists and Anarcho-Syndicalists. Insults were traded back and forth, with syndicalists calling their critics followers of Nechaev,* and being likened to bourgeois socialist parliamentarians. There were also contrasting traditions of Tolstoyan pacifist anarchism, and individualist anarchism. Libertarians were frequently set up by Russia's secret police, and betrayed by infiltrators. Some were executed and other suffered long terms of imprisonment. Kropotkin and co-thinkers (including a young Alexander Schapiro) opposed terror tactics but had limited influence.

Before the coming of the internet international contact and discussion was largely facilitated through the press. Ideas were, and would continue to be, exchanged through a series of journals, including: *La Protesta* (Argentina); *A Plebe, A Voz do Trabalhado,* (Brazil), *Arbeter Fraint, Freedom,* (Britain); *¡Tierra!* (Cuba); *Combat Syndicaliste, Le Libertaire, Temps nouveaux, Vie Ouvrière,* (France); *Der Syndikalist, Die Internationale,* (Germany); *Pensiero e Voluntà, Umanità Nova* (Italy); *A Batalha (Portugal); Revista Blanca, Solidaridad Obrera, Tierra y Libertad* (Spain);[31] *Le Reveil/Risveglio* (Switzerland); *L'Adunata dei Refrattari, Cronaca Sovversiva, Dielo Trouda-Probuzhdenie, Industrial Pioneer, La Huelga General, Marine Worker, Mother Earth, Solidarity, Industrial Worker,* (USA); and *Studi Sociali* (Uruguay).

Some of these publications survived for many years. At the other extreme, one-off issues of a journal might also serve a purpose, as one-off publications could not easily be banned. Conferences and congresses might be facilitated by the circulation of preparatory discussion bulletins. Sometimes seafarers facilitated the distribution of this press. New nodes of South American libertarian activity – along the Atlantic and Pacific coasts, and through some river basins – owed much to their activity. Libertarians

---

* A nihilist briefly close to Bakunin, he died in prison in 1882.

in smaller states would welcome the attention of the libertarian press from larger neighbours – sometimes disseminating such journals when they lacked a capacity to produce their own, or whenever the local press was supressed. Common to the movement, through Latin America and Europe, were campaigns calling for the release of prisoners – Sacco & Vanzetti, Francesco Ghezzi, Simón Radowitzky – and the commemoration of the martyrs – in Barcelona, Chicago, Iquique, Ludlow, Patagonia, Tokyo, etc.

Some of this press came in the form of a review, and was devoted to the discussion of social and scientific ideas. Often a lead essay discussed some new concept or theory and such content might take up the first few pages, followed by shorter columns on key topics. The pre-war weekly *Temps nouveaux* frequently featured anti-militarist comments. Critical comments on the politics of Social-Democracy, news of abuses of human rights, international news, notes on strikes begun and finished, mentions of events, correspondence (often very brief) and comments on new books, some of which were sold by periodicals' publishers. *Revista Blanca*, publishing less frequently in the 1920s and 1930s contained frequent theatrical sketches; *Studi Sociali* usually contained a reprinted item from Malatesta.

Some journals catered for readers of more than one language: for example, *Le Reveil/Risveglio* had pages in French and Italian; *La Protesta* might have a page in Italian or Yiddish. After 1945, French syndicalist journals had pages in Spanish. Public activity might attract attention rapidly when it was conducted in the language of the state. But if publication was in a language of a migrant community – one poorly understood by authorities – it might escape notice. The USA had a flourishing press – much of it sponsored by the IWW – servicing particular communities. The aggregate circulation of this non-English libertarian press far exceeded its English-language counterpart. In Brazil, too, there was a pattern of multi-lingual publishing – it took time for immigrants to learn and prefer Portuguese to their first language.

The more solid journal publishers also took on the translation and publishing of books – both political books by well-known activists and radical fiction. Journals survived where they could build up subscriptions. The receipts of donations from supporters might show the geographical contacts that were sustaining particular journals – one random example – for the Italian language review *Studi Sociale* showed donations from: Alès, France; Brighton, Mass.; Buenos Aires; Geneva; Geelong, Australia; Ingham, Australia; La Plata; Montevideo; Needham, Mass.; Nice, France; Peckville, Pa.; Rio de Janeiro; Scranton, Pa.; San Francisco, Ca.; Sommerville, Mass. and Youngstown, Ohio;[32] such a spread does indeed support the perspective of Italian anarchism as a transnational movement.

Emigration had a great impact: Italian and Spanish anarchists looking for work found their way all over the Americas and beyond. In new countries new space for reflection might open, as more repressive home conditions were left behind.[33] Migration, deportation, exile, all led activists to compare experiences between one land and another and consider if there might be advantages to using tactics and policies developed in one place in another location.

A huge range of libertarian journals were published, sometimes taking material, translating it and recirculating it, for particular trades, regions and communities. This press might help activists fleeing repression and provide some income for refugees. When publications were censored and banned by authoritarian regimes in some areas, publication might continue elsewhere. Space for reflection and publication might open and close: before 1930-31 the space for the libertarian press was greater in Argentina than in Spain; the balance was then inverted as the Spanish Republic replaced an authoritarian regime, while in Argentina the change was in the opposite direction. Together, this press facilitated an intercontinental dialogue among libertarians.

Anarchism and International Labour Congresses

International labour congresses in the 1890s had been contentious events. Anarchists and other anti-parliamentary socialists denied the potential and rejected the priority that Social-Democratic parties demanded for electoral and parliamentary tactics. Libertarians doubted the effectiveness of parliamentary legislation and criticised the view that parliamentary influence could effectively promote workers' interests. Some young socialists[34] were won over to co-operate with anarchist-communists and libertarian syndicalists and would eventually see themselves as anarchists.[35] Radical Marxists and libertarians found common cause working together to promote forms of direct action, anti-militarism and the social general strike.

Anarchists and libertarians sought to influence international labour conventions while German Social-Democrats – the leading party of the Second International – sought to exclude them. Libertarians did not object to Social-Democrats organising congresses, but they did object to Social-Democratic congresses setting themselves up to speak for labour as a whole, insisting that they too were socialists and part of the labour movement. The London-based journal *Freedom* had argued in October 1895: 'We have no objection to a Social-Democratic congress as such, or to a congress to which only believers in political action are admitted, provided no attempt be made to claim that such a congress is representative of and *speaks in the name of labour*.'[36]

Several unions had nominated Malatesta as a delegate to the London Universal Workers' Congress of 1896.[37] Some 650 persons attended the congress, among them veterans from the First International. Joining the conflict on one side were Élisée Reclus, Paul Robin and Errico Malatesta – confronting Bebel, Liebknecht and members of the Marx family. Some twenty of the forty-three delegates representing French syndicates were anarchists. Invitations to the conference had been sent to all workers' bodies. Despite having credentials as delegates of unions, those who denied the priority of parliamentary electoralism[38] were nevertheless excluded.[39]

Up to this point the term 'socialist' had been commonly used by Marxists and libertarians alike, and was not a partisan term. For some anarchists – including Malatesta – the term Socialist 'party' designated, all socialist tendencies, statists and anti-statists alike. Malatesta argued that anarchists were undoubtedly socialists, and that the Second International should not become a forum for one, partisan, tendency. 'It is in the interest of all enemies of capitalist society that there should be unity and solidarity in the struggle against capitalism.' 'Politics is naturally a great cause of division.' So, 'in consequence, an entente between all workers fighting for their emancipation, can only take place in the economic field'. And, thus, without asking any tendency to renounce their opinions: 'We demand only that that divisions are not carried over into a terrain where they have no reason to be; we demand for all workers the right to fight against the bourgeoisie hand in hand with his brothers, without the distinction of political ideas.'[40]

Malatesta argued that workers could form common organisations in the workplace, whatever their philosophical or political ideas. Workplace unity might also facilitate a pluralist model of socialism, one that admitted 'political' differences but rejected the imposition of a single strategy. Such arguments had some resonance among radical and anti-parliamentary socialists. The expulsion of anarchists from the London congress and from the Second International was a milestone marking a long-term breach between conflicting partisan organisations.

One commentator, in an Independent Labour Party (ILP) report on the congress (jottings section), commented that German Social-Democrats – it named Liebknecht and Singer explicitly – were intolerant: 'They alone, they believe, hold the key to all wisdom in the Socialist movement.' Furthermore, matters were managed to suit them; for example, when they were not present, the congress 'was not allowed to meet'.[41] Louise Michel commented that the

Social-Democrats were pretending to defend an infallible orthodoxy, which she likened to a state religion.[42] French libertarian syndicalists would shortly identify the exclusionists – one of whom was Millerand[43] – as betrayers of the workers' movement.

Some British labour leaders did not endorse the exclusion of anti-electoralists. On 28 July 1896, an anarchist-socialist and anti-parliamentary committee announced a meeting to welcome congress delegates. Some thirty personalities were to speak, including Keir Hardie, the leader of the ILP, Ben Tillet and Tom Mann. Several libertarians attended: Amilcare Cipriani, Pietro Gori, Peter Kropotkin, Gustave Landauer, Errico Malatesta, Louise Michel and Élisée Reclus. Some radical socialists from the Netherlands and Germany continued to work with anarchists. Dissident currents were emerging in the Dutch, German, Italian and other socialist parties and some of these evolved, over time, towards anarchism. Present also in London were Christiaan Cornelissen and F. Domela Nieuwenhuis of the Dutch *Socialistenbond*, (an anti-parliamentary Socialist League) and Paul Delesalle, Fernand Pelloutier and Émile Pouget from the French CGT.

Between 29-31 July an anarchist-socialist conference met in the evenings in St Martin's Hall. It drew in delegates who had been the excluded and others who had retained the right to attend the congress. It discussed a diverse agenda: the land question received some extended discussion; there was little time to discuss other matters such as propaganda – including the criticism that electors were voluntarily depriving themselves of the right of direct control over the corrupted machinery of state, and economic organisation. There was a proposal that if the state was not abolished, it should at least be deprived of its rights to direct the economy. Rather communal mass meetings should meet and vote on budgets, war credits and taxation.[44] (This idea of 'communal mass meetings' seems not too distant from the Council/Soviet concept). Some individualist anarchists were not so happy with such co-operation. The conference was attended by an incorrigible Stirner sympathiser who greeted every decision taken with cries of 'not another decision'. Others responded if you had stayed at home no one would have disagreed with you, why did you come here to bore us? The ILP report concluded that it was 'a most interesting Conference, which only lack of time, due to the fact that it could only sit when the official Congress had risen, prevented from being a complete success'.[45]

In 1900 Paris was announced as the venue for a Revolutionary International Workers' Congress. The event had been planned as a broad meeting inviting workers organisations, anarchists and non-parliamentary Marxists, with invitations from Domela Nieuwenhuis, Fernand Pelloutier* and Émile Pouget: 'Revolutionary groups of various countries had recognised the necessity of separating themselves from a Social-Democracy, which in its intolerance sought to impose the necessity of legislative and parliamentary action on all organisations, even union ones.'[46] Kropotkin wrote a short essay on international labour organisation for *Temps nouveaux* reminding readers of recent history and concluding rather sharply that there had been two currents in the Fisrt International (IWA), Latin revolutionaries and among the Germans, counter-revolutionaries.[47]

Some thirty-six of the delegates that were expected to arrive made it to Paris in September, after the assassination of American president McKinley. Over 200 pages of texts from various contributors had been published in preparation for the meeting.[48] Some delegates were able to meet together privately, but the congress was banned by the French government.[49]

Emma Goldman records in her memoirs her disquiet at a decision made to prohibit a public discussion on sexuality – only a closed meeting was envisaged – to prevent 'misconceptions'. She protested: 'I could not co-operate with a congress that attempted to silence opinion or suppress views that failed to meet the approval of certain elements.'[50] In France and elsewhere there were diverse views among women radicals and libertarians

---

* Pelloutier led the *bourses* section of the CGT.

on gender issues. Some women, such as Madeleine Vernet, advocated free love,[51] but still condemned abortion and called for rights for maternity.*

Earlier, between 4-6 August, there had also been a non-public meeting held in Paris of the *Ligue de la regeneration humaine*, a Neo-Malthusian network. Involved in that earlier meeting were Francisco Ferrer, Emma Goldman, Paul Robin, Nelly Roussel and others – a dozen or so persons in all. The organisation would promote family planning and discuss means of contraception. Family planning was portrayed as a means of giving women control. It was described as a *grève des ventres*, a strike of wombs. It was noted that the state wanted bodies for cannon-fodder.

This meeting in Paris found echoes elsewhere. In Spain for example, a pamphlet of the same title, *Huelga de vientres* (Practical methods to avoid larger families) by Luis Bulffi de Quintana, went through several editions and was distributed in Spain and Latin America. Other individualist anarchists, such as Émile Armand and Jean Marestan, wrote popular texts that were widely circulated, translated and reprinted.[52]

Abortion and contraception were banned in many countries. The law portrayed discussions of these topics as obscene in the USA; free speech was denied and circulation of material in the post criminalised. In France, contraceptive advice might be passed from mothers to daughters, but Catholic morality prevailed in public spaces. Many women did not find as friendly a space in the CGT as Emma Goldman was able to find in parts of the libertarian and feminist networks in the USA. Her disagreements with others over the planning of discussions for the anarchist congress in Paris reflected disparate attitudes, sexist contexts, and the small numbers of women involved in libertarian organisations.

---

* 'Vernet' was an alias for Madeleine Cavelier (1878-1949). She was a convinced pacifist, after 1914 she supported Sébastien Faure and his review: *Ce qu'il faut dire*.

2
LATIN AMERICA BEFORE 1907

Of all the countries where anarchism gained a foothold, it was Argentina that was most shaped by migrants. But here and throughout the Americas indigenous peoples were frequently, disenfranchised, marginalised and abused. State frontiers had been drawn up disregarding ethnic affiliations, for example the Mapuche people were split by state lines between Argentina and Chile. Large scale industrial agriculture used, or rather abused, indigenous peoples with little restraint, treating indigenous workers – for example sugar workers in the El Chaco region of Argentina – as non-citizens and/or slaves and subjecting them to military force.[53]

Millions of Italian and Spanish people settled in Argentina. Its labour movement also included sizable communities from neighbouring countries travelling along nearby coasts and rivers and from further afield (including Russia). Argentinean electoral and parliamentary politics was largely a male elite concern, with some concessions to more prosperous urban layers. Non-citizens – who formed a very large part of the population – had little prospect of acquiring the vote. Such factors helped shape a vibrant labour movement. While the economy prospered and labour was in demand, workers' organisations had a relatively strong bargaining position. Strikes and general strikes were frequent occurrences; there were twelve general strikes during 1903-4. The state responded with measures declaring a state of siege on several occasions, banning labour organisation, targeting aliens and using violence.[54] Many non-citizens were targeted: some kept their heads down, some fled to Uruguay, others – perhaps some 400 labour activists – were deported. A law for 'social defence' facilitated the exclusion and deportation of 'criminals'; it outlawed anarchist propaganda, the red flag and public meetings held without permission. However, repression did not quell the labour movement. Campaigns against the threat of deportation of 'foreign agitators', or to repeal anti-alien legislation became a central concern for libertarians all over Latin America. Libertarians and others might reply to cases of blatant abuse with campaigns calling for the boycott of goods and trade from the most offensive states.

In terms of numbers the Argentine libertarian movement was the third largest in the world, after the Spanish CNT, and the Italian USI; in terms of press activity, it was second to none. Its leading publication was *La Protesta*, which changed to daily publication in February 1904, aiming to draw support from 2,500 subscribers. By December it had a print-run of 8,000. It developed weekly supplements discussing literature and the arts (incorporating the review *Martín Fierro*) as well as anarchist theory. A huge range of radical journals and books were published in this era, with libertarian thinking appearing in many forms. Much of this literature was profoundly international, interrogating events that affected peoples from different lands who had settled in Argentina. One of the influential figures in the development of Argentine anarchism was Pietro Gori, the founder of an influential journal on modern criminology.

The first review of anarchist women, *La Voz de la Mujer*, was published in Argentina in 1896, with the watchword *Ni dios, ni patrón, ni marido* (Neither God, Nor Boss, Nor Husband). This short-lived journal, written by women for women, sought to explore their situation as the most oppressed layer in society. It advocated free love. It condemned bourgeois marriage, and challenged contemporary machismo – which sought freedom for men but confined women to housework.[55] A series of pamphlets was published exploring these issues. 'We, awkward women, we take things in our own hands, our initiative is the product of our own thinking – do you know, we too can think.'[56] An Anarchist Feminist Centre was formed in 1907,[57] working with striking tenants, protesting against deportations and leafleting women as they left factories. Salvadora Medina Onrubia became a notorious labour personality; Josefina América Scarfo was another, and she summed up a militant commitment in 1920 as follows: 'Create: the impossible; Conquer: the intangible; Love: life; The Goal: the ideal.'[58]

There were two major labour federations in Argentina – the Labour Federation of Argentina, (FOA), soon to be renamed Labour Federation of the Argentine Region (FORA), and a General Labour Union (the UGT). The latter had 7,500 members in 1904, compared to 11,000 in the FORA.[59] There were also Catholic unions, and industrial unions in rail and maritime industries not closely tied to national federations. The rail unions had some 15,000 in 1907,[60] perhaps much larger than any other union, and organised the first effective national strikes. The UGT was linked to the Socialist Party, but, as with the Italian labour movement, a syndicalist current grew within it and reformists and syndicalists began to diverge.

If the press is a good guide, socialism and anarchism had differing profiles: socialists were more often professionals and privileged workers, anarchists were more often in less skilled occupations. The anarchist press allowed women more space – on front pages and elsewhere; it articulated demands for 'equal pay [for women] for equal work'.

The FORA had a Federal Council at the national level, and a central office with members from local federations. It grouped members by local area, for the most part with trade 'societies of resistance'. It had members in the liberal professions. Women were encouraged to join, without having to pay dues. The FORA developed a distinct anarchist identity. Its pact of solidarity of 1904 noted:

> Our organisation, being purely economic, is different and opposed to all labour political parties, because while they organise for the conquest of political power, we organise to render down current juridical and political States, reducing them to purely economic functions, replacing them with a free federation of free associations of free producers.[61]

All resistance societies committed themselves to practice the fullest moral and material solidarity between themselves, mobilising such force as circumstances might dictate to obtain success.[62] Eduardo Colombo comments that such resolute views were held only by a minority – he quotes from the FORA journal *Organizacíon Obrera* that there were two tendencies in resistance societies, 'the one represented by the minority which, without neglecting the present seeks future well-being and another which emanates from the majority and is concerned only with the present'.[63]

FORA's fifth congress resolved to campaign against new laws that facilitated the expulsion of foreign labour activists.[64] There was also a discussion of methods of struggle: boycotts, sabotage, and a new method, the 'label' (a mark designating production by FORA labour), which might – in the future – be a powerful weapon in the armoury of labour if it was spread and widely recognised.[65] The congress also defined its end-goal as libertarian communism. It resolved to support educational work to spread a culture in workers' communities: 'This education, by preventing them from concentrating merely on achieving the eight-hour day, will emancipate them completely and consequently lead to the hoped-for social evolution.'[66]

The FORA condemned social vices, such as gambling and prostitution. It sought to define a radical community at odds with Catholic patriarchal norms. It recognised that marriage might not last for ever. It blamed capitalism for impoverishing women, depriving them of the ability to make free choices. It criticised the macho brutality of many husbands.

The seventh FORA congress, held in 1907, attempted to build bridges with the UGT, drawing in representatives from 30 UGT and 36 independent workplace organisations. A resolution sought to recommend discussion of all ideas and propaganda for direct action and libertarian communism. It considered political (parliamentary) struggle as prejudicial to the proletariat. The vote for this resolution was 62 in favour, 9 against, and 38 abstentions. The event provoked some discussion internationally. Luigi Fabbri commented on 28 May 1907, in *Vita Operaria* (Rome): 'I believe that labour organisation, to avoid being authoritarian, dogmatic or sectarian, should avoid all ideological affirmations, which might divide the proletarian masses along the lines of party preoccupations ...'[67] The FORA campaigned against laws facilitating the expulsion of foreign 'agitators' and called for a general strike in January 1908, condemning the criminal and barbaric action of the state as a negation of human rights. In the same year, a Local Workers' Federation was founded in La Paz, Bolivia.

Cuba

In 1900, Cuba obtained a sovereignty that was precarious and subject to ongoing pressures from the USA.

Anarchists looked for a 'Cuba for all', breaking with the exploitative and exclusive patterns of Spanish colonialism,[68] and supporting justice, freedom, and equality. They envisioned a Cuban identity – a *cubanidad* – that was 'internationalist but localized to Cuban reality, and as based upon gender, race, and national origin equality.'[69] In Cuba, and elsewhere in Latin America, memories of slavery were very much alive. Modern forms of employment were viewed as wage-slavery. Campaigns for the eight-hour day were motivated not just in terms of improving workers' conditions at work, but also of allowing time for self-education. Some libertarians also looked back to certain pre-colonial societies – those that had promoted communal and co-operative cultures – viewing them as alternatives, particularly where settler land-owners were treating indigenous peoples as serfs, providing unpaid labour. Social relations in many Latin American societies were rather different from those in Europe. The urban working class was relatively small, rural workers, besides being exploited, were geographically isolated in pockets and estates, entrepreneurs might rely on their ability to use and abuse indigenous peoples or imported labour. The youth of privileged layers had fewer openings or prospects. There was some potential here for some form of cross-class politics in opposition to a capitalism run by foreigners. Manuel González Prada, a Peruvian liberal turned libertarian, riled against foreign capital: 'All these great robbers together form an international masonic body, scattered all over the globe, sworn together and closely united to struggle against their common enemy: the proletariat.' González Prada proposed a bloc between all sorts of manual and intellectual workers – but without any sort of privileges for the latter.[70] He also wrote that Peru's so-called democratic republic was a big lie, 'in the interior the violation of every right under a blatant feudal regime is palpable'. Big hacienda owners more or less owned local government.[71] The subsequent influence of Manuel González Prada spread among radical and left movements in Peru, tending to redefine politics to include the interest of indigenous peoples disrespected by the 'Aristocratic Republic' and elites and businesses wanting a cheap source of labour.

The tomb of Florencio Aliaga, killed in a docks strike, 1904

Malatesta gave some lectures in Cuba, after a spell in Patterson in the USA. In his view, the Cuban labour movement still had to confront US power, if it was to secure its liberation. (American troops would intervene and 'pacify' Cuba from time to time.) He advised:

> Today Cubans aspire to be liberated from the intervention of the American government – that, under the lying mantle of liberator, has

come to dictate and tyrannize as in a country under conquest ... But this will not be realised – either by the rich class that needs American protection, in order to be able to safely exploit the energetic Cuban worker, or by the merchants of patriotism who beg their share of the interventionists' spoils.[72]

Malatesta was ordered by the US governor, Leonard Wood, not to lecture on anarchism. Anarchists 'challenged the Cuban elite for abandoning the social reforms that they had promised to the popular classes in return for their war-time support'.[73] Anarchists helped foster educational facilities – both formal and informal – drawing an enthusiastic response from women and men deprived of literacy and culture. Some such efforts targeted racist ideas and prejudices, at a time when white-on-black violence was not uncommon; others helped promote improvements in the health of women.

Anarchists esteemed secular homes and family life – with women nurturing children – in contrast with the corruption fostered by capital and the poverty it helped create.[74] An alternative set of values was articulated in works of anarchist fiction: 'women of color and the relationships they had with men of different colors provided a means by which to celebrate anarchists' preferred relationships, and as a means of propaganda, to attract followers of all races.'[75] Such fiction might have a paternalist tone, celebrating healthy 'revolutionary' motherhood, and viewing abortion as a by-product of misery, exploitation and corrupted values.[76]

In 1912, the Cuban government forced through the disbandment of an Independent Party of Coloureds (Blacks) and killed some 6,000 Afro-Cubans. Anarchists had little sympathy for that party's project, suggesting that politicians whatever their colour, were all as bad as each other.[77] Anarchists had praised Afro-Cuban culture and made some effort to integrate Afro-Cubans into labour organisations, but many libertarians had Spanish origins and propaganda for racial equality had only a limited impact.

Some forty anarchist journals were published throughout the Caribbean. ¡Tierra! was the most influential Caribbean libertarian journal, circulating in Cuba, Florida, Panama, Puerto Rico and occasionally further afield.[78] It circulated in US territories – the Panama Canal zone and Puerto Rico – where US political models, state officials and trade-unionism were wholly opposed to anarchism.

¡Tierra! drew support from agricultural workers and cigar-rollers, who might pay to have radical papers read to them while they were working. ¡Tierra! addressed a broad agenda. It spread rational education, drawing on the thinking of Francisco Ferrer. It attacked health care systems denied to those who could not pay. Alternative lifestyles were promoted – simpler living, vegetarian food, and homeopathic remedies.[79] ¡Tierra! also sought to harmonise relations between locals and incomers (Italian and Spanish workers).

¡Tierra! highlighted racism in Tampa, Florida. It demanded equal wages for American and non-Americans. It articulated critical perspectives on American-style 'democracy' and imperialism working to corrupt successive governments in Cuba, and exploit Cuban labour. AFL leader Samuel Gompers attempted to find support in Cuba, but found few takers. 'Anarchists believed the AFL favored US workers and business interests. They urged workers either to avoid the AFL or challenge its conservatism from within AFL-affiliated unions.'[80]

Both ¡Tierra! and the movement it helped to articulate, were hard hit after the outbreak of the First World War; the paper was prosecuted and suspended, and the authorities also adopted a policy of deporting activists. In 1915, Juan Tenorio, Vicente Lípiz, and Román Delgado, all three accused of promoting sugar worker strikes in Camagüey and Guantánamo, were deported to Spain; some 300 Spaniards would be sent back to Spain in the next twenty years. Cuba joined the First World War in April 1917.

3
ITALY BEFORE 1907

'Italy' in 1900 was a recent creation, a monarchy in which few could vote. There were acute social and geographical disparities and tensions within the country, between north and south, between city and rural areas, and between social layers and classes.

Anarchism had deep roots. Bakunin had had an enthusiastic reception in Italy. Errico Malatesta provided a link to these earlier times. Born in 1853, he had attended the congresses of the First International, (IWA) in St. Imier in 1872, and in Bern in 1876. He wrote persuasively and had a wide range of experience.

Troubles broke out in the more prosperous north in 1898 over rising food prices and excessive taxation. Official figures acknowledged that the military had killed some eighty persons in Milan, and wounded 450 more.[81] A wave of state repression followed, with unanticipated results: the shared solidarity of internment and prison provided opportunities for dissidents to discuss strategies.

Labour leadership was frequently shaped by social position. In sectors where literacy was limited – particularly among precarious unskilled workers and day labourers – educated and literate persons acquired weight as against illiterate or uneducated labourers. Such disparities shaped the internal dynamics of many labour organisations. Labour organisers were targeted by the state – sometimes travelling abroad until an amnesty allowed their safe return. Many workers had experience of living in neighbouring countries, or in the Americas.

Among many organised anarchists there was a turn towards activity in workplace unions, and this appeared to have positive results. Local general strikes broke out in several cities. One historian has asserted that the first two decades of the twentieth century were 'the best years the anarchists experienced since their heyday in the 1870s'.[82] Malatesta did not expect that an anarchist revolution would come soon – but did hope for the overthrow of the Italian monarchy. In 1899, he wrote that it would be best to take part in movements for change – even if they did not fully share anarchist goals – because such participation would enhance progress 'as far as possible', build popular sympathy, and facilitate anarchists' moral and armed strength.[83] In September 1901 he commented on priorities after the recent election:

> It's good, when our propaganda obstructs the people sending to parliament socialists or republicans (given that it is these who we can most easily reach with our propaganda and it is especially these who, without us, would vote for anti-monarchist candidates), if we have the capacity, with those we have wrenched away from electoral fetishism, to facilitate them becoming active and conscious fighters for true and complete liberation. If not, we would, and will, serve the interests of conservatives and the monarchy.
>
> Think about it, all of you. At stake is the interest of our cause, and our honour, as men and as a party. Isolated occasional propaganda, which is often carried on to ease the conscience or to give free play to one's passion for discussion, such propaganda is of no value, or almost none. Before one person's effort can be added to another's, it is forgotten, it is lost; given the masses' unconscious and miserable conditions, and moreover, given all those forces which it opposes, it cannot become fertile. The ground is too ungrateful for seed randomly sown to germinate and grow roots.
>
> Continuous, coordinated, patient work is needed; adapted to particular circumstances and environments. We all need to be able to count on the co-operation of all others, so that in all places where the grain is sown, the work of the gardener is not lacking – to look after it, and to protect it, until such time as it can live on its own, and can in turn generate new fertile grain. In Italy, there are millions of proletarians who are blind instruments in the hands of priests, there are millions who hate their bosses with an intense hatred, [and] yet are persuaded that they cannot live without bosses, and who cannot imagine or wish for any liberation, other than that they, in turn, should become bosses to exploit their companions in misery.
>
> Our voice has not been heard in immense regions, in the greater part of the surface area of Italy to be exact, and there is no notable trace that it has ever been present. In some workers' organisations (it may in truth be in only in a few) we are [still] strangers. For the lack of foresight and preparation, when strikes break out, we can neither help workers in their struggles, nor can our propaganda profit from the excitement. Riots,

quasi-insurrections break out, and none of us knows about them. And then there is persecution, imprisonment, deportations by the hundreds and thousands, and yet not only are we powerless to react, but we are unable even to attract public attention to the infamy of our sufferings. To work comrades! There is much to do! To work, one and all!

Malatesta criticised those who used the label of anarchism, but forgot morality. Such people erred in thinking that because they rejected bourgeois morality and the state they could therefore abjure any morality or use violence as if it was the only or predominant form of struggle. He also criticised a reaction that had been occurring due to the abuse of violence – Tolstoyan non-violence, or passivism. As a revolutionary party, anarchists could not renounce violence; but it was the lesser evil, to be used as little as possible.[84] Luigi Fabbri, a close friend and colleague of Malatesta, criticised two libertarian tendencies: one that was individualist, Nietzschean or Stirnerist, and another that supported violent direct action by the individual, through bombings and assassinations.[85]

When in 1900, King Umberto was assassinated the action was disavowed by a group in Rome in the name of the Anarchist Party* because such methods had been rejected.[86] Malatesta criticised individual action. He preferred collective action and argued that individuals using such methods generally did more harm than good. He set out criteria for judging the effects of direct action, by an individual or group, in a text first published in 1892. Such action might be 'good when it helps to bring the revolution nearer and makes it easier, when it helps to gain for the revolution the conscious co-operation of the masses and to give it that character of universal liberation without which we might, indeed, have a revolution, but not the revolution that we desire.'[87]

Anarchists, he thought, did not love violence, even if it was somewhat inevitable. The state provoked wars and organised repression. Desperate tactics flowed from authoritarian politics – organisation and propaganda having been prohibited – when people concluded they had no hope. One had to understand what provoked violence. The assassination of King Umberto could be traced back to anger arising out of the king's endorsement of repression in Milan; if such oppression ended violence might relent.[88]

Unskilled male labourers formed the larger part of the Italian labour movement abroad, but women were also present in migrant communities. In the Americas gender relations were more open than in much of Italy. Cities in New England witnessed the emergence of a female Italian anarchist

* This 'Party' denoted a broad swathe of tendencies, rather than an electoral organisation.

scene, where radical circles of women explored new ideas and expressed themselves through groups, cultural associations, drama, publishing and bookselling. Often, there was some disconnection between anarchist identities abroad and patriarchal relations at home. One woman named 'Titi', wrote:

> There is a beautiful saying: I am an anarchist, I am free in my house, I benefit from my freedom and don't believe that a father, brother, or husband should exercise physical or moral coercion over me. All of this would be true to say, but in the end, when we can't have bread without the say of men with whom we live, if we can't have a roof, a bed, clothes without the money of our comrades necessary to buy them, we are slaves and we must suffer for better or for worse to the will of those who keep us ... We should take a glance not only at the bourgeois society but at ourselves, workers who are part of the anarchist family.[89]

Some prominent women anarchists had connections or professions: Virgilia D'Andrea,* an Italian anarchist poet, qualified as a teacher before becoming the partner of the syndicalist leader Armando Borghi; Emma Goldman was a nurse and lecturer; the journalist and future anarchist minister, Frederica Montsenny could rely on her Urales family for support; another Spaniard, Lucía Sánchez Saornil, was an editor and poet, before becoming a secretary of *Mujeres Libres* organisation. Perhaps the precarious and insecure circumstances of many other libertarian women reduced their capacity to play a part in leading radical campaigns.

The anarchist movement had some impact in promoting the idea of the general strike in Italy. Armando Borghi, the future syndicalist leader, wrote that this was an era of development and progress, and the unions believed that they would be able to win what they wanted through collective pressure. Some parts of the labour movement were under the illusion that whatever economic conditions prevailed, reforms would be easy to come by, and could be extended ad infinitum.[90] 'Alibrando Giovannetti, secretary of the USI's metalworkers' union, and a believer in nonviolence, saw peaceful occupations of factories as a substitute for insurrection.'[91] Malatesta wrote about *armed* strikes, rejecting the illusion that revolution might come peacefully.[92]

Although progress was made, this was not a liberal golden age for labour. Anarchists were targeted by the state and threatened with years of *domicilio coatto* – a form of house arrest where activists were directed to live in remote

---

* She was a frequent speaker at anti-fascist meetings in the USA before her death in 1933.

locations, under police supervision. The police could impose conditions on public meetings or ban them outright. Persons who would become fascists some years later were already using violent repression against anti-militarist agitators.

There were many critics unhappy with the leadership of the Italy's Socialist Party (the PSI), and disparaging its politics. Critics thought the PSI was seeking to build an electoral base by building cross-class alliances, compromising on socialism. A few critics may have moved towards anarchism, but generally Malatesta's call for the development of a serious anarchist organisation met with a limited response. Collectivist anarchism was strongest in north-eastern Italy, in the centre and Sicily, and weakest in the south of the peninsular and in Sardinia. In later years, libertarians had a strong presence in a band of country bordering the Adriatic, from Ravenna and its neighbourhood in the north, towards Ancona in the south.[93] Collectivist anarchists confronted individualists. Armando Borghi called such people called pseudo-anarchists; they argued for unlimited absolute freedom (for themselves).[94] He also commented: 'One should always distinguish between the anarchism of persons who wish neither to command nor obey, and those who, from arrogance, do not wish to obey because they intend to command.'[95]

A conference of Italian anarchists was called to meet in Rome in 1907, in preparation for the Amsterdam international anarchist congress. A hundred persons took part.[96] It formed an Anarchist-Socialist Federation and discussed strategy and goals in the workplace labour movement – it was indispensable, but it was not the one and only lens through which the energy to change society might be focused. The congress prioritised anti-militarist work, which it linked with anarchist principles: anti-authoritarianism and anti-patriotism. It brought together 37 groups and federations from 43 localities, with a majority in favour of organisation. Fabbri recognised that there had been much discussion and some publishing. He noted a strong – if not always predominant influence in Ancona, Carrara, La Spezia, Livorno, Pisa and Rome – but lamented the lack of influence of anarchists in recent events.[97] It was not easy to organise coordinated and effective action given the lack of common agreement on the necessity of organisation. In a report Fabbri said:

> And, on the contrary, I have realised for some many years that we tear at each other precisely because we are too close, and we are close artificially. There are enormous differences beneath the common varnish of three or four ideas – abolition of the state and private property, revolution,

anti-parliamentarianism – in each one of these theories. Such differences that we cannot travel on the same route without quarrelling, without the mutual undermining of each other's work, or if you wish – remaining at peace – without either of us neglecting the truth …

The walls of Jericho, said Fabbri, would not fall down at the sound of anarchist propaganda. New life would spring up, only if it could find 'adequate organs ready to meet the needs of social life which can be substituted for the old organisations.' Failing that authoritarian organisations might fill the gap left by an absence of libertarian organs.[98]

Luigi Galleani was an influential leader of an anti-organisational anarchism. He was critical of those who might work for an Anarchist Party or who might work in the labour movement, because they bred programmes, government, hierarchy, discipline, excommunications and expulsions. In the perspective of Galleani and the anti-organisation current, such a party could not help but become a party like the others: conservative when it grew up, reactionary as it became older.[99]

The Amsterdam congress was told that the Italian anarchist movement was polarised between the organised and the unorganised, and between pro- and anti-syndicalists. There were also libertarians who prioritised local, educational or anti-militarist activity,[100] but nothing would ever be done if one waited for perfect conditions and perfect coherence.

4
FRANCE AND THE CGT

France had a history of syndicalist labour organisation consolidated in the CGT (the General Confederation of Labour). Anarchism too had deep roots in France – from the era of Proudhon onwards, sometimes taking a rather individualist form. There were many anarchist journals articulating various viewpoints.

From the Commune to the 'Charte d'Amiens'

Labour organisations took some years to recover after the defeat of the Paris commune in 1871. Local all-trades *bourses du travail* (labour councils) and trade organisations developed despite the hostility of the new Third Republic. Laws forbidding union organisation was repealed in 1884, and trade organisations were legalised. A syndicalist influence was growing and was shortly to become preponderant. Libertarian ideas were circulated in a lively press: in Paris, the most important journals were *Le Révolté/La Révolte* with its literary supplement, Le *Père Peinard,* Les *Temps nouveaux* and *L'Endehors*; followed by *Le Cri typographique, Le Riflard, Le Pot-à-Colle, La Revue Anarchiste* and *La Revue Libertarie.* Provincial cities had many other journals.[101]

The CGT was founded in 1895. One of its key concepts was the revolutionary general strike. The general strike was defined as the best, most efficacious means of forwarding social liberation; it was widely viewed as an alternative to the socialist perspective that looked for change through legislation and parliament.[102]

Radical syndicalists held transitional perspectives, linking current struggles to broader change: 'In the present syndicalists' action aims at the conquest of gradual and partial advances, which are far from being goals and can only be considered as a means to demand more, to seize further improvements.' Syndicates looked forward to a non-capitalist future.[103] Anti-militarism was widespread within the French labour movement – many young people hated the prospect of two years of compulsory military service.

In 1905 Kropotkin's stance – as set out on the front page of *Les Temps nouveaux* – was:

> If France is invaded by some military power, the duty of revolutionaries is not to stand with their arms crossed leaving the invaders to do as they might wish. It is to launch the social revolution and to defend to territory of the revolution in order to continue it. The formula 'conscripts should strike' is insufficient. It has this deficiency, that of being silent on the essential goal of propaganda and it allows a space for erroneous interpretations. It says nothing about revolution …

Les Temps nouveaux carried several articles by Kropotkin on the Great French Revolution, and these had set out the prospect of a reprise of a revolutionary-people-in-arms. Charles Albert responded to Kropotkin that 1905 was not 1792. A new revolution would not have old features. Now was a time for syndicates to organise working people. Rather than French revolutionaries fighting other workers – brother [workers] from Britain, Germany or Russia – it would be better for French revolutionaries to let themselves be shot by the French bourgeoisie.[104] (Kropotkin did not say what should be done if the strength to launch a social revolution was lacking?)*

Syndicalists, and socialists who doubted the parliamentary tactic, de-prioritised electoral and parliamentary politics. Not infrequently they felt contempt for tactics that made little or no headway in improving the lot of workers. If laws were enacted for the benefit of labour (such as laws to reduce working hours or to protect women and children) it was easy for employers to circumvent them.

Georges Sorel criticised the state model. He wrote against 'socialist' officials who behaved like officers in the army, maximising discipline, disregarding the spirit and élan that had empowered common people in the great French revolution: 'Syndicalists do not propose to reform the state, as the men of the eighteenth century did; they want to destroy it, because they want to realise this idea of Marx's that the Socialist revolution ought not to culminate in the replacement of one governing authority by another minority.'[105]

The CGT was not always progressive as regards the rights of women.[106] At its 5th Congress, in 1900 it noted that all (male) workers concurred in viewing the introduction of woman workers into waged labour force as harmful to the working class – from a moral and physical viewpoint and

---

* Anti-militarism and the nature of syndicalism and are considered at below, pages 127-135

from a wage perspective. Such conservative viewpoints were challenged, for example by Nelly Roussel, who wrote in *Le Libertaire* that women's situation was not so much a matter of law, rather:

> [I]t arose out of the inevitable conditions in which, nine times time out of ten, a woman had to live, forcing her to depend on a man to live; someone who often abused circumstances to enslave and humiliate her. A regular marriage, an unregistered union, or 'gallantry' … in the end all such things were alike for women, her situation – surrendering her body to a man in return for her daily bread – was always as humiliating as it was perilous.[107]

Some years later Sophia Zaïkowska, wrote:

> Among anarchists the [question of] women's emancipation is, in my opinion wrongly set out. Women are barely considered, except as wives or lovers, as complements of men, and incapable of living by or for themselves …[108]

Attempts were made to establish women-only unions in 1910 and 1913, as a response to the discrimination that obstructed women joining unions. The matter was placed on the agenda of the CGT's congress of 1914, but the outbreak of war prevented that congress from meeting. Meanwhile there was a growth in the numbers of women in unions; at the turn of the century they were twenty or thirty thousand, twenty years later their numbers were approaching a quarter of a million. Towards the end of 1918 the proportion of women in paid employment was rising towards a third of the labour force.

Sabotage and the General Strike

Libertarians were prominent among the leadership of the CGT. The general strike was seen as the best and ultimate means through which workers might mobilise their power, to promote change and to initiate a social revolution.[109] The CGT's General Strike commission believed that in current miserable conditions the majority were most often unconscious and sheep-like, but that active minorities could play key roles in breaking log jams and provoking struggles.[110] The CGT 'Charte d'Amiens' of 1906 set out activist priorities: direct action, strikes and sabotage. It sought to build unity through 'economic' activity and worked to prevent divisive conflicts between advocates of particular political philosophies. Georges Yvetot argued that labour found its strength through direct action in or around the workplace: 'For the future, what is set out is that the general strike is the one and only means that the working class can chose to employ to quit waged-work and to overthrow the capitalist order and the government.'[111] [and]:

> Direct action is that which, without any extraneous help, without counting on some influence with the powers that be or with parliament, is exercised by those involved, with the aim of finding substantial satisfaction, be it partial or complete. Results are always both more durable and better, if they depend completely on the spontaneous and methodical energies of the workers concerned.

Victor Griffuelhes wrote:

> Direct action is for us nothing other than the expression of our continuous efforts. We say that those concerned have to struggle every day. Thus, in our eyes there is a daily practice that may grow, to the point that it transforms itself into a conflagration, which we call the general strike that will become the Social Revolution.[112]

Direct action might take on diverse forms – where food was scarce soup kitchens might be provided and the children of strikers might be cared for by other syndicalists.

Sabotage was another tactic adopted by the CGT. Rich and powerful employers were, syndicalists said, free to conspire together to intimidate, bust and destroy unions; workers needed to counter-plan, to find effective counter measures. Sabotage was designed to cement unity, by bringing quick results in conflicts. It worked to prevent the victimisation of conscious minorities, the employment of scabs and the intimidation of the rank and file. Sabotage was to the class struggle, what guerrilla warfare was to armed conflict, a means of levelling up the scales of power between the weak and the powerful.

New forms of industrial action travelled from Britain, where the go-slow or 'go cannie' was adopted at the end of the nineteenth century, to the USA and back to France. 'Go cannie' prescribed bad labour for bad wages. At its simplest there would be a withdrawal of co-operation or just a simple slowing down in production. Railway workers might carefully work to rule, observing every procedure meticulously, insisting on every safety measure.

If workers were threatened they might consider taking action to damage machinery by way of deterrent or reprisal. Employees might also pay back employers in their own coin. Instead of cheating consumers the boot would be put on the other foot: work would be done to a standard that was 'too good'. Workers were enjoined to inform consumers of sub-standard ingredients wherever shoddy goods were produced. A union stamp was designed to indicate products produced in CGT workplaces, its presence or absence may not have had a great impact, but it was perhaps good for CGT morale. These labels did not indicate anything about the quality of products. So, CGT labels indicated that the conditions of labour in production were respected, but perhaps not the interests of the consumers.

Label indicating goods produced with CGT labour

Perspectives and structures

In 1909 Griffuelhes wrote that syndicalism – revolutionary syndicalism – had quite another perspective to that of the church, the socialists or the state.

> In the face of any usurpation of rights, which is the very essence of management, syndicalism arises proclaiming for the proletariat the absolute right to work by all means at its disposal towards reducing managerial authority, to diminish managerial privilege, to make the atmosphere of the workplace healthier, to conquer new rights and guarantees, insofar as these may be considered as so many steps bringing closer its complete liberation. Syndicalism arises in the face of the state and its imperatives proclaiming the absolute right of the proletariat to think, act and struggle on lines that it itself sets out, to take into account state regulations only insofar as such legal rulings are helpful and work for it. So, for the worker, syndicalism asserts that nothing can be expected from management.[113]

The CGT sought to promote workers' organisation both in metropolitan France and in its colonies and looked towards the goal of total emancipation.

In 1902, a reviving labour movement began to consolidate as the CGT merged trade (syndicate) federations and local labour councils. A federation of *bourses* – 65 labour councils – joined the CGT.[114] This dual form – a local all-trades combination and a wider organisation of a trade or industrial sector – was one of the characteristics of syndicalism. Some unions operated as united national bodies, but much labour activity was centred on local organisations, *bourses du travail* and small syndicates (many of them had 100 to 200 members). A syndicate usually had three interlocking structures: an assembly of members, an administrative council, and a smaller bureau or executive.[115] Syndicates had considerable autonomy to make decisions at a local level. In this they contrasted with the pattern of trade union organisation developing in Germany, the UK and the USA, where national executives had much more power.

Where there were large industrial concerns it might be more natural to prioritise industrial organisation; where there were smaller concerns, especially in small towns, it was natural for organisations to take on a local character across many trades and workplaces. In the era before the First World War much of the population lived in rural areas and small towns. *Bourses du travail* might help job seekers find work, and help itinerant workers to find temporary accommodation. Many *bourses* had libraries of radical writers, and supported educational and cultural activities. Later, new forms of organisation developed: departmental* unions which organised all trades within their area, and industry-wide structures that organised workers in various trades working in particular industries (e.g. construction, railways).

Emma Goldman paints this rather rosy picture of the work of *bourses* and *mutualités*:†

> these Syndicalist activities are permeated with the spirit of educational work, carried on systematically by evening classes on all vital subjects treated from an unbiased, libertarian standpoint – not the adulterated 'knowledge' with which the minds are stuffed in our public schools. The scope of the education is truly phenomenal, including sex hygiene, the care of women during pregnancy and confinement, the care of home and children, sanitation and general hygiene; in fact, every branch of human knowledge – science, history, art – receives thorough attention ...[116]

---

* The department was an administrative area, there were some eighty departments in metropolitan France.
† Forums discussing educational and social issues.

At times, the CGT looked to counter education administered by the French state for capitalist interests.[117]

On a national scale, the CGT brought together representatives from two networks: one a network of *bourses,* the other a network of syndicates in trades or an industrial sector. It is difficult to measure through any organisational study the specific nationwide weight of the CGT or of its affiliates. Both large and small bodies might have equal representation at a national congress, with larger unions lacking influence in proportion to their numerical strength.[118] The disparity between membership and influence was such that 23 organisations with 22,550 members had greater weight in the CGT than 20 others with 114,000 members. It was argued[119] that the many organisations of the active minorities – in the smaller trades – were worth some extra weight, because they represented the most active groups.*

Although CGT congresses supported ant-militarist positions, the majority that voted these resolutions through was a majority of syndicates. If the vote had been counted in terms of the membership weight of each syndicate, a smaller number of syndicates with larger memberships might have prevailed over the larger number of syndicates with smaller numbers.[120]

The historian Jean Maitron saw the period between 1902 and 1908 as the apogee of the CGT. Between 1904 and 1906 the number of bourses (almost all CGT affiliated) increased from 110 to 135, and the number of syndicates increased from 1,792 to 2,399.[121] For some time, three of the CGT's main figures were libertarians: Paul Delesalle, Émile Pouget and Georges Yvetot. Pouget headed the union section and edited *La Voix du Peuple*; earlier he had published *Père peinard*, which campaigned for an independent unionism, and against colonialism† and imperialism; Delesalle and Yvetot headed the *bourses* du travail section of the CGT.[122] In a polemic on direct action, written in 1910, Pouget wrote:

> So, direct action implies that the working class should affirm and believe in freedom and autonomy, rather than lying down before the principle of authority; because it is on account of this pivotal principle of authority – the latest articulation of which is democracy – that people are tied down a thousand times over by moral and material chains, deprived of initiative and will at every opportunity.

* This principle was also applied in the CNT and in the IWA.
† The French libertarian press remarked on atrocities in French colonies and elsewhere, for example the Groupe d'études sociales of Autun protested against 'abominable crimes committed by so-called civilised countries against the Chinese people' *Les Temps nouveaux*, 13-19 July 1901.

The syndicalist method arises entirely out of this negation of hypocritical, mendacious 'democracy', which is the last word in the crystallisation of authority...

... the work of social transformation must start at the bottom... [as was affirmed by the IWA]. It therefore prioritises action by collective organisations. It naturally affirms and legitimates direct action. It needs direct action to live; direct action is nothing other than the process of its development.

Direct action is in fact the everyday business of the union, it is the essential element in its constitution. It would be an abomination if such bodies were to limit themselves to bringing wage earners together, the better to make them fit to produce for others – the fate which would they would be condemned to by bourgeois society.

Obviously, in a union, some people with no clear cut social ideas will come together, for their self-defence to struggle directly and in person. Common interest attracts them; instinctively they gravitate together. There, in this living nursery, unfolds the work of fermentation, elaboration and education. Workers, hitherto inculcated by the ruling class and blinded by prejudice, are raised to consciousness by the union. Eyes are opened wide, the overriding necessity of struggle, of revolt is demonstrated. Through its cohesion, through its concerted work, it prepares them for social conflict. From such knowledge, it becomes plain that all should act; neither failing to pull their weight, nor passing the buck. The consequence of these gymnastics, the productive energy of direct action, resides in this increased personal self-assurance and in self-confidence. Human resourcefulness is strengthened, character is tempered, energy is refined. Self-confidence is being taught! And self-reliance! And self-mastery! And acting for oneself!

Now compare the above with the methods in use in various groupings, bodies [and in the structures of] democratic politics! One sees that they have nothing in common: neither with the ongoing tendency [work] to raise consciousness, nor with being adapted to and preparing for action, action being the life and breath of economic associations [unions]. And it should not be supposed that methods in everyday use in the latter can be decanted into the former. Direct action is an empty phrase outside the economic [union] arena, because activity is in contradiction with the workings of the constituent structures of 'democracy'; the representative system is the compulsory mechanism of democracy. *Democracy demands at grass-roots level the inactivity of all.* Everything becomes a matter of trusting representatives! Of relying on them! Of counting on them! Of leaving them free to act!

... Direct action develops the human personality and at the same time the spirit of initiative. In contrast to democratic spinelessness, which is satisfied by sheepishness and following, it shakes up an individual's torpor and raises them to consciousness. It neither regiments workers nor brands them. Quite the opposite! It awakens their sense of value and power, and the groupings that it forms and inspires are alive and vibrant bodies, in which, the weight of gravity, of unconscious immobility, of numbers does not translate into a decisive force. Persons with initiative are not suffocated, and minorities – which are and always have been the progressive element – can develop without being shackled, and through the effect of its propaganda can accomplish the work of coordination that precedes action.[123]

Pouget portrays direct action – led by active minorities – as wholly positive. He was speaking in a workplace context where there were some checks and balances – if active syndicalists went out on a limb or disrespected the majority of their fellow workers, they might be ignored. In strikes, active minorities might lead and propose, but an assembly of workers might dispose and make final decisions. The power of initiative was therefore limited and depended on the preparation (propaganda) that might explain and justify action. Pouget made clear – it was not a case of all or nothing – he had in mind wholesale change, but sought to win such partial improvements as would make the life of working people easier.

Pouget also drew a distinction between elections in which politicians sought to win power and the selection procedures of the CGT:

The functions of syndicate's council are strictly limited and only administrative. The council does the work assigned to it without ever neutralising those by whom it is mandated, without substituting itself for them, without acting for them.[124]

The CGT distanced itself from both bourgeois democracy in general and the politics of the various socialist parties. The Amiens CGT congress resisted the calls for a regular institutional relationship between the CGT and the Socialist Party (SFIO) proposed by Victor Renard. Renard argued that it was better for relations between party and union to be conducted properly, in the full light of day, rather than behind the scenes. The document below became one of the historic definitions of French syndicalism.

The Charter of Amiens

The Charter of Amiens was endorsed by the CGT by 830 votes to 8 at its congress in October 1906:

> The Confederal Congress of Amiens reconfirms article 2 of the CGT constitution: 'Whatever their political schooling, the CGT unites all workers conscious of the struggle to be conducted for the disappearance of the system of wage-earning and management. Congress considers that this declaration is recognition of class struggle. In the economic field, workers in revolt are opposed to all forms of exploitation and oppression, material as well as moral, used by the capitalist class against the working class.' Congress defines this theoretical affirmation by the following points: in its day-to-day demands, syndicalism seeks to co-ordinate workers' efforts, to improve workers' well-being by the achievement of immediate improvements, such as the reduction of working hours, the increase of wages, etc. But this task is only one side of the work of syndicalism: it prepares for complete emancipation, which can be achieved only by expropriating the capitalist class; it proposes as a method for its action the general strike and it considers that the union, today an organisation of resistance, will be in the future the foundation for social reorganisation for the organisation of production and distribution. Congress declares that this is the double duty in the present and for the future, that emerges from the position of wage-earners, falling on the working class and charging all workers, whatever their political and philosophical opinions and inclinations, with the duty of belonging to indispensable organisations such as unions. As for individuals, Congress consequently affirms, the complete liberty of members to participate, outside the union, in whatsoever forms of struggle conform to their political or philosophical views, and limits itself to requesting, in reciprocity, that they should not introduce into the union opinions held outside it. As for organisation, Congress resolves, that since economic action must be conducted directly against employers for syndicalism to achieve its maximum effect, the organisations of the confederation, insofar as they are unions should not concern themselves with parties and sects, which, outside and alongside, may pursue social transformation in complete freedom.

Pierre Monatte wrote a polemic published in *Les Temps nouveaux* after the congress. He took issue with socialists of the *départment du Nord* (around Lille), allies of Guesde, and advocates of an electoralist strategy. There was no correlation between winning votes and the strength of the

CGT. Anarchists could, he asserted, serve the CGT better because they did not have divided loyalties:

> As for our energies, they are not divided into two parts, a part reserved for political action and a part for union action. All our strength is devoted to the union movement which we wish to see progress and develop to such strength that the autonomous action of the working class should be broadly sufficient for all struggles …'[125]

Many libertarian syndicalists looked on syndicalism as an alternative to parliamentary-political action, as a body that had an agenda that included economic issues but also went beyond a purely economic agenda. In this view, the CGT was itself a major 'political' actor. There were some supporters of various Social-Democratic and Socialist parties hoping that the CGT, through the Amiens charter, would distance itself from 'politics' – especially the politics of anti-militarism and anti-parliamentarianism. There were also some libertarian syndicalists who were glad that *anarchist* politics were kept *out* of the CGT. Some CGT members prioritised labour and workplace issues and thought 'politics' – even anarchist politics – might be a distraction. However, the CGT did address both workplace issues and a 'social' agenda with some pretty 'political' themes – especially anti-militarism. Just where the social agenda stopped and the political agenda started was a moot point. The 'Charter of Amiens' did not close the door on all 'politics'. There was a certain amount of ambiguity: there was talk of syndicates not being involved in disputes between parties and sects, but congress resolutions did not condemn these bodies outright. 'Apoliticism' might be interpreted by some as *chacun chez soi*, 'sticking to one's own patch', for the CGT acting in the economic field and others in a party-political-field. For some, 'the complete liberty of members to participate, outside the union, in whatsoever forms of struggle conform to their political or philosophical views,' meant that they were free to pursue state-socialist politics. Yet the socialists were frequently criticised in the CGT journal *Voix du Peuple* and the CGT adopted anti-militarism. There was some space for differences of opinion. For some, certain distinct and particular concerns might still be viewed as complimentary to activity in the CGT, provided they did not 'intrude'; for others, the CGT had its own stream of distinct politics – participatory, workplace-focused and anti-militarist. For the latter, the CGT formed, in its own right, a party of sorts – *Le Parti du Travail* (the Party of Labour).[126] Over and above these varied perspectives, the CGT was not a monolith, and it contained a variety of perspectives and politics.

5
THE AMSTERDAM CONGRESS OF 1907

The congress that met in Amsterdam, in August 1907, brought together some seventy activists from different backgrounds – anarchists, syndicalists and anti-parliamentary socialists – and from many countries. Persons present included:

Argentina: Aristide Ceccarelli (from Rome, for the FORA).

Austria/ Britain: Rudolf Grossmann (alias Pierre Ramus) *Die freie Arbeiterwelt*, *Die Freie Generation*; Siegfried Nacht.

Belgium: Henri Fuss-Amoré, Émile Chapelier, Maurice Heyman, Hamburger, Henri J. Janssens, Sergher Rabauw, Victor Resseler, Schouteten, Georges Thonar, Henri Willems.

Bohemia: Ladislav Knotek, Karl Vohryzek, (Anarchist Federation of Bohemia).

Britain: Otto Schreiber and Jean Wilquet, (*Kommunistische Arbeiter-Bildungs-Verein* London); Thomas Keell (*Freedom*), Rudolf Rocker, and Alexander Schapiro (*Arbeter Fraint* and *Germinal* of London; Jewish Anarchist Federation); Karl Walter (*Voice of Labour*); Guy Aldred(?), Flatt, Carlo Frigerio, Solo Linder, Otto Schreiber.

Bulgaria: S. Velev.

France: Henri Beylie, Brille, Léon Clément, Louis Coriol, Benoît Broutchoux (North Africa); Amédée Dunois (Francophone Switzerland); H. Margoulis, René de Marmande (*Temps nouveaux*), Pierre Monatte (CGT), Albert Zibelin.

Germany: Paul Frauböse, Raphael Friedeberg (FVdG), Rudolf Lange, Ludwig, Sepp Oerter, Wagner.

Italy: Ennio Enrico Belelli, Silvio Celestino Corio, Luigi Fabbri, Errico Malatesta.

The Netherlands: Altink, J. L. Bruijn, Christiaan Cornelissen (NAS), Hesp,

Klein, Koekoek, Nelly Korver, Johan. J. Lodewijk, Domela Nieuwenhuis (*De Vrije Socialist*), Gerhard Rijnders, Bernard Reyndorp (Rijnsdorp), I. Izak Samson, Nicholas Schermerhorn, Stad, Jacob Van Rees.

Poland: Joseph Schweber, Iza Zielinska (Paris).

Russia: Nicolas Rogdaev (*Burevestnik*), Emilie Wetkov, Sophie Wodnef, Vladimir Zabrezhnev (*Khleb i Volia*).

Serbia: Peter Mougnitch.

USA: Max Baginsky, D. A. Bullard, Emma Goldman.

Some regions were represented by comrades living elsewhere.

The life of someone like Carlo Frigerio was so complex that it is difficult to say to which country he 'belonged'. Frigerio was born in Switzerland in 1878, grew up in Milan, was expelled from Italy in 1898, came to London in 1901 and Paris in 1905, was expelled from France in 1905, and he would be expelled from Belgium in 1908. Malatesta lived for many years in London, and his views were informed by his experience there.

Various libertarian, Maximalist and mixed tendencies and organisations existed in Poland, Lithuania and other parts of the Russian Empire. With repression falling on revolutionaries the 'Russian' presence was somewhat indirect, through exiles. The Amsterdam congress only brought together a scanty representation of the diverse 'Russian' tendencies.

Naturally enough the Low Countries were well represented. The Belgians and the Dutch had taken the initiative to call the congress and looked forward to the creation of some sort of international organisation. The Belgian federation had organised international pre-congress discussions through *Le Bulletin de l'Internationale Libertaire*. The Dutch federation facilitated the anarchist congress. It coincided with the second anti-militarist congress, also held in Amsterdam and many Dutch activists attended both meetings. The meeting of an anarchist congress was possible in the Netherlands but would most likely have been impossible and or dangerous for the participants in most of the rest of Europe.

Attendance from Southern Europe and the Americas – being further off – was less numerous. The Spanish movement was absent, would-be participants failed to arrive in time because of travel problems. Fundraising efforts helped pay for fares and living expenses. Emma Goldman was able to attend because groups and individuals helped raise sufficient funds for the trip. *Les Temps nouveaux*, solicited funds to support delegates from France. A few anarchist federations were represented: in Belgium, an ephemeral *Groupement communiste libertaire*,[127] in Bohemia the *Česká Anarchistická*

Federace and in Francophone Switzerland the *Fédération Communiste-Anarchiste de la Suisse Romande*. Italy had regional federations and a national federation, but the latter was a new body, only launched in Rome to prepare for the Amsterdam congress. A congress of a German national anarchist federation congress was called to prepare for Amsterdam but was banned. Repression hampered discussions and communication in Polish, Lithuanian, Latvian and Russian networks (a congress had met in eastern Poland in 1906). There was no national French anarchist federation. Many French libertarians invested their energies in syndicalist organisations or labour councils. Pierre Ramus commented that the opinions and perspective discussed at the congress were those of the individuals present.[128]

The French syndicalist confederation, the CGT, was present in the person of the young Pierre Monatte, but older and better-known CGT leaders did not attend. This signalled that despite differences, the CGT had not abandoned links to the International Secretariat of National Trade Union Centres (ISNTUC), and would not endorse anarchism. The discussion of syndicalism that would take place at the congress had been preceded by a series of texts from various personalities (including A. Girard, Jean Grave, Kropotkin, Marc Pierrot) on the subject published in *Les Temps nouveaux*. Kropotkin had concluded that the proletariat, being now disgusted with Social-Democratic parliamentarianism, had returned to older ideas of direct internationalist action against capital.[129]

Many participants would be key figures in the future, but there were some absences: Galleani (in the USA), Jean Grave,* Guillaume, Kropotkin, Landauer, Mühsam and Nettlau. Kropotkin was ill perhaps,[130] but some member of the *Khleb i Volia* (Bread and Freedom) group did attend. The congress had been prepared by partisans of organisation – perhaps this preference dissuaded Galleani from attending. Landauer and Mühsam may have had little interest in discussions of syndicalism. They and other individualist currents may have felt little enthusiasm for this congress.

Malatesta commented: 'Many comrades, perhaps the majority, regarded the preparations with an indifferent or hostile eye.'[131] So, the organisational preparations and deliberations preceding the Amsterdam congress might have been expected to have given rise to only limited and tentative beginnings.

There were regional reports on activities. One of these, 'The Situation

---

* The editor of *Les Temps nouveaux* was absent but at least two frequent contributors were present (de Marmande, Dunois). Grave commented later, in the issue of 21 September 1907, that in his view, anarchists were more likely to find life in everyday events, rather than in congresses.

in America', was printed in *Mother Earth*. It began by stating that 'Properly speaking, there is no American Nation; what is usually called by that name is a conglomeration of members of all European nations, with a considerable proportion of Asiatic and African races'.[132]

Malatesta viewed organisation as the most important subject at the congress,[133] and Emma Goldman termed the debate lively.[134] Malatesta was perhaps looking for cohesion among various sorts of libertarians. He wrote of his own opinion that:

> In reality, we are all in agreement in practice, we all want more or less the same things, and are agreed more or less on same means ... In reality, one can be 'disorganised' only if one does nothing – or if one does those few things for which the strength of an isolated individual suffices. ... What is most important – I repeat – is the desire for common struggle, and the intention to maintain relationships – so that when key moments for action come – one does not have to go in search of them, taking the risk that the moment will pass before those relationships are found.[135]

A resolution was passed that organisation complimented and clarified anarchism, but with a proviso that associations should seek neither to diminish initiative nor to impose one view. Amedée Dunois had presented the argument that anarchist organisation would not unite all anarchists, but 'It would be enough for it to rally around a program of practical action all those comrades subscribing to our principles ...'[136] Rights of individuals, groups and federations were acknowledged – each deserving autonomy.[137] Conference also noted that organisation facilitated rights and that rights could not be obtained except through organisation.[138] In practice there were varied judgements as to what organisation might achieve and which forms of organisation best suited particular aims, or sets of aims.

Another important discussion focused on the new model of syndicalism represented by the CGT. Christiaan Cornelissen, a leader of the small Dutch syndicalist union federation, the National Labour Secretariat, spoke about problems of workplace organisation. He referred to some skilled typographers' organisations that refused to admit women. (Given the lack of representation of women in the conference, this was a telling point.) He talked of diamond workers in Antwerp and Amsterdam who prioritised direct action for their own corporatist, trade interests (these workers supported a liberal-reformist labour confederation, the *Nederlands Verbond van Vakvereinigingen*, NVV;[139] so this point had particular partisan importance). He reminded listeners that in the USA and Britain, trade unions were wont to use direct action to defend the interests of privileged layers of workers. Professional and skilled workers might act against the unskilled, the unqualified and the immigrant. He referred to events in the USA, where there was a threat of war with Japan, and where the American Federation of Labour (AFL) refused to admit Japanese manual workers.[140] He also referred to strikes against technical improvements in production. In this view, some workers' organisations had only sectional interests; syndicalism needed to take in and promote solidarity among the working class a whole.[141]

Cornelissen lived in a context of conflicting labour confederations. His own organisation had never managed to organise the wealthy diamond workers and had lost the support of some other sectors. The syndicalism he espoused came to be in competition or in conflict with other Christian/Catholic and Social-Democratic union centres.[142] His critical perspectives highlighted circumstances where there were multiple, diverse and conflicting unions, and union centres, brought together for ideological as well as for professional reasons. In this context, the CGT model of one all-encompassing, big union was inoperative. A challenge to the CGT concept of union unity was indeed perceived and led CGT leader Louis Niel to write, after the congress, that anarchist unions would not be useful.[143] *Action-directe* of Liège replied that all Amsterdam congress attendees were united in opposition to a specifically anarchist unionism, except possibly in unusual circumstances where unions were controlled by a political party.[144]

Pierre Monatte, as an unofficial representative of the CGT, made a keynote speech on the subject of relations between anarchism and syndicalism. Monatte spoke in Amsterdam against 'scholastic and sectarian quarrels', and for class unity. He spoke from a context where the CGT was a hegemonic confederation working to defend and unite French workers in their everyday struggles in workplaces and local labour councils.[145] Monatte spoke out of experience in a rising labour movement that had recently been involved in an unusually high level of strike activity.

Pierre Monatte: Speech at the International Anarchist Congress, Amsterdam, August 1907

My wish is not to give you a theoretical account of revolutionary syndicalism, but to show you its workings, to talk about facts. Revolutionary syndicalism, in contrast to the movements that came before it – socialism and anarchism – has asserted itself not so much by theories as in action, it is in action rather than in books that it has to be found.

One would be blind not to see the common ground between anarchism and syndicalism. Both work for the wholesale destruction of capitalism and of the wage-earning system by the means of social revolution. Syndicalism proves that the workers' movement has revived; it has recalled anarchism back to feel its working-class origins. And further, anarchism has in no small measure contributed to drawing the workers' movements into revolutionary path popularising ideas of direct action. So, in this way, syndicalism and anarchism have reacted with each other, for the benefit of each.

Revolutionary syndicalist ideas have been born and developed in France, in the ranks of the CGT. The Confederation occupies a unique place in the international workers' movement. It is the only organisation that, while clearly declaring itself revolutionary is without any link to political parties, even the most advanced of them. In most other countries, Social-Democracy leads the way. In France, the CGT leaves the Socialist Party far behind both in terms of numbers and in terms of its influence. It claims to represent the working class alone, and resolutely repels all advances that have been made to it in recent years. Autonomy has made it powerful, and it intends to remain autonomous.

This claim of the CGT, its refusal to relate to parties, has won from its exasperated enemies an anarchist tag. But nothing could be more false. The CGT, a vast grouping of workers' unions and syndicates, has no official doctrine. But all doctrines are represented within it and are equally tolerated. There are on its confederal committee a certain number of anarchists, meeting and working together with socialists, of whom the great majority, and this should be noted in passing, are no less hostile than the anarchists to any idea of collusion between unions and the Socialist Party.

The structure of the CGT deserves recognition. In contrast with structures of so many other workers' organisations it is neither centralised nor authoritarian. The confederal committee is not, as is imagined by managers and reporters of bourgeois newspapers, a directing committee bringing together in its own hands legislative and executive powers, it has no authority. The CGT is governed from bottom to top; the union has no master but itself, it is free to act or not to act; no outsider can intervene to launch it into action.

At the base of the Confederation is the union [In the original French text, *syndicat*.] But the latter does not belong directly to the confederation; it can do so through its corporate federation [of unions] on the one hand [and] on the other hand through its [federations of] *bourses du travail*. The CGT is constituted and brought together by the organisation of union federations with the organisation of the *bourses*.

The life of the confederation is co-ordinated by the confederal committee composed alike of delegates from both trades' councils and [union] federations. Alongside and within function commissions: the newspaper commission (*La Voix du Peuple*), the control commission with financial responsibilities, and the commission for strikes and for the general strike.

For the regulation of business, the congress is sovereign. Every union, however weak, has the right to be represented by a delegate, which it chooses for itself. The confederal budget is very modest. It has less than 30,000 francs each year. Ongoing agitation, which culminated in the widespread movement of May 1906 for the eight-hour day, absorbed less than 60,000 francs. Such a niggardly sum, when it was divulged, astonished journalists. What! With only a few thousand francs how could the confederation have undertaken such an intense workers' agitation for months and months! French syndicalism, although poor in terms of money, was rich in terms of energy, devotion, enthusiasm, and these are riches which carry no risk of bringing enslavement.

The French workers' movement did not become what it is today without long years of effort. Multiple phases have passed over thirty-five years since the Paris Commune. The idea that made the proletariat, organised through their 'organisations of resistance', into the (active) agency of the revolution was the basic mother idea, the fundamental conception of the International Workers Association founded in London in 1864. The motto of the International was, you will remember, 'the emancipation of workers will be the accomplishment of the workers themselves', and this is still our motto, for all of us partisans of direct action and opponents of parliamentarianism. Ideas of autonomy and of federation, that are so esteemed among us, were formerly the inspiration of all those who in the International revolted against the abuse of power by the General Council, and after the Congress at The Hague,[146] adopted overtly the party of Bakunin. Indeed, the very idea of the general strike, which is so popular today, is an idea of the International, which was the first to understand the power that it mobilised.

The defeat of the Commune unleashed terrible reaction in France. The workers' movement was stopped dead, its militants having been assassinated or forced abroad. However, after a few years it recovered; at first nervously, later with some vigour. The first congress took place in Paris in 1876. The pacific spirit of co-operativists and mutualists was dominant at first. At the next congress the socialists were vocal, talking about abolishing the wages system. Later, at Marseilles in 1879, the newcomers triumphed giving the congress a markedly revolutionary and socialist character. But there soon arose disputes between scholastic socialists and various other tendencies. At Le Havre, the anarchists were on the back foot leaving the field open to the partisans of a minimum programme and the conquest of power. Left to themselves collectivists couldn't work together. The struggle between Guesde and Brousse tore the nascent *Parti Ouvrier* apart, leading to complete schism.[147]

Moreover, neither the followers of Guesde nor those of Brousse (from whom the followers of Allemane later split off) were able to speak for the proletariat. The latter was rightly indifferent to scholastic quarrels, and reformed unions, which were given the new name of syndicates. Abandoned to itself, out of the limelight of internecine conflicts, because of its very weakness, the syndicalist movement gradually developed in confidence. It grew. The federation of trades' councils (*Bourses*) was founded in 1892, the General Confederation of Labour [CGT] which from the first carefully declared its political neutrality, in 1895. Meantime a workers' congress of 1894 (in Nantes) voted for the principle of the revolutionary general strike.

In these times, numerous anarchists, perceiving that philosophy was not enough to make revolution, entered into the workers' movement and there those with vision were inspired with the greatest expectations. Fernand Pelloutier was the man who at this time best incarnated the evolution of the anarchists. All subsequent congresses further accentuated the divorce between the organised working class and politics. At Toulouse in 1897, our comrades Delesalle and Pouget adopted tactics of boycotts and sabotage. In 1900, the *Voix du Peuple* was founded with Pouget as its chief editor. It was evident that, after its beginnings, the CGT's strength was growing day by day. It now became a power to be reckoned with, by both the government and the socialist parties.

The new movement was then subjected to a vicious assault from the government, which had the support of all reformist socialists. Millerand, once he became a minister, tried to governmentalise the unions, making each bourse into a branch office of his ministry. He had paid agents working in the organisation. Attempts were made to corrupt loyal militants and they were in great danger. It was averted through the mutual understanding that now developed between all revolutionary fractions; between anarchists and revolutionaries, followers of Guesde and Blanqui. When the danger passed, the entente remained. Today it draws strength from within itself. Revolutionary syndicalism was born out of this entente, the doctrine which makes the union the organ, and the general strike the means, of social transformation.

But, and on this point I call for the complete attention of our non-French comrades to something of extreme importance, neither the achievement of workers' unity nor a revolutionary coalition would have been able to promote the influence or progress of the CGT by themselves, if we had not remained faithful, in union life, to this fundamental principle: one union for each trade and each town, excluding in fact unions based on opinions. The consequence of this principle is the political neutrality of the union, which must and should be simply of workers, neither anarchist, nor Guesdiste, nor Allemaniste.* In the union differences of opinion, which may be so subtle, so artificial, become of secondary importance and thereby unity becomes possible. In everyday life, interests come before ideas: thus, all scholastic and sectarian quarrels will not so determine things to prevent workers, insofar as they are all equally subjected to the law of wage earning, having identical interests. This is the secret of the common unity which was established, creating the power of syndicalism, and this is what allowed it, last year at the Congress of Amiens, to proudly affirm that it was sufficient unto itself.

I would be gravely at fault if I did not make plain to you the means on which revolutionary syndicalism relies to accomplish the emancipation of the working class. These means can be summarised in two words: direct action. What is direct action? For a long time, under the influence of scholastic socialism, that of the Guesdiste tendency for the most part, workers relied on the state to realise their demands. Remember workers' processions, with socialist deputies at their head carrying to the public authorities the aggregate demands of the Fourth Estate! [The press.] This manner of activity brought a load of deception with it; little by little one comes to understand that workers obtain only the reforms that they were able to impose *for themselves*; or, to put it another way, that the motto of the International that I have cited earlier should be understood and applied in the strictest manner. Act for yourselves, rely on yourselves: that's direct action. And it goes without saying that this can take on the most varied of forms.

The strike is its principle form, or better its most conspicuous form. As has been said earlier, it is a two-edged sword: a solid, well-tempered weapon we say, which, when cleverly used by workers, can hit the bosses in the heart. Through strikes, the mass of workers join the class struggle and become familiar with strategies on which it relies, through strikes

---

* References to competing Socialist party leaders – Allemane and Guesde. Notes on individuals mentioned in the text will be included in a later volume in this series..

they acquire a revolutionary education, thereby it measures its own power and that of its enemy, capitalism; thereby it acquires confidence in itself, it learns audacity.

Sabotage has, if only by a little, a smaller impact. It is summed up as: 'bad work for bad pay'. As with the strike, it has been in use forever, but only in the last few years has it acquired a truly revolutionary meaning. Already there are important results from sabotage. In places where strikes lacked force, it has broken the resistance of the bosses. One recent example was given after the defeat of the Parisian builders' strike of 1906. Builders returned to sites resolved to put in place a peace that they would influence bosses with a force greater than that of war itself. By unanimous tacit agreement a slow-down in daily production was begun. As if by chance, spoilt sacks of plaster and of cement were found, etc, etc. This war is ongoing now, and I repeat, results have been excellent. Not only did bosses most often give in, but also after a campaign of several months the building worker came out of it all more aware, more independent and more willing to revolt.

But, if I [only] considered syndicalism as a whole, without commenting further on its particular features, I should have to make some apology! In France, the spirit of revolution was dying, or was getting thinned out at the least, as years went by. For example, Guesde's revolutionary phrases became just words, or worse were electoralist and parliamentary. Jaurès's 'revolutionism', for its part, went further, but it was simply and frankly ministerial and governmentalist. As for the anarchists, their revolutionism took up a superb refuge in the ivory towers of speculative philosophy. Syndicalism emerged in the midst of such incompetence, and through the effects of this incompetence. Revolutionary moral revived as it manifested itself; and for the first time since the grand voice of anarchist dynamite was silenced, the bourgeoisie trembled!

Well then, it is important that the syndicalist experience of the French proletariat should benefit proletarians of all countries. It is for anarchists to work so that this experience is renewed wherever a working class exists and works for its emancipation. Anarchists should set up the French manner of syndicalism, neutral syndicalism, or more exactly independent syndicalism in opposition to syndicalism of ideas, which have produced in Russia, for example, anarchist unions, and in Belgium and Germany Christian and Social-Democratic unions. Just as there is only one working class, so in every trade and in every town, there should be just one workers' organisation, and only one union. Class struggle now breaking free from the jealousies of scholastic bickering of rival sects, can, if this one condition is observed, develop fully to maximum effect.

The 'Charter of Amiens' proclaimed that syndicalism sufficed unto itself. I know that this motto has not always been well understood even by anarchists. However, what can it mean, if not that the now fully grown working class intends to be rely on itself, not depend on anyone for its own emancipation. What could any anarchist have to add to a commitment to action, so richly asserted? Syndicalism does not wait to promise workers an earthly paradise. It asks them to set about conquering it, assuring them that their action will never be entirely wasted. It is a school for commitment, energy and fertile thinking. It opens new hopes and perspectives to an anarchism which has for too long been shut in on itself. So, let all anarchists come to syndicalism; their work will be more effective, and the blows against the regime will be more decisive.

As in all human creation, the syndicalist movement isn't devoid of some imperfections, and far from hiding them I think it is useful to have them present in mind, in order to deal with them. The most important is the tendency of individuals to take care to fight in their unions, federations and in the Confederation, calling for collective power when individual effort would have been sufficient. We anarchists who constantly appeal to individual will, initiative and audacity, can vigorously react against the damaging tendency to appeal to collective force for small as much as for big things.

Union functionaries also excite lively criticism, which moreover are often justified. It can happen, it does happen, that militants no longer use their posts [in the union] to fight for what they believe in but because they can earn their crust in this way. However, one should not deduce that union bodies should entirely forgo the use of full-timers. Many organisations can't do without them. This is a necessity whose disadvantages can be corrected by an ever-watchful critical spirit.[148]

Errico Malatesta made a critical reply. He said he would save time and speak only on points where he had *differences* with Monatte. Malatesta first drew a distinction between the labour movement on the one hand and syndicalism on the other. The movement was a fact, but syndical*ism* was not. The doctrine of syndical*ism* being sufficient *in itself* was radically wrong. Maybe Malatesta was implying that the portrait painted by Monatte was too ideal, too rosy, too much the product of favourable circumstances, and not so appropriate where the labour movement had other traditions. He also spoke of potential conflict within the working class and viewed all unions or syndicates, as potentially conservative. While he supported activity in the workers' movement he argued that in general, those who worked as union officials were lost to the movement,* because they came to be indebted to the unions that paid them rather than to the wider movement. If they followed their conscience they might lose their job in the union, if they followed their self-interest to preserve their job in the union, they lost their politics. As with parliamentary socialism, unionism led to corruption. 'In the workers' [union] movement, the official is a danger, one that can only be compared with parliamentarianism: both lead to corruption and from corruption to death there isn't far to go.' In terms of danger, it was not just that particular individuals might be corrupted, rather that structures and relationships engendered corruption.

Later, he would write of syndicalist inebriation, noting that former anarchists, once they became officials, would soon cease to be anarchists.[149] Malatesta in Amsterdam spoke as someone active in a union, but primarily as an anarchist. For him common economic interests were neither as powerful, nor as strong, as solidarity born of a shared ideal.[150] He wrote later, in one congress report: 'Workers and the oppressed can feel solidarity with one another, only when there a prospect of a complete social transformation. It is the role of anarchists to keep the fire of ideals burning, and to work as much as is possible towards sign-posting any movement in the direction of future conquests, towards revolution itself, if necessary to the detriment of those small gains that may be obtained today by some fraction of the working class, which moreover are most often obtained at a cost to other workers and public consumers.'[151] In another report he argued that 'Certainly, syndicalism … can emancipate a part of the workers but not all', also syndicates make a serious division of the workers.[152]

Malatesta had worried in the past that too many comrades were isolated from the labour movement, now his worries ran the other way, that too many comrades might be absorbed by the labour movement. Monatte had suggested that it was possible to build syndicates that were radical, supported direct action and maintained workers' unity. Like other speakers, he could not disregard particular interests – racism and sexism in modern parlance – within the labour movement. He was careful in qualifying his support for unions. He noted that as well as conflicts between workers and capital there were conflicts within the working class, so that unions might represent workers in conflict with each other. He argued that while unions were small they might remain radical, but as soon as they grew they would

---

* He suggested that anarchists should abstain from taking paid positions in unions. *Les Temps Nouveaux*, 5 October 1907.

begin winning privileges for their members, and unions would become conservative, hostile more towards the unskilled and un-organised than towards capital. He did not want anarchist unions, or red unions, because their development might offer a pretext for yellow, or partisan unions. 'I want, on the contrary, unions that are open wide to all workers, without distinctions as to their opinions, unions that are absolutely neutral.'[153] Malatesta did wish that unions should be drawn 'as close as possible towards anarchist tactics'. He also spoke of the inevitability of strikes engendering conflict and of the need to prepare for insurrection. The general strike might be a means of opening the social revolution, but sooner or later a broader confrontation would develop into a revolutionary insurrection.* Unions would need to prepare and keep the economy going after an insurrection.

He concluded:

Once again, the workers' movement, strikes, general strikes, direct action, boycotts, sabotage and armed insurrection, all these are just *means*. Anarchism is the *goal*. The anarchist revolution that we desire goes far beyond class interests, it targets humanity as it is actually enslaved from three perspectives: economic, political and moral, [and] aims at complete liberation.[154]

If a stress was placed on going 'far beyond class interests' this made syndicalism a means, but not the only one, and in Malatesta's view syndicalism was not *the* goal. Perhaps because he did want to dissuade anarchists from becoming paid officials Malatesta did not challenge Monatte's assertion that the CGT was led from bottom to top. Subsequent events would show that national office-holders had space to encourage – or discourage – action being taken. Syndicalists active in a large confederation like the CGT, might perhaps have been more concerned about how national leadership functioned. The means of communication of the CGT – its journals – gave a lead and would shape the agenda for discussion. How could the CGT as a whole be lead from bottom to top if the mass of its membership had little say in the running of its press? Malatesta, as someone with little experience of working in a union, was ill-placed to challenge Monatte's too rosy, and unrealistic picture of syndicalist democracy. Malatesta's comments about unions did not address the point that unions were not all the same. Talking about organisation in the workplace in general terms did not get to grips

---

* Monatte commented all this was outdated, and reflected the thinking of Blanqui. Russian anarchist-communists fought syndicalists, seeing them as actual or potential compromisers.

with varied conceptions and practices – between the AFL and the IWW, or within a big confederation like the CGT or TUC.

Resolutions agreed at this congress were for guidance rather than 'law'. Libertarians had early taken the view that the purpose of a congress was not to designate one policy that all should have to follow, but rather to bring together the views that existed and to attempt to harmonise them. Some 35 years earlier, in September 1872, the Saint-Imier congress of the IWA recorded these federalist organisational norms in the first sentences of its resolutions:

> Considering that the autonomy and independence of workers' sections and federations is the first precondition for labour emancipation; that all power accorded to a Congress to regulate and legislate would be a flagrant negation of that freedom and autonomy; Congress repudiates as a matter of principle, that congresses, be they regional or general, should have legislative power; it recognises as the mission of congresses only that they should bring together the ideas, needs and aspirations of the proletariat in various places and lands, in order, as much as is possible, to facilitate their harmonisation and unification; but not in any case that some Congress majority should impose its resolutions on a minority.[155]

The congress passed the four motions below on the question of unions. Close and careful reading was needed to grasp particular nuances and the potential or actual divergences between resolutions.

Motion by Cornelissen, Vohryzek and Malatesta (approved by 33 votes to 10).
The International Anarchist Congress considers that syndicates are, on the one hand, fighting organisations of the class struggle working for the improvement of conditions in workplace, and also producers' unions, which will serve to transform capitalism into anarchist communist society. Further, while recognising the future necessity of creating various revolutionary syndicalist groups, congress recommends that comrades support general union organisations open to workers in the same line of work. Congress considers that it is the responsibility of anarchists to build the revolutionary element in these organisations facilitating the development of forms and examples of direct action – strikes, boycotts, sabotage – which within them have revolutionary characteristics and which work towards social transformation.

Anarchists consider the union movement in the workplace and the general strike as powerful revolutionary means, but not as substitutes to revolution. It is also their recommendation in the case of the proclamation of a general strike aimed at the conquest of power, that comrades should support strikes. Further it is their suggestion that they should simultaneously encourage those unions that they influence, to make their economic demands heard. Anarchists believe that the destruction of authoritarian and capitalist society can be achieved only by armed insurrection and violent expropriation, and that the general strike and the union movement should not overlook or forget more direct means of direct struggle against the armed forces of the state.

The Dunois Motion countersigned by Monatte, Fuss-Amoré, Fabbri, Walter, Nacht, Zielinska, (approved by 28 votes to 7).
Noting that the contemporary legal and economic regime is characterised by exploitation and the slavery of the mass of producers, and that between the latter and those who benefit from the existing regime there is an absolute and unavoidable conflict of interest, which is the source of class struggle; moreover, taking note that union organisation encourages solidarity, resistance and revolt in the economic area, beyond the preoccupations over [questions of] doctrine, and that it is the fundamental and specific organisation of the proletarian struggle against the bourgeoisie, and further that it is important that an ever more daring revolutionary spirit should direct the work of union organisations, towards the expropriation of the capitalism and the suppression of all forms of power; also that expropriation and taking possession of the instruments and produce of work can only be accomplished by the workers themselves. [Congress considers that:] The union is called on to transform itself into a productive force, and is already in [this] society the living germ of the society of tomorrow. [Congress] recommends that comrades from all countries engage themselves in an active participation in the autonomous movement of the working class, without losing perspective, keeping in mind that anarchist action is not contained entirely within the limits of the union, developing in unions the ideas of revolt, individual initiative and solidarity, which is the essence of anarchism.

The Nacht Monatte Motion countersigned by Fuss-Amoré, Dunois, Fabbri, Zelinska and Karl Walter. (Approved by 25 votes.)
The Anarchists meeting together in Amsterdam from the 26-31 August, declare: they consider that, in today's society, the expropriating general strike is a remarkable stimulant to organisation and the spirit of revolt,

and the form in which the emancipation of the proletariat may be achieved. The general strike should not be confused with the political general strike (*Politischer Massenstreik**), which is nothing other than an attempt, by politicians to turn the general strike away from its revolutionary and economic goals. Local, regional and trade general strikes will progressively uplift the working class, leading it towards the expropriating general strike, which will accomplish the destruction of this society, the expropriation of goods and of the means of production.

The Motion of R. Friedeberg (Approved by 36 votes to 6).
Class struggle and the emancipation of the proletariat is not identical with the ideas and aspirations of anarchism, which works – over and above the immediate aspirations of classes – for the moral and economic deliverance of the human personality, for an environment with no authority, and not for a new power, that of a majority over a minority. Nevertheless, anarchism considers the abolition of class oppression, and economic dependency of the majority of human beings as absolutely necessary and essential stage in the road towards its final aim. Anarchism must always oppose that the struggle for proletarian emancipation should be conducted by means which contradict anarchism, and which are an obstacle to the precise aim of this movement. So, it opposes conducting this struggle by those means advocated by Marxist socialism, that is to say by parliamentarianism, and by a corporatist union movement which looks only to the improvement of proletarian conditions. These two means can only facilitate the development of a new bureaucracy, of a more or less patent intellectual authority – leading to the oppression of the minority. Anarchist means for suppressing class oppression can be only those that emerge directly out of an affirmation of individual personality: 'direct action', and, 'the non-consenting individual', that is to say of an individualism that is active and passive, either of one person alone, or of a mass [inspired by] collective commitment. The Libertarian Communist Congress therefore rejects strikes for political rights (*Politischer Massenstreik*),† whose goal is unacceptable for anarchism, but recognises in the revolutionary economic general strike, or in other words, in the rejection of work by the whole proletariat as a class, the appropriate means for dismantling the economic structure of contemporary society and for the emancipation of the proletariat from the oppression of the wages system. The penetration of unions by the anarchist ideal must be

---

* A formulation much used by German Social-Democrats.
† Differing conceptions of strikes in Germany are discussed below.

considered as indispensable for the realisation of such a general strike. A union movement full of the anarchist spirit may, through the means of a revolutionary general strike, destroy class oppression opening the way towards the final goal of anarchism: the arrival of a society without any authority.[156]

Although it does not say so explicitly, the Cornelissen/Vohryzek/Malatesta resolution implied that big unions were unlikely to remain revolutionary – but that libertarians and revolutionaries should choose to work in them. The motion mentioned syndicates making economic demands and noted that general changes should come from armed insurrection overthrowing capitalism and the state. Were unions to manage 'economics' while the wider community armed itself and managed general or 'political' change?

The Dunois motion saw syndicates as 'the fundamental and specific organisation of the proletarian struggle against the bourgeoisie'. Syndicates had revolutionary potential. Even if anarchists had broader concerns and perspectives, unions needed no mentoring from the outside. No role is mentioned for revolutionary syndicalist groups. Nonetheless Dunois thought that anarchists might have an inspirational role. In a debate on anarchism and organisation he argued that anarchists in unions needed a support network outside, so that they did not feel abandoned: 'we wish to create this link, to provide this constant support; and I am personally convinced that our union activities cannot but benefit both in energy and in intelligence. And the stronger we are – and we will only become strong by organising ourselves – the stronger will be the flow of ideas that we can send through the workers' movement …'

Syndicates were proposed as the nexus for managing the society of the future, rather than parliaments or top-down bureaucracies. The Dunois motion might be read as an anticipation of 'anarcho-syndicalism' – if the priority was placed on 'the germ of the society of tomorrow'.

Some syndicalists were more go-ahead and would come to be defined by their overt opposition to other less radical forms of labour organisation. In contrast, the pre-war CGT model was one of unity, in one all-inclusive, all embracing confederation, avoiding overt splits between radicals and reformists, disregarding internal tensions. Other syndicalists would argue for not running too far ahead of, or beyond, the mass of union members; theirs would be a more cautious syndicalism. Such more cautious syndicalists easily became disenchanted with an anarchism that they viewed as extremist and exaggerated; and with the anarchism of older personalities who refused to see in syndicalism the key to social progress.

The Italian labour historian, Maurizio Antonioli writes: 'Amsterdam did not lead to the definitive liquidation of "traditional" anarchism as the syndicalist anarchists had hoped, in order that anarchism could regain its leading role in the process of the proletariat's emancipation.'[157] The resolutions that were passed no doubt reflected circumstances at the time – and particular pressures and concerns in particular places. No congress like Amsterdam was convened for many years, so, at an international level, the questions and nuances which arose there were debated only in the form of articles exchanged in the libertarian press. Some syndicalist anarchists would turn towards syndicalism and eventually communism. Maurizio Antonioli comments that Amsterdam was also a turning point in the sense of who organised with whom. Monatte went on to found *La Vie Ouvrière*, and found an initial nucleus of contributors among persons (Dunois, Fuss-Amoré and Léon Clément) who had been present in Amsterdam.

In November 1907 Malatesta wrote that organisations like the CGT, going under the name of revolutionary syndicalism, were a great advance. They sought to promote direct action by workers and to exclude bourgeois political influences, but nevertheless they contained 'elements of degeneration which have corrupted labour movements in the past'.[158] In the 1925-6 period Malatesta would write that he hoped anarchists 'should not want the unions to be anarchist', rather unions, so long as they were open to all, should be 'neutral', and 'anarchists [should] remain, *when they can*, within the largest possible groupings'.[159] But, it should be noted, circumstances in 1926 were rather different to those earlier. At this later point a concerted response to fascism was needed. Perhaps he had in mind these new circumstances and a timely wish to promote workers' unity, which might be weakened where unions were allied to one or another tendency.

The agenda of unions might vary, depending on timeliness, on the level of activity among working people and their readiness – or unreadiness – to adopt direct action, form assemblies and take control of struggles. So, for example, if a situation was hotter and radical change might be nearer, then a more radical agenda might be more appropriate. Perhaps the circumstances that obtained in Argentina in and around 1917, in Italy in 1920, and in Spain after July 1936 demanded sharper agendas, to help encourage forward movement. If one takes out of context – a statement such as this one, from Malatesta – 'A union, [one] that is revolutionary initially, because founded on revolution and composed of the most pugnacious minority of the most developed areas, *would become ever more moderate or reactionary, as it developed and expanded*.' – that statement* might appear to set out universal

---

* See below, page 117

and eternal tendencies, rather than timely judgements, fitting particular circumstances.

Debates at international meetings and congresses highlighted the viewpoints of libertarians and syndicalists, in particular circumstances, and locations. Differences of perspectives might be viewed not as a problem but as an advantage, if they helped highlight different aspects of a problem and thereby facilitated solutions. Libertarian organisational norms, respecting autonomy, might better facilitate the emergence a set of complex solutions rather than one generalised solution, as was sometimes prescribed by leaders shaped by a Jacobin or Marxist tradition.

Returning to the Amsterdam Congress, its agenda also included discussion of education, a world language, alcoholism, literature, religion, the role of the individual, the 1905 revolution in Russia, militarism – issues of gender seemed not to have been discussed.[160]

A resolution against militarism proclaimed that comrades should revolt and refuse to serve in its armed forces: army, navy, or police:

> We engage our comrades, and all those who aspire to freedom generally, to struggle as circumstances and temperament allows, by every means: by individual revolt, by individual and collective refusal of [military] service, by passive and active disobedience and by military non-compliance; and by the root and branch destruction of instruments of domination. We express the hope that the people of all countries affected by a declaration of war will respond with insurrection, proclaiming our belief that anarchists will set the example.[161]

Anti-militarists attempted, with limited success, to build an international campaign against war. They had some impact in Italy, the Netherlands and France, perhaps among students and young people, who were motivated to revolt against being compelled to spend years in the armed forces.

Meetings in and around the Anarchist congress had implications for future exchanges between syndicalists. Cornelissen was made responsible for setting up a press bureau to exchange news and opinion on international union developments. This continued to function until 1915. The *Bulletin international du mouvement syndicaliste* which he edited was financed by European syndicalists, with occasional contributions from the IWW.[162] (In the years that followed translations of the writings of Cornelissen[163] – and of other French syndicalists – would influence the development of new movements in Italy, Spain, Portugal, Russia and Scandinavia.) The congress also took steps to set up a five-person international anarchist bureau, with diverse responsibilities: for correspondence, to maintain archives, and for liaison with individuals and organisations. Errico Malatesta, Rudolf Rocker, Alexander Schapiro, John Turner and Jean Wilquet were appointed to this bureau, which survived until 1911.[164] Thirteen issues of a *Bulletin de l'Internationale anarchiste* were published between 1908 and 1910.

The Amsterdam Congress also agreed to call for solidarity with workers and the revolution in Russia. One detailed report on events was delivered in Russian and published in *Les Temps Nouveaux* under the signatures of Orlovsky and Rogdaev.[165] Anarchist groups, it reported, had formed only recently so that when events began in 1905 anarchists were weak and were able to make their presence felt only in a few places. They worked with others to accomplish the destruction of Tsarist autocracy, although they had no wish to see a new provisional revolutionary government or some democratic republic arise in its place. 'Because, indeed, one cannot fight capitalism without demolishing its watchdog – the State' – they strove towards a broader goal, social revolution. The report mentioned activity in many cities and regions: Moscow and St Petersburg, the (now Polish) city of Bialystok, Ekaterinoslav (now Dnepropetrovsk) and Zhytomyr in the Ukraine, and in the Caucasus.

Anarchists had organised defence units in the face of government attacks on Jews and had campaigned against racial animosity. Innumerable 'isolated political terrorist acts' also took place – against various government agents. Many of those killed were known for being especially cruel in their own areas. In Ekaterinoslav in three months of the summer of 1906, anarchists killed or wounded thirty spies, Cossacks and police agents; such acts made an impact and some police agents resigned. Bombs were used in Vilnius (Lithuania), Warsaw, St Petersburg and many other cities against police and government targets.

There were also many urban economic struggles in which anarchists played a part, for example the report mentions that anarchists organised mass expropriations of food when a mass textile workers' strike resulted in widespread hunger in Bialystok. Bombs were thrown against managers who refused to concede demands. Sabotage was frequently used. In Warsaw vitriol was thrown to damage textiles and petrol to ruin foodstuffs. Bombs were placed to stop the trams running in the course of a strike in Riga (Latvia). There were also individual attacks on sundry members of the bourgeoisie – not because some persons targeted were notoriously bad, but principally because of their position as members of that class. In one village in the Caucasus a peasant commune was established.

New traditions were created or reasserted – of collective armed resistance, as had previously been promoted by *Narodnaya Volya* (Peoples' Will) populists. There were innumerable acts of armed resistance – both collective and individual. The number and spread of anarchist expropriations was remarkable. Other tendencies imitated anarchists, especially Maximalists and Polish socialists. Occasionally printing workshops were seized long enough to print leaflets. Anarchists also organised prison escapes. A hundred anarchists died in armed confrontations. Sixty more, well-known in labour circles, had been executed – but the full total was not known exactly. Similar numbers had been condemned to hard labour.

Although this report discussed action by collectives it did not comment much on the particular forms of various collective. Unions were organised, but what was most distinctive was the formation of Soviets. Where Soviets were non-party assemblies they were widely praised. (The executive committee of the St Petersburg Soviet, however, voted to exclude anarchists).[166] Anarchists were hostile to Social-Democratic party-run soviets. 'Many of the councils, in fact, became true representatives of labor during the heady days of 1905.' Syndicalists approved of Soviets such as these and saw them as akin to *bourses du travail*. Anarchist-communists were not impressed by syndicalists – they were seen as 'legal anarchists'.[167] Violent struggles continued – with individuals taking matters into their own hands although sometimes using party political labels. '… open struggles between revolution and reaction mostly take the form of individual acts, individual acts in terms of activity of course, because they arise most often from the decisions of groups and parties.'[168] Subsequently an epidemic of lock-outs was reported – an attempt by management to recover from and reverse any gains won over the previous two years. Thousands were being condemned to hunger and unemployment.

Rogdaev wrote later that workers were responding to this challenge: 'Faced with locks-out which condemn them to new suffering – famine, prostitution, begging – they respond with a mass or individual anti-bourgeois terror.' Rogdaev spoke of workers advancing towards a social revolution ignoring the appeals of Social-Democratic and other parties. Although he concluded one article with a question – as to how soon the Gordion knot might be cut – he seemed to be suggesting that there were high hopes for change in the near future.[169]

Controversies over the use of 'legal' or 'terror' tactics continued and would affect developments in 1917. There were no opportunities for such matters to be discussed before an international audience in the Amsterdam congress, and no other international anarchist congress came close to meeting other than the ill-fated and abortive congress of 1914.

6
SPAIN

Syndicalism had a long history in Spain. It has been said that 'the CNT was not merely "founded", it developed organically out of the Catalan Workers' Solidarity …' and the remnants that survived from the First International in local and trade organisations.[170] This *Confederación Nacional del Trabajo*, (CNT, National Confederation of Labour) developed through the coalescence of a range of newer and older workers' organisations in Barcelona between 1907 and 1910. An older UGT union had been unable to take root there. The new CNT soon began to offer a different set of priorities and practices contrasting with the reformism of the Second International. James Baer writes that the formation of the CNT drew some inspiration from Argentina – so, international experience from the Americas could influence movements in Europe.[171] Many Spanish workers emigrated to the Americas in the early decades of the twentieth century, so there was some interaction between movements across the seas.

The CNT organised in workplaces and communities. Supporters were also invited to educational activities. Its hostility towards alcoholism and commitment to educational work are evidence of its broad modernistic spirit, which encompassed cultural as well as 'political' values, competing with and offering an alternative to reactionary Catholicism. Libertarians sought to teach through experience: 'We will learn how to live in libertarian communism by living in it.'[172]

Although its practice was nowhere near perfect in this respect, it allowed some challenges to gender oppression. The first CNT congress called for equal wages for men and women, also recognising that when a working woman returned home, often, 'instead of rest she came up against another bourgeois: her *compañero*, who calmly expects her to take care of all domestic work'.[173]

There was also a network of co-operatives that orbited the CNT. Experience with co-ops might facilitate change in the future. José Prat made some critical comments about them in 1900:

And the proletariat has to work: firstly, through its trade unions to fight class interests that oppose social progress, and then to establish by means of co-operation the foundations of a new society. It is true that co-operation, as it is today incarnated in workers' co-ops is far from that which one might want for the new society but it is the germ of one, despite all the failings that arise out of its social environment. It does not resolve problems in their entirety, it does not produce a harmony of interests, nor the good life, nor can it win through to that, because the monetary impulse, competition, property, etc., transform it into a commercial concern like any other. Co-ops may become [somewhat] bourgeois – shutting themselves off from the collective ideal of comprehensive socialisation. Already the co-operative foundation has been invented, the push towards free co-operation has been launched, a basis for a new society – the model of how a new society might function has been primed.

Workers' co-ops cannot fight against bourgeois capital. Given their existence as a society of workers' capital – the benefits of which can extend only to members – co-ops limit the practice of solidarity. But the worker is educated; he learns administration, the running of production and the distribution of goods without tutors and without a class of directors.[174]

Spain lost its last major colonies, Cuba and the Philippines, in 1898, in a war with the USA, but it retained large territories in North Africa. Spanish anarchists refused to support these colonial wars – they were widely seen as tyrannical. Some Spanish libertarians supported the work of the Anti-Militarist International.[175] The CNT was banned when it approved a resolution calling for a general strike to protest against colonial wars. Working people in Spain were urged to ask why their sons should be sent off to fight in the colonies, while the sons of their rulers stayed at home.

There was little respect for a decrepit state that used men as cannon fodder in colonial wars. A military setback in Morocco, became the occasion for a 'tragic week' in July 1909. The city of Barcelona was taken over and barricades were built. Workers confronted the forces of reaction: army, church and state. A hundred or so people were killed in state-terror reprisals by the 'forces of order'; another two or three thousand were imprisoned.

Francisco Ferrer, a libertarian educator, was found morally responsible for these troubles. He had been living in France, and had no connection with these events, but was made a scapegoat by the church and state. He was executed in October. Emma Goldman wrote that 'had he [Ferrer] hurled a hundred bombs, he could not have been so dangerous to the Catholic church and to despotism, as with his opposition to discipline ...' Defending progressive values threatened order and for these reasons, he had to die.[176] He became a victim of a backward-looking Catholicism that felt threatened by democracy, modernism and all manner of new things. Freethinkers viewed his execution as an anti-clerical martyrdom and built a coalition of protest with liberals and socialists, who ordinarily would have little sympathy for anarchism. In the protests that followed on from his execution the church was portrayed as a reactionary assassin. In Rome, the Vatican had to be surrounded by armed forces to keep angry crowds at bay. Protest demonstrations, strikes and meetings were held in Algeria, Amsterdam, Antwerp, Berlin, Buenos Aires, Brussels, Chicago, Geneva, Ghent, Lisbon, London, Milan, Montevideo, Naples, New York, Paris, Prague, Río de Janeiro, Santiago (Chile), St Petersburg, Sheffield, Trieste, Vienna and elsewhere. While Ferrer the man was killed, something of his spirit survived in Ferrer schools that blossomed in many countries with support from libertarians and free thinkers. Thousands of radicals left Spain, some 600 anarchists settled in for France.[177]

In Spain, the life of the CNT was punctuated by efforts to engage, confront, radicalise or master its rival, the UGT union, linked to the Spanish Socialist Party. In 1910, the CNT congress adopted policies on the general strike similar to those of the French CGT. It reacted critically against a reformism that privileged skilled workers and noted: 'it is not possible to abolish privileges with organisations in which privilege exists.'[178] The CNT also faced episodic repression – with syndicate offices closed and its press banned; for three years from 1911 it was unable to operate in public, but it re-emerged and expanded after 1914 becoming larger than its UGT rival.

7
ARGENTINA AFTER 1907

Libertarians were the leading current in the labour movement throughout Latin America before the First World War, and for some years thereafter. Radical syndicalists campaigned for the eight-hour day, using partial and general strikes to press for their demands. The eight-hour day was first conceded in particular trades and regions: to carpenters in Paraguay in 1905; to some trades in São Paulo in 1907, to day labourers in Callao (Peru), in 1913; and later enacted into law, in Ecuador and Uruguay in 1915-6, in Mexico in 1917, and in Peru in 1918.

In 1909 forces commanded by police chief Ramón Lorenzo Falcón, killed twelve workers celebrating May Day in Buenos Aires. A 'Red Week' of protests followed, with further repression of protests and the destruction of left and anarchist printing presses. That year the largest strike, organised by the FORA, brought out 220,000 workers. Eight persons were killed and many more wounded in the course of a transport workers' strike in Buenos Aires. Strikes might take on aspects of mass counter-cultural festival with music and celebration, all part and parcel of a labour counter-power.[179] Strikes were also viewed as 'schools of rebellion'. There was also a spontaneous strike of some 20,000 workers in Buenos Aires later in the year, over the judicial murder of Ferrer. Many Ferrer memorial schools were formed. Some of these networks were quite extensive – for example, in Uruguay some thirty *Centros de Estudios Sociales* were created. FORA supporters helped support a network of rationalist schools and educational facilities.

There were periods in Argentina in which labour centres, bookshops and print-works were attacked and destroyed, but despite repression, the movement was able to revive, rebuild, and sustain some strength over a thirty-year period. In November 1909, Simón Radowitzky, a FORA supporter acting on his own initiative, carried out a reprisal killing of Falcón. He was sentenced to indefinite imprisonment. There were ongoing campaigns for his release.

In 1910, there were more violent confrontations with the Argentinean state, coinciding with celebrations for the centenary of the war of independence. Anarchists reshaped the national anthem: they substituted a call for 'anarchy and solidarity' to replace the call for 'freedom, freedom' of its third verse. In the same spirit, Easter was recast as the Red or Labour Festival. That same year the morning libertarian paper, *La Protesta*, became a daily, complimented by an evening paper *La Batalla*. Such influence was demonstrated in events such as May Day; in Buenos Aires crowds in tens of thousands were attracted to anarchist celebrations, significantly more than the rival socialist events (in 1910, the centenary year of the Argentine state, 70,000 came, and *La Protesta* doubled its print-run to 16,000 copies).

In 1912, new legislation gave the vote to male Argentine citizens. Two-thirds of the adult population, however, immigrants, who formed between a third and a half of the population, and all women were still disregarded. Immigrants – some of them activists seeking to escape persecution in their native countries– faced deportation in times of trouble.

A syndicalist tendency developed in the Socialist Party, and later re-focused activity towards workplace organisations. In 1914, the FORA Federal Council commented that every labour body might be admitted that was in agreement with its pact of solidarity. It declared libertarian communism – as set out at its 5th congress – as an end-goal and a means of propaganda. But this was not an imposition, and affiliated bodies had freedom to propagate it (or not).

The FORA developed a distinctive organisational pattern – organising in and beyond the workplace, promoting a broad, hegemonic project. A distinct specific or political libertarian organisation was viewed as unnecessary. It supported calls to re-establish the First International,* and plans were set out for a South American congress in Montevideo – or Buenos Aires – as a step towards that goal. In 1913, the FORA sent envoys to Peru to support the formation of a Regional Workers' Federation of Peru (FORP). The FORP, like FORA, 'espoused the principles and goals of anarchism and syndicalism and was committed to both short term improvements and social revolution.'[180] Peru had had its first general strike in 1911, with textile workers obtaining the suppression of night work. Some unions in particular trades (e.g. bakers) had a greater resilience than national structures.

---

* Organisations like the FORA emerged in Bolivia, Paraguay, Peru and Uruguay. The FORA had planned and prepared a continental congress in 1910. Government repression – a state of siege – prevented the congress taking place.

8

THE INDUSTRIAL WORKERS OF THE WORLD

The IWW was based in the USA, but had an international influence and was a multilingual body. Bill Haywood set out twelve differences between the IWW and the American Federation of Labor (AFL), one of them being that:

> the AFL in all of its branches stands ready to divide against itself and enter into contracts and agreements with the employing class, thus dividing labor's great force into smaller groups or sections. The Industrial Workers of the World recognize that these contracts are the death warrants of labor. No time agreement has ever been entered into by any part of the organization. The settlement of any difficulty between the workers and the employing class is but an armed truce.[181]

The IWW advocated organisation on the basis of industry rather than craft, and had a greater degree of centralisation than obtained in European radical syndicalist organisations where decentralisation was common. It also articulated a critique of bureaucratic union organisation:

> [I]f you look to labor leadership to solve your problems, the outcome is large union office buildings, with larger desks and larger swivel chairs, presumably with even larger and larger labor leaders occupying them. If you look to the joint action of yourself and your fellow workers to cope with your problems, you move forward with time into situations where steadily you and they cut a larger role in life ... We think it means a powerful lot of difference what means you select, not only for the here and now but for the generations to follow.[182]

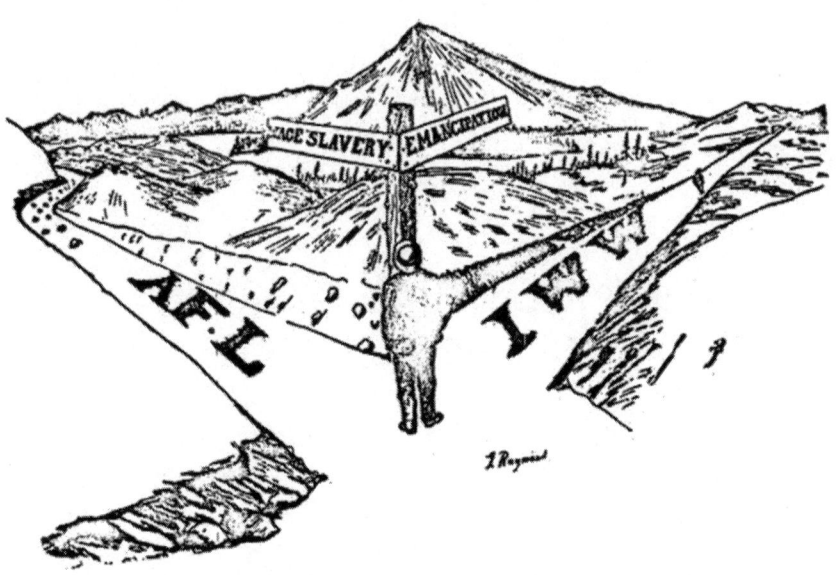

AT THE FORK OF THE ROADS

Attention to linguistic and community affinities was evident in IWW organisation, for example, in 1912, in a textile strike in Lawrence, Massachusetts, the strike committee was organised to draw in representation from diverse communities and language groups, with each community being represented on the committee.[183] The song *Bread and Roses* recalls these struggles and a short-lived victory in 1912 of striking women:

> As we go marching, marching, in the beauty of the day,
> A million darkened kitchens, a thousand mill lofts grey,
> Are touched with all the radiance that a sudden sun discloses,
> For the people hear us singing: Bread and Roses! Bread and Roses!
> As we go marching, marching, we battle too for men,
> For they are women's children, and we mother them again.
> Our lives shall not be sweated from birth until life closes;
> Hearts starve as well as bodies; give us bread, but give us roses.

The IWW challenged the racism found in much of the labour movement, organising black and white Americans together. One inspirational IWW leaders was Benjamin Harrison Fletcher (1890-1949), a black dock worker who managed to promote a waterfront union in Philadelphia. It had to confront AFL labour 'fakirs' and police forces using violence – ready to murder whites, and hating black unionised labour most of all. In 1919 the IWW published a pamphlet, *Justice for the Negro*, highlighting frequent lynchings and saying that the IWW was 'not a white man's union, not a black man's union ... but a working man's union. All the working class in one big union'.[184] It adopted the old motto that 'an injury to one is an injury to all'; it aspired to ensure that 'in the IWW the colored worker, man or woman, is on an equal footing with every other worker ...' Eugene Debs, a prominent IWW supporter, was a remarkable leader, eloquent in his advocacy of industrial unionism and passionate in his condemnation of racism:

> For myself, my heart goes to the Negro and I make no apology to any white man for it. In fact, when I see the poor, brutalized, outraged black victim, I feel a burning sense of guilt for his intellectual poverty and moral debasement that makes me blush for the unspeakable crimes committed by my own race.[185]

In the USA migrants and non-citizens attracted to the IWW were particularly vulnerable.[186] An IWW membership card could be represented as a ticket for deportation from the USA.[187] The IWW organised children – if they were old enough to work, they were old enough to join the IWW.

The IWW published routinely in twelve to fifteen languages to cater for and organise a diverse labour constituency in North America, and this press also circulated further afield.[188] Migrants carried the IWW model back to their homelands and elsewhere. IWW ideas impacted in surprising places. The preamble to the IWW constitution, advocating workplace organisation and the development of industrial democracy, was used in many countries. As revised at the fourth IWW convention of September 1908 it read:

> The working class and the employing class have nothing in common. There can be no peace so long as hunger and want are found among millions of working people and the few, who make up the employing class, have all the good things of life. Between these two classes a struggle must go on until the workers of the world organize as a class, take possession of the earth and the machinery of production, and abolish the wage system. We find that the centering of the management of industries into fewer and fewer hands makes the trade-unions unable to cope with the ever-growing power of the employing class. The trade-unions foster a state of affairs which allows one set of workers to be pitted against another set of workers in the same industry, thereby helping to defeat one another in wage wars. Moreover, the trade-unions aid the employing class to mislead

the workers into belief that the working class have interests in common with their employers. These conditions can be changed and the interest of the working class upheld only by an organization formed in such a way that all its members in any one industry, or in all industries, if necessary, cease work whenever a strike or lockout is on in any department thereof, thus making an injury to one an injury to all. Instead of the conservative motto, 'A fair day's wages for a fair day's work', we must inscribe on our banner the revolutionary watchword, 'Abolition of the wage system'. It is the historic mission of the working class to do away with capitalism. The army of production must be organized, not only for the everyday struggle with the capitalists, but also to carry on production when capitalism shall have been overthrown. By organizing industrially, we are forming the structure of the new society within the shell of the old.

The IWW had some affiliates in Australasia and Latin America, and some influence in Southern Africa in the Industrial and Commercial Workers Union (ICU).[189]

When revolution broke out in Mexico many IWW members took the side of the revolutionaries and sided with the rebels associated with the anarchist Ricardo Flores Magón. Eugene Debs did not. He once opined patronisingly that 'Mexicans were too ignorant to fight for freedom ...'.[190] Jean Grave, also doubted the libertarian credentials of the Liberal Party, and a polemic commenced in the French libertarian press.[191]

9
GERMANY

Germany was a rapidly changing society in the era before the First World War. A patchwork of small states had come together in an imperial Reich, and rapid industrialisation was drawing people from rural to urban areas and from agriculture to mining and industry. Bismarck, the Iron Chancellor, who dominated the state until 1890, had persecuted the labour movement and trade unions, but in subsequent years the Social-Democratic Party (SPD) and its trade unions allies obtained a measure of tolerance from the state. Jean Grave wrote that Social-Democrats might have managed to dragoon three million voters to support Bebel, Liebknecht and their consorts instead of Bismarck, but all that had happened was that they had substituted one idol or Messiah for another, they had not changed voters' mentality, in effect change was equated with having new leaders in power.[192]

Unions were best able to organise where skilled labour had some scarcity-value; here unions could have some weight, but in mines and in other sectors of large scale production, unions were very weak, and often employers – helped by police forces – worked to inhibit their organisation. There was limited waged work for women – especially for young women and for some widows – but after marriage many women worked only in the home. The labour movement was stronger in the north and weaker in many rural, southern and Catholic areas. The organisations and ideas of labourism and liberalism might be confused in such areas.

Social-Democracy and its critics

Voting was the easiest way to express dissidence in Imperial Germany. Candidates for legislatures did better where coalitions were built, so pressure grew to fashion electoral pacts and coalitions between workers, artisans, traders and professionals. Radicals might view SPD politics as being left-liberal rather than socialist, neglecting the interests of parts of the labour movement. In the era of Bismarck, repression fostered some solidarity between radicals and reformists. After 1890, radicals of various sorts, especially youth, became discontented with labour passivity, and promoted alternatives. Internal conflicts developed.

Friedrich Engels wrote of the Social-Democrats that 'the two million voters whom they send to the ballot box, together with the young men and women who stand behind them as non-voters, form *the most numerous, most compact mass, the decisive shock force of the international proletarian army*'. He went on to hope that 'we shall grow into the decisive power in the land, before which all other powers will have to bow, whether they like it or not'.[193] The Social-Democratic press grew and had a combined circulation figure of over one million, but this left many working people beyond SDP influence.

August Bebel, a veteran Social-Democrat leader, opposed deploying the Social-Democratic 'shock force' to oppose warmongering. He argued in 1906, that any mass strike called to resist war would bring only military rule over all Germany, and that such talk was empty-headedness.[194] In debates on opposing and preventing war, he warned against direct action that might draw the attention of the state; he thought any action that promoted desertion from the armed forces would be harmful to the spread of socialism. The SPD leadership agreed to hinder any discussion of the general strike.[195] Bebel also justified a preference for centralised organisation with the argument that capital was concentrating and that a concentrated workers' response was needed, something that localism could not achieve.[196]

Karl Kautsky, a leading Social-Democrat theorist, also stressed unity and discipline: 'The social revolution requires high intelligence, strict discipline and complete organisation of the great mass and these must exist simultaneously with and be indispensable to economic life if it is to attain strength to overcome so powerful an opponent.' He wrote that the process of struggle against capital and the pressure of capital itself were together creating a talent for organisation and 'discipline in every way... it is only through the unanimous co-operation of the great body of mankind that the proletariat can assert itself against capital and the capitalist state.'[197] Kautsky disregarded the diversity that was a facet of the German labour movement.

Gustav Landauer wrote that there was no real democracy in the trade unions or in the SPD; both were characterised by demagogy and bureaucracy.[198] Rudolf Rocker commented that this singular discipline was excessive and doubly dangerous.[199]

Experience came to suggest that Engels' prognosis that there was an electoral and parliamentary road to socialism was inaccurate. For example, in France, Alexandre Millerand was one of the first socialists to become a minister; he was instrumental in deploying the army to break the 1910 railway workers' strike. (Louis Lecoin, then an army recruit, later a prominent anarchist, refused orders to help break this strike and was imprisoned for six months.)

In Germany, young radicals accused the SPD of preferring small reforms rather than wholesale change. They evolved towards libertarian politics and began organising outside the SPD. Some were expelled from the SPD: Rudolf Rocker in 1890, Dr Raphael Friedeberg in 1907, others, like Fritz Kater, left in 1908. Radical activists faced the prospect of imprisonment for agitation, the circulation of banned literature, or for refusing military service. Rudolf Rocker saw friends being sentenced to terms of two to nine years. He viewed the army as a body that 'suffocated every feeling of resistance and which transformed living men into dead machines'. He left Germany to see the wider world, forgoing training in mass murder.[200]

The 'free' trade unions – allied with the SPD[*] – chose to work within the law, notably within the terms of reference of legislation that set out that trade-unions operating on a national level should refrain from discussing and organising around political issues. This prohibition was not applied to local workers' organisations. A minority of trade unionists – 'localists' – preferred local organisation particularly since it facilitated some wider opportunities to engage in politics. There were also objections to centralised, national contract negotiations. A minority began to adopt syndicalism, stressing direct action and the general strike.

The Localists and the 'Free' unions

In 1901 localists formed the *Freie Vereinigung deutscher Gewerkschaften* (Free Union of German Trade Unions, FVdG). Friedeberg was a prominent member. The FVdG brought together many skilled workers: jewellery workers, masons, carpenters and makers of musical instruments, with some concentration in Berlin. The FVdG became advocates of the general strike, earning the ire of the leaders of the 'free' *Generalkommission* trade unions. Friedeberg was largely isolated at the 1903 SPD congress when he proposed discussion of the general strike as a step towards a socialist revolution. In the following year, the FVdG observed that the separation between politics and economics, between the SDP party and the trade unions, had led to a growing neutrality in the unions, a neutrality that impeded class struggle.[201]

One historian saw the German labour movement as 'more like a fraternal

---

[*] There were three major trade-union centres in Germany. The *Hirsch-Dunckerschen Gewerkvereinen* were somewhat liberal, the *Christlichen Gewerkschaften*, were largely Catholic and the 'Free' (Social-Democratic) unions were united by the *Generalkommission der Gewerkschaften Deutschlands*, founded in 1890.

society than a fighting force',²⁰² a huge contrast with Engels' image of a Social-Democratic 'shock force'. Arnold Roller, an anarchist journalist, called Social-Democrat labour leaders professional collaborators and sleep-inducing-hypnotists,²⁰³ suffocating the revolutionary spirit in Germany. Roller believed that the general strike would arise naturally, as smaller strikes grew and spread. He looked forward to a social revolution, with unions taking production into their own hands.* Otto Rühle, later a left communist, commented that through the priority afforded to insurance 'the class struggle character of the organisation is systematically undermined ...' and that most trade unions had become, 'the most loyal shield-bearers of the bourgeois class ...'²⁰⁴ Many if not most trade union leaders opposed general strikes, arguing that they needed 'peace' to develop their organisations. Rosa Luxemburg, on the left of the SPD, thought the base of the movement was animated by healthy class struggle instincts – even in slow moving times. She castigated radicals for 'schoolboy errors'. She argued in her book, *The Mass Strike*, that when workers chose to join the 'Free' *Generalkommission* trade unions, instead of Catholic or 'apolitical' Hirsch-Dunker unions, workers made a choice for modern class struggle. She wrote:

> ... the enormous strides taken by the labour movement in *all capitalist countries* during the last 25 years are the most convincing evidence of the value of the tactics of political struggle, which was insisted upon by Marx and Engels in opposition to Bakuninism; and *German Social-Democracy, in its position of vanguard of the entire international labour movement* is, not the least, the direct product of the consistent and energetic application of these tactics.²⁰⁵

She wrote that 'the historical career of Anarchism is well-nigh ended'.²⁰⁶ This was not how things turned out in the aftermath of the Russian Revolution: 'the first time in years, anarchist speakers appeared on [German] Socialist platforms by invitation.'²⁰⁷

Although they differed in the matter of what mechanism would bring it about, both Luxemburg and Roller shared rosy expectations for change. Subsequent events suggested that their hopes that class struggle would soon bring great changes were somewhat misplaced. The leaders of the 'free' *Generalkommission* trade unions and SPD had no use for a general strike. Trade union leaders had insisted that the party should take financial

---

* A pamphlet on the *Social General Strike* by Arnold Roller (alias Siegried Nacht) had a wide circulation in and after 1905, circulating in translation as far away as Japan. Roller also wrote an anti-militarist text – a *Soldiers' Breviary*, or handbook

responsibility for the costs of any strike action, something which the SPD was not prepared to contemplate. Bebel used socialist rhetoric and contemplated the possible use of the general strike in some emergency, but the SPD leadership had an understanding that the general strike or any other form of sustained illegal activity was impractical. Karl Legien articulated the views of many union leaders in describing general strikes as 'general nonsense'.[208] Union leaders said the general strike was too sharp a weapon, and that one should not allow 'children' to play with sharp knives. (A formulation that says something about the paternalist attitude of union leaders.) Resolutions passed by a 'free' *Generalkommission* trade union congress meeting in Cologne emphasised the weight of conservative thinking. The congress resolved to oppose the general strike. It even sought to prevent any discussion of these ideas:

> all attempts to set up a definite line of tactics by preaching the political general strike should be repudiated; it recommends the organised workers to resist such attempts energetically. The congress regards the general strike as it is represented by Anarchists and people without any experience in the sphere of economic struggle, as beneath consideration; it warns the workers not to let the acceptance and circulation of such ideas distract them from detailed daily work of strengthening their trade organisations.[209]

Les Temps nouveaux reported on the Mannheim party congress of 1906. It noted the 'socialist pontiff', Bebel, had set out that the way of revolution through a general strike was not for the SPD. Bebel conceded that there might be an eventuality for a revolutionary struggle if the government attacked 'universal suffrage', otherwise – for example in the event of war – it would be a utopian folly. Rosa Luxemburg rose and asserted that this was just what French [CGT] had resolved on, for such an event. Furthermore, added this article, such a resolution was already 38 years old, it had had first been endorsed in Brussels, in September 1868, by the International Workers Association.[210] Bebel's reference to universal suffrage was telling – it suggested that the SPD leaders believed that it was just a matter of time before the fruits of their patience would deliver SPD domination. Subsequent events might suggest that such a prospect was never on the cards, given that a majority in one parliamentary chamber did not provide power over the diverse levers of the polity, society or economy. Moreover 'universal suffrage' did not exist – what the SPD enjoyed was an unequal right for male citizens to elect deputies in one chamber of the German state – a very circumscribed and limited right, and one that disregarded the interests of non-citizens and women.

James Guillaume commented, in early 1907, that he saw in debates in Germany on the relationship between unions, socialism and the state a reprise of what had been seen earlier, in 1872; once again socialism was engendering two tendencies – one that was bourgeois, parliamentary, democratic, reformist or, one might say, conservative; another that was a workers' tendency, syndicalist and truly revolutionary.[211] The first looked for an extension of democracy, something that would result only in a socialism of the state, a caricature; the second was anti-statist. About this time, in France, Bakunin was hailed as a syndicalist before the fact. Guillaume went on to publish a six-volume anthology of Bakunin's writings and a four-volume anthology of texts and documents on the First International in the years after the Amsterdam congress [212]

Rosa Luxemburg denounced opportunist SDP tendencies in her pamphlet *The Mass Strike*, but there was no effective challenge within the Social-Democratic movement to the rightist tendencies of the 'free' *Generalkommission* union leaders, or to their allies in the SPD.[213] It was indicative of the way the wind was blowing that localists were expelled from the SPD while rightists were not. Such expulsions symbolised that the party was not open to rethinking its general position. Some areas of debate were off-limits; any practical discussion of revolutionary tactics might result in expulsions.

Looking back some years later, another leftist, Karl Korsch, suggested that SPD critics (he had in mind Luxemburg, and other left figures, Lenin included) misdirected their criticisms of the Second International. In Korsch's view it was not just the thinking of SPD's revisionists – Eduard Bernstein and co-thinkers – that undermined socialism; it was the everyday practice of the labour movement. Georges Sorel, writing years earlier, criticised social relations within the German labour movement:

> ... Bernstein saw quite plainly that the dictatorship of the proletariat corresponds to a division of society into masters and servants, but it is curious that he did not perceive that the idea of the political strike (which he now to a certain extent accepts) is connected in the closest manner with the dictatorship of the proletariat which he fears. The men who had managed to organise the proletariat in the form of an army, ever ready to obey their orders, would be the generals who would set up a state of siege in a vanquished society; we should therefore have, on the day following the revolution, a dictatorship exercised by these politicians who in the society of today already form a compact group.[214]

Sorel was suggesting that the organisational structure of the labour movement – a relationship of masters and servants – was antithetical to its socialist purpose. Change – socialist change at least – could not be directed by generals.[215] Both Sorel and Kautsky viewed the labour movement as a school of a sort, promoting a new socialist culture; but between them there was some difference of emphasis. For Kautsky, workers had little or no leisure, and hence technology and culture tended to come to them from the bourgeoisie* and through the mediation of the party. For Sorel and the CGT, working people needed to fashion new social relations for themselves.

There were attitudes and characteristics that set the FVdG at odds with the centralised *Generalkommission* trade unions. The FVdG had a federalist structure, with autonomous local unions. Local structures controlled funds and might launch strikes. FVdG comrades practiced mutual solidarity, promoting offensive struggles; they articulated class interests, promoted direct action – strikes and sympathy action. They criticised militarism and worked to undermine capitalism, promoting mass and general strikes.[216]

These FVdG norms challenged prevailing social culture – indeed the FVdG saw the 'free' *Generalkommission* trade unions as part and parcel of that culture. Authoritarian and hierarchical organisational forms were present in school, in the church and in the workplace; these norms were reproduced (and not challenged) in the centralised 'free' *Generalkommission* trade unions. These unions might work to defend pay and conditions in the workplace, but were content – even proud – to accept a subordinate status; they were the Non-Commissioned Officers of a state directed by an officer class. Consequently, no radical change was possible, so long as the 'free' trade unions embraced their NCO status, managing labour in an orderly manner.

In 1906, the localists' fortnightly newspaper revealed details of a secret entente reached by the SPD and the trade union leaders. Behind the backs of their members these leaders had agreed among themselves to obstruct discussion of a general strike. When their entente was revealed these leaders were embarrassed but resolved to denounce their critics and obtain revenge. Luxemburg, in her speech at the Mannheim SPD Congress of September 1906, had defended anarchists, arguing that since no rightists or revisionists had been expelled, none of the far left should be expelled either; no one should be expelled for their opinions. After 1908 membership of localist trade unions became grounds for expulsion from the SPD. Many longstanding members of the SPD, members who had chosen to support localist unions, members who believed that the free *Generalkommission* unions

---

* Such themes were also present in Lenin's *What is to be done?* Lenin relied on Kautsky and his theories for over a decade, breaking with him, partially, only after 1914.

had given up on class struggle, were now expelled from their party.[217] A few FVdG members were offered, and took permanent paid positions as officials in *Generalkommission* unions. As something of an anomaly, some FVdG members remained in the SPD (and later in the USPD and KPD).

Pierre Ramus, who lived for many years in Austria, set out perspectives on the general strike and labour tactics in a work published in 1910. He condemned the parliamentary tactic as a waste of energy and failed to develop workers' power.[218] He argued that it was through direct action, as in the general strike, that solidarity and workers' power was promoted. The general strike was not in itself the revolution, but it was a means to an end. The political mass strike (*Politische Massenstreik*) advocated by Rosa Luxemburg and her co-thinkers might have placed the economic power of the organised proletariat in the service of a parliamentarianism long recognised as totally bankrupt.[219] Franz Pfemfert – the editor of *Die Aktion* – criticised Luxemburg for her loyalty to Social-Democracy.[220]

The leaders of the 'free' *Generalkommission* trade unions initiated a campaign of character assassination against their libertarian critics, denouncing the FVdG as a discussion club for anarchists and sowers of confusion.[221] These measures halved the membership of the localist movement, which fell from 17,000 to 9,000. They lost the affiliation of the Berlin masons. The organisation also suffered from frequent attacks against its newspaper: the names of responsible persons changed frequently in the face of repeated state prosecution targeting editors as subversives.

Localists drew inspiration from events and movements in France and elsewhere,[222] but relations between the localists and the French CGT were not very close. In 1911, some CGT functionaries travelled to Berlin for a study tour. They encountered the solidity – even some luxury – in the establishments of the SPD and their union allies; they also joined a FVdG demonstration. Jouhaux asked why the latter did not work with the former in a mass movement. Fritz Kater thought it was impossible to work within the SPD movement: federalism was incompatible with centralism, the union bureaucracy was too entrenched, and resorted to intimidation and expulsions. The FVdG had adopted another approach, not the conciliation practiced by the CGT in these years, but rather ideological criticism and confrontation.[223]

A small anarchist movement had evolved out of the SDP back in the 1880s inspired by Johann Most, a rebel SDP-turned-anarchist. This tendency published *Neues Leben* (New Life), from 1897. It evolved into the *Anarchistische Föderation Deutschlands* (German Anarchist Federation, AFD) in 1903. It had at best some 500 members. It propagated the idea of a social general strike and worked for a labour-led social revolution, but it left it to members to decide whether they should join the FvDG or the 'free' *Generalkommission* unions. It faced regular police harassment especially when it attempted to carry out any anti-military propaganda. (Anything that might demoralise the national armed forces might be judged as attempted treason). Its journals, *Der Freie Arbeiter*, and *Revolutionär* had print runs of 2,000 to 5,000 copies, but were subjected to police scrutiny, with whole editions frequently being seized. Editors were repeatedly imprisoned, and some faced accusations of high treason.

Anarchist ideas were unwelcome in the FVdG before 1904, but sympathies changed after 1908.[224] The FVdG was not very close to the anarchist sympathisers around Gustav Landauer, although they had some things in common – internationalism and the belief that direct action worked for the creation of freer communities. The FVdG did not turn its back on industry, whereas Landauer, in the aims of the *Sozialistische Bund* (Socialist Federation) set out a call for workers to leave the cities and resettle in the country.[225] The Socialist Federation published a fortnightly periodical *Der Socialist*.

The *Anarchistische Föderation* distanced itself from the anarchism of Landauer and the *Bund*, which it saw as somewhat utopian. The latter saw the *Anarchistische Föderation* as excessively bureaucratic, and was suspicious of theories of class struggle. Gustav Landauer, 'though he thought revolutions and strikes were a long way off, defined them in view of particular ends, as active, constructive and pre-figurative beginnings in which workers would work for themselves, and for their own needs, inspired by a new spirit:

> A general strike, yes! but an active one, with a very different activity than is sometimes associated with the revolutionary general strike, which in plain language is called 'plundering'. The active general strike will be victorious only when the working men were able to refuse to give one bit of their activity, their work, to others, but work only for their own needs, their real needs.[226]

Rudolf Rocker – based in London at this time – also distanced himself from certain fractions of German anarchists: both those who rejected on principle all organisation predicated on goals and opinions and others who recognised the need for small groups but rejected co-ordinated activity because it would create restrictions on individual freedom. For Rocker, such opinions were born of confusion and a lack of understanding of the meaning of anarchism.[227]

The SPD leadership faced growing discontent as the First World War came closer. The politics of direct action gained some influence. Opposition currents were articulated through local and regional SPD newspapers. Kautsky accused militant minorities of violating well-tested tactics and accused radicals of indulging in 'revolutionary gymnastics'. Anton Pannekoek, later a left communist, replied that the leaders had given up the fight and that these well-tested tactics achieved little: 'they shunned the fight more and more in order not to endanger this precious organisation.' The trade union apparatus was 'in service', for capital. Every independent initiative of the masses breaking out against the wishes of union leaders was branded as a 'lack of discipline' and 'anarchism'.[228] Pannekoek, 'though he criticised anarchism, supported the syndicalist principle of revolutionary activity, which was both good and necessary'.[229]

There was growing dissatisfaction and impatience among rank and file trade unionists. One such instance occurred on the docks at Hamburg and Bremen in July-August 1913 when dockers and shipyard workers went on strike without the official approval of their trade union. Hundreds were sacked. There was also some conflict among miners in the Ruhr. Dissident members of the SPD facilitated the formation of oppositional groups which eventually joined the FVdG. By 1914 some 450 miners were involved. Dissidents criticised 'discipline', the watchword of trade unions:

> Success of mass movements depends on their capacity for autonomous action, their unquenchable ardour for battle, and the boldness and initiative of the masses. But it is precisely these qualities, the primary condition of the struggle for freedom that are repressed and annihilated by trade union discipline.[230]

There were emerging patterns of disrespect for trade union officialdom. Life was no longer so easy for the trade union official; the latter felt an 'unhealthy atmosphere'; a new syndicalist feeling was present; the trade union was no longer successful enough for many workers, tactics were too cautious, leaders too circumspect.[231]

The profile of the FVdG changed in the run up to the First World War. It lost members in construction and metal industries, but gained some presence among Ruhr mine-workers. In 1912, there were 2,384 strikes involving a million workers, a peak year for industrial unrest.[232] The German trade union movement was quite strong, in numerical terms the equal of the British TUC.[233] But it was still absent from some industries and had little presence outside urban areas.

By 1914 numbers in the localist unions had declined to 6,000 members,[234] as against two to three million in the free (SPD) trade unions, and 600,000 in an independent railway workers' union. The localists' paper, *Die Einigheit* (Unity), had a circulation in the region of 30,000.

FVdG members paid dues towards strike action funds but received neither health or unemployment benefits, nor funeral expenses as provided by the centralised trade unions. When industrial conflicts broke out, the FVdG campaigned for solidarity strikes to broaden support, criticising the reformist trade union movement if they obstructed solidarity. The FVdG's 1912 congress declared that it worked for regular improvements in wages and conditions, but was not restricted to corporate interests; it worked also for class interests and a wider agenda: for a general strike, for anti-militarism, anti-patriotism, for freedom to refuse to pay the church tax, and for libertarian socialism. The FVdG congress affirmed its decentralised and federal method of organisation, with local union bodies having the right to begin and end strikes. Crucially, funds, and the power to dispense funds were not centralised, in contrast with the Social-Democratic unions and party, where a central leadership had powers to allocate or remove funds from local strikes and journals. The FVdG supported the international conference of syndicalist union centres that met in London shortly before the outbreak of the First World War.

The FVdG noted that the Reich was a multi-lingual polity, with large numbers of non-German speakers. Its paper *Der Pioneer* described the SPD's internationalism as humbug. Ernst Toller noted that the German worker was used to blind obedience, wanted to follow orders, and confused the suppression of freedom with discipline. Blind submission was taught in schools, in barracks and at work.[235]

When the FVdG campaigned against militarism it confronted hostility both from the state and from large parts of the labour movement. In December 1911, the FVdG attempted to distribute 100,000 copies of a banned pamphlet, 'The Abolition of War by Self-determination of the people: questions to the German Workers', by Gustav Landauer.[236] In it he commented: 'I cannot stand pomposity. It is easy for a few party bureaucrats to exchange a few meaningless phrases.' Landauer saw Marxism as a nationalist ideology. He thought that nothing would come from the Social-Democratic anti-war congress held in Basel, in November 1912. He recalled: 'Marx always saw revolution as a process of war between states, having as its purpose the consolidation of a single Social-Democratic centralised state.'[237] In April 1914, Fritz Kater commented in *La Voix du Peuple* that it would be as easy for FVdG members to work for syndicalism in the centralised unions as it would be for soldiers to campaign for anti-militarism in military barracks. The officials of the centralised unions practiced 'close surveillance' over their members. All sorts of rebels, if they refused to be silent, would inevitably be excluded from the centralised *Generalkommission* unions for some infraction of rules. Centralised unions practiced 'terrorism', going as far as to denounce FVdG members to the police or having them sacked. Their 'discipline' imposed hunger and starvation. The centralised unions had one key asset – their ability to provide benefits – three-fifths of their dues went towards health or other benefits.[238]

A fixation with order and organisation was displayed by the *Generalkommission* trade unions when war was declared in 1914. A special issue of *Korrespondenzblatt* was issued setting out that:

> It is not in vain that Germany is the nation where in all fields organisation is most strongly developed. Organisation means the promotion of social forces through the subordination of personal interests to common interests and of individual will to the collective will. A well organised people is always ready for war, and in case of need is always stronger than one lacking organisation. And the strength of organisation of German workers is also an essential factor for national defence.[239]

Rudolf Rocker wrote that the socialist movement was 'completely emasculated by long years of parliamentary routine and was no longer capable of a creative act'. Socialist parties became, without their members knowing it, 'buffers in the fight between capital and labour working for the security of capitalism'.[240] Leaders and followers had been seduced by the fantasy described by Rosa Luxemburg, as 'nothing but parliamentarianism as the sole panacea'.[241]

10

SYNDICALISM AND ANARCHISM IN FRANCE AFTER 1907

Emile Pataud and Emile Pouget, two leading CGT members, published a portrait of a revolution entitled *Comment nous ferons la revolution* in 1909.* They suggested that a revolution might begin when sparked by government repression and popular anger. An active minority would act as a catalyst, encouraging workers to join a mass general strike. The old government would be overwhelmed – unable to move troops. Means of communication and transport would not function. On the railways signals would be set at danger, points would not operate, locomotives would lack key components. Most of the army would be subverted and support the revolution.

Bakeries would operate only under the licence of unions, and all would come to depend on the union-organised system of food supply. That system would be generalised, unions becoming effective organising centres for the new society; the less radical unions would be swept on by the wave of changing sentiments. A new society and polity would be created: politicians would recognise that the parliamentary system had served its time, now was the time for something new, for a unionised or syndicalised commonwealth, where each union managed its own affairs and coordinated with the community and with other unions. Workplaces would initiate contracts for the exchange of their products.

All share and share alike. Some products would be available on demand. Other scarcer commodities would be rationed, with their price reflecting scarcity, the costs of inputs and the working time that they embody. Prices help manage demand for such goods and, as these are products less widely desired, supply and demand fall into balance. The arms industry would

---

* Translated into English and published in 1913 with an introduction by Tom Mann as *Syndicalism and the Co-operative Commonwealth*. Re-published under the title: *How we shall bring about the Revolution*.

find new products. Members of useful liberal professions form syndicates like any other groups of workers, they would lose out on their privileged incomes, but gain in other ways. A syndicalist bank would open. Private capital – in whatever form: estates, buildings, warehouses, factories, titles to rent, or shares – would be suppressed. Money might play a role in exchange beyond the borders of the new society, but would matter little internally.

Those whose jobs henceforward would have no use – such as stock exchange speculators – would have to find new more productive employment. Most small business people would join the syndicalist commonwealth voluntarily, but there would be no forceful compulsion. Some, a proportion of shopkeepers for example, might wish initially to remain outside the new society; they might do so, but at the cost of not being able to draw on social solidarity and on not having supplies from union-run distribution centres. Faced with this limited choice, the recalcitrant would reconsider. The new society would be defended from within by bonds of social solidarity, rather than by police forces. If perverts attacked children, they might face collective rage and the possibility of immediate execution. Communal determination to punish such crimes would act as a forceful deterrent. If the revolution were attacked from abroad, its new technologies, and its general determination, would soon destroy the morale and the fighting capacity of invaders.

In this scenario, it is the unions that provide the framework for change. It is within unions that active minorities play a role. New circumstances compel parliamentary parties to recognise that they have no future role, and they would 'abdicate'. The mass of people would sweep repression away and give life to new structures.

Subsequent experience would suggest that it would easier to imagine revolution than to sustain that imagination and make it into reality. The CGT promoted a *La Bataille Syndicaliste*, with a circulation of some 27,000, falling to 8,000 in 1913, when the Hachette chain stopped selling it at its station kiosks (Jean Jaurès's socialist *L'Humanité* sold some 70,000).[242]

The character of the CGT changed after 1909. The new secretary of the CGT, Léon Jouhaux, had been initially influenced by libertarian priorities. He remarked in *L'Humanité*, in September 1909, that the Amiens Charter was maybe not so much against politics, as against politics in the CGT. It was not for leaders of a socialist party to be a general staff and to order about workers in their unions: 'Perhaps for you the political organisation is a great ship and the economic organisation a little boat in its tow. For us, the great ship is the union organisation; it is necessary to subordinate political action to union action.'[243] But parts of the CGT, including Jouhaux, were gradually moving towards more cautious forms of syndicalism.

A 66 per cent pay rise (to 15,000 francs per year), which deputies voted themselves in 1910, provoked widespread protests. Parliamentary politics was presented as part and parcel of a system of lies, cheating, fraud, brigandage and so on, and the CGT posed itself as the alternative to bourgeois corruption. It also opposed pension plans prepared by the Socialist Party. In 1912 preparations for an anti-electoral campaign were put in place by a network involving supporters and editors of various radical journals: *Le Battaille syndicaliste, Germinal, La Guerre Sociale,** *Le Libertaire*, and *Les Temps nouveaux*. A large poster was prepared noting the inability of municipal councils to limit rents. Electors were called on, not to vote, but to join the CGT and/or other revolutionary educational groups. Twelve thousand copies were printed.[244]

The political nature of the CGT is surrounded in controversy. Latapie, a delegate to the Amiens Congress declared that 'syndicalism should be between anarchist and socialist theory. Moreover, this doctrine should be sufficient unto itself.' In this view syndicalism would became the force that led, and syndicalists would prioritise unionism and union organisation above Marxist or anarchist politics.

Some historians have noted conflicts between French socialists – followers of Jaurès who voted for the Charter, and followers of Guesde who voted against. Ariane Miéville says that Amiens charter was the consequence of a circumstantial alliance between a majority of revolutionary syndicalists and one reformist moderate syndicalist current, against the Guesdist current led by Victor Renard, who wished to build bridges between the CGT and the Socialist Party. Pierre Monatte, had written in *Les Temps nouveaux* shortly before the Amiens congress met that the Socialist Party had had 'a desire to replace anti-parliamentary confederal officials (or persons who abstain from parliamentary propaganda) with men who have the confidence of the party'. It was seeking to place the confederation in tow behind the party.[245] After the congress Monatte saw himself among anarchist syndicalists, and denied that there was any split between anarchist syndicalists and syndicalists-without-adjectives.[246] Interestingly however, talk of 'keeping politics outside' the CGT, also served, after the congress, to keep anarchist propaganda out of the unions.[247] Four years later, in 1910, Victor Serge, criticised union or syndicalist organisations in general and the CGT in particular:

> In their organisation, they are a perfect copy of the parliamentary farce. Not even the clowns are missing. Delegation of power, votes, decisions

---

* Most associates of *Guerre Sociale* dropped out; the paper called for CGT members to vote Socialist.

having force of law, as well as half-hidden combinations, personal competition, kitchen squabbles: we can find in the CGT the exact, though reduced, transposition of parliamentary hideousness ...

At their beginning all parties, all groups (even all individuals) are combative. Age comes, and with it a potbelly and wisdom. This is the story of many men who we are today permitted to admire raised to the top of the social machine ... Very revolutionary during the blessed period of their youth, the English trade unions have become what we know them to be. The same thing happened to many German unions, and is now happening to the Belgian worker's movement, which is losing all energy as it grows. In certain places in the United States, in Australia, in New Zealand, in England, where the unions have reached their heights, they have only managed to create a caste of privileged, conservative workers, lined up under the protective shield of the state, and are hardly worth more than the more official bourgeois.

Having seen the evolution of the French unions and observed the incoherence of the CGT, I don't think it's possible to foresee a different destiny for it.[248]

Serge's comments came as the CGT began the process of reforming local and craft bodies unto industrial organisations at its congress in Toulouse in 1910. Monatte, Dunois and Fuss-Amoré prioritised support for *La Vie Ouvrière* rather than the libertarian press.[249]

Luigi Bertoni, a Swiss union activist was invited to Paris to lecture on the politics of the CGT in the spring of 1910. A report in *Temps nouveaux* on 11 June 1910 says he was invited as part of the work of the paper and its support group, because in their view he was the anarchist best placed to talk about the usefulness and failings of syndicalism – on a theoretical level, and a practical level too since he had kept his independence, being a worker (a typesetter) and not a union official. He spoke to an audience of 650 syndicalists and anarchists. He had critical comments to make – he talked as revolutionary – but was not an opponent of syndicalism. Syndicalism facilitated organisation and within it there was a space for revolutionary propaganda; but accepting subsidies for *bourses du travail* (trades councils/ centres) and focusing on working for laws for labour protection impeded broader objectives. There was no difference between reformist and revolutionary syndicalism, both worked only for reforms; libertarians would show that any reforms were precarious and exploitation was ongoing; they needed some other organisation beyond workplace union – a specifically revolutionary organisation.[250] Direct action – for reforms and employee (corporate) benefits – was insufficient to make revolution; those who are satisfied with such things forget to work for a general strike and general expropriation. The larger labour unions were becoming prey to bureaucracy and centralisation. In Zurich typesetters were being asked to pay 2.20 francs a week to their union – a level of dues that might be demanded by some aristocratic club. Often – to get numbers up – members were recruited indiscriminately. With such measures, the issue was one of getting a monopoly on the sale of labour, to have labour paid as high a price as possible, for whatever jobs workers might get, be it making weapons or constructing prisons. Bertoni concluded by asserting that the goal of propaganda was to build the strength of active labour organisations – with their own power rather than with a power delegated to others.

A follow up meeting met in a restaurant and extended the discussion. Yvetot did sustain some anarchist views, but Léon Jouhaux and A. Boudet demonstrated that although they used revolutionary labels, they were 'entirely reformist'. 'For Jouhaux, everything is right in the CGT', he defended centralisation, the better to fight management. Boudet asserted that in strikes workers needed officials to argue with management. 'Boudet did not see that he was defending a serf morality. If workers are incapable of freeing themselves, who will do it for them?' Bertoni was reported as saying that as unions become bigger, management and officials have an incentive to get together behind the backs of workers. For officials, a state of 'peace' is preferable, thus reformism would gain ground. Yvetot perhaps saw this as all too ideological, and insufficiently rooted in practical everyday unionism.

This controversy spluttered on over the next four years until the outbreak of the First World War. There was some accord between *Temps Nouveaux* (Paris), *Le Réveil-Il Risveglio* (Geneva) and *Voluntá* (Ancona).

In *Vie Ouvriere*, and *Battaile Syndicaliste* Guilluame cited texts from Bakunin to support the general position of the CGT; in February 1914 Guillaume went so far as to present Bertoni as an element of disorganisation undermining the strength of labour.[251] Circumstances and developments in France, Italy and Francophone Switzerland inspired perspectives that emanated in part from these contexts. In Italy Armando Borghi put a question to Malatesta:

> Perhaps there persists, between us two, a different manner and a different degree of appreciating the function of key ideas ... should key ideas be alive within the kernel of the class, or – contrariwise – should that class kernel not fall in with every initiative that promotes those key ideas?[252]

What came first, ideas or organisation? Without 'ideas' would the movement regress? What was the chicken and what was the egg? Was the CGT being transformed, institutionalised and compromised? Should revolutionary elites develop within syndicalist organisations, with their consciousness emanating from within, or would that consciousness develop better or more easily outside the workplace in some anarchist organisation? For a time, it seemed that the arguments of James Guillaume flowed in the first vein and those of Errico Malatesta in the second vein.[253]

Within unions some libertarian officials became 'prisoners' of their conquest of the CGT. They were institutionally constrained: they became less, or not at all, able to express wider concerns, and were poorly connected or accountable. Anarchist critics looked to change relationships between officials and ordinary syndicalists, suggesting that after a year or two in office, officials should not be eligible for re-election. Such a measure – it was suggested – would deter officials from being permanent fixtures with distinct interests. Several arguments opposed such a reform: that there were not so many persons willing to become officials and so an ordinance disqualifying existing officials would help to destabilise syndicates. (This was denied. It was also asserted if there were insufficient candidates for posts this was because there was a lack of preparation or education to help.) It was also said that former officials would be placed on lists of undesirables by management. CGT congresses would decisively reject moves to limit the terms of officials.[254]

Pierre Monatte wrote on the success of his journalism (for *La Vie Ouvrière* and other press) and on developments in the CGT, in a text he first published in 1959.[255] He suggests that reformist citadels were being dismantled one after another in this period. He asserted that syndicalist were, in a healthy fashion, re-examining their practice. He highlighted attacks made against CGT leaders by Aristide Briand and the state. He commented that conservative and royalist journalists found employment in one or another labour journal. The paper *Le Libertaire* was, in Monatte's view, somewhat rabid and over optimistic. He supported a syndicalism that sought an even course between revolutionary rhetoric that was inappropriate in these times, and reformism.*

Differences also emerged among libertarians. There were two central concerns around which libertarians who prioritised workplace action might become polarised: some 'libertarian syndicalists' were particularly concerned with class and CGT unity, other 'anarchist syndicalists' were concerned more with promoting the action of lively minorities. Guillaume Davranche writes that around the first pole were such figures as Monatte,

---

* Monatte's perspectives on the approach of war are discussed further below.

Jouhaux and Pouget, and around the second pole Broutchoux, Janvion and Yvetot.[256] With the exception of Yvetot, most of the second group did not take key positions in national CGT structures.

Jean Maitron noted the scale of syndicalist representation within *anarchist* organisation and the presence of experienced union leaders in the organised anarchist movement; perhaps four out of seven or eight of the commission nominated by the national anarchist congress of 1913 were also important union leaders.[257]

A French anarchist congress met on 15-17 August 1913. It helped consolidate the formation of the Anarchist-Communist Federation (ACF). It came together as Gustave Hervé and his paper *Guerre Sociale* made a right turn in favour of an alliance between the CGT and the Socialist Party. Some of his supporters moved away from him and towards the new federation. Congress heard a declaration from Sébastien Faure, which sought to define a consensus for the new ACF, one that condemned individualism.[258] Sébastien Faure spoke of an inseparable abyss separating the organised anarchist movement from the individualists. No doubt he had in mind the activities of the Bonnot gang and the sympathetic reception it received in the individualist weekly *L'anarchie*, and contributions such as those of the recalcitrant Victor Serge (alias Le Rétif). The congress was attended by 130 delegates from sixty French groups.[259] It was the first such event since the international congress that had been called to meet in Paris in 1900. It received two international visitors – from Germany and Italy. Some individualists attended the congress but retired in the face of general hostility. *Le Libertaire* and the ACF were far from representing the entirety of French libertarians. Jean Grave had written in *Les Temps nouveaux* two years earlier that 'it is not desirable that anarchists should come to a common view in order to establish a common programme, such a thing would only be detrimental to the birth of original thinking and new initiatives'.[260] In 1914 in a small propaganda pamphlet he rejected dogmatic perspectives and endorsed anarchist pluralism: 'there may be as many targets to attack as there are perspectives.'[261] It might be admitted that organisation was useful – both for reflection and for organising action – but this led only some anarchists towards forming coherent collectives where there was some accountability and democratic control among editors and activists and collective agreement as to goals, targets, means, and how activists might best support each other.

A congress report noted that anarchists were advised to get involved in union work, to seed revolutionary feelings and ideas. (One writer in *Les Temps nouveaux* asserted, somewhat mischievously, that most 'anarchists' were not CGT members.)[262] There were discussions on a general strike

– allied to expropriation and insurrection. A key speech by a relatively unknown building worker activist, Dominique Lagru, dared raise the concept of scission between revolutionaries and reformists in labour organisations. He spoke of centralisation, and the bureaucratisation of national structures,* even where base organisations remained democratic; he noted recent experience and false hopes: reforms had been won, sometimes with violent means, but meanwhile revolutionary perspectives had been dissipating. He called on radicals to prioritise inter-union educational work at grass-roots levels; turning away from working for and in posts in national CGT structures. Pierre Monatte was aghast at the prospect of any split and Lagru's ideas were too much for most delegates. Some wondered why the ACF should spend such time on CGT affairs.[263] But Lagru's comments were not unreasonable. An article entitled 'Crisis of Syndicalism', published in *Le Mouvement anarchiste* in October 1912 on the recent CGT congress in Le Havre had concluded: 'Irresolution and backsliding. A triumph of bureaucracy. That is the balance sheet of this congress.'[264] Another article had poked fun at Jouhaux for asserting that campaigns for the half-day off on Saturday were the extent of the CGT's ambition. 'From Jouhaux through Monatte to Desplanques, anarchism is something that no longer exists, it need not exist now, once in the past it might have been a good thing, but now the *syndicate* is all that matters, and anarchism has died.'[265] Jouhaux, however, was still prepared to explain CGT policy to a closed meeting with a hundred ACF members in January 1913.[266] One 'congress impression' in *Les Temps nouveaux* commented that the anarchist-communist congress should not expect too much from the CGT, it could not launch a general strike every six months, or whenever the government tried to provoke labour; if the CGT reacted too quickly it would have setbacks and that would provoke a negative reaction.[267] Another, from Pierre Martin, an editor and administrator of *Le Libertaire*, commented: 'The congress did good work in being careful not to fall into some form of dogmatic petrification; doors have been left wide open for initiatives.'[268]

The ACF congress adopted the following Manifesto:

Manifesto of the Revolutionary Anarchist-Communist Federation

WE REPUDIATE INDIVIDUALISM

The congress has clearly delineated the separation between revolutionary anarchist-communist movement and the erroneous practices and misleading theories of individualism. The antagonisms that opposed the

---

* See also below, comments by James Connolly on amalgamated British trade unions.

one to the other being always so profound and so irreducible, there never was, nor could there ever be the least solidarity between revolutionary anarchist-communism and individualism. Recent sensational acts, wrongly termed 'anarchist', have engendered a fatal confusion which the congress had to counter. So, this has been done. Henceforth – excepting persons who are deplorably ignorant and those who might thereby show bad faith – no one will be able to entertain this detestable equivocation, no one can confuse these two doctrines without manifesting deplorable ignorance; unless they are ignorant or dishonest, no one will be able to deny the abyss that separates the one from the other.

OUR ORGANISATION

The Revolutionary Anarchist-Communist Federation of the French language* is founded. Being faithful to the principles of freedom and federalism which form the basis of anarchism, its charter respects the independence of individuals within groups, and the autonomy of groups within the federation. It has already received the backing of many individuals and of numerous groups; it exists, it is ready to act.

WE ARE ANTI-PARLIAMENTARIAN

Anarchists remain determined opponents of parliamentarianism. Parliamentary action always deceives; anti-parliamentary agitation is an ongoing necessity. Anarchists will decide, in each area or region, if electoral periods may provide opportunities to intensify abstentionist propaganda – and what forms it might take.

AGAINST MILITARISM

Struggles against militarism must be promoted, now, more than ever. Anarchists will ardently participate in any and every agitation against the furies of nationalism, currently encroaching through armament, through war sensation, through military service [being extended to] three years, through military parades, and, in the barracks, through savage repression along with grassing and snitching.

ANARCHISTS AND SYNDICALISM

The Revolutionary Anarchist-Communists, being convinced that syndicalism – even if is not entirely sufficient unto itself – still remains the most powerful means of liberation of the working class, urgently urges

---

* *Temps nouveaux* had carried many reports on developments in Belgium and Switzerland, but the RACF appears to have had few French speaking members outside France. A Belgian ACF was founded in 1913, but its journal *L'Emancipateur* was repressed after publishing an issue opposing militarism

all workers to join syndicates affiliated to the CGT. They invite friends to take an ever more active part in the life of syndicates, in order to promote revolutionary ardour, and to spread the spirit of revolt. It advises them to work constantly to increase wages, to reduce working hours progressively, to promote a healthier and stronger labour organisation; but it also reminds them that these achievements are not the *goals* of syndicalism, and they should be considered only as moral victories, as provisional, passing improvements, obtained by direct action and by the violent pressure of wage earners on management; above all they constitute a form of indispensable revolutionary gymnastics. They are, through their very limitations, destined to impact on the consciousness of all, to make clear the necessity of a profound, complete revolution liberating the world of labour.

THE GENERAL STRIKE

Congress affirms the revolutionary value of a violent and expropriating general strike of short duration. In every situation, in all fields, and above all within labour organisations, anarchists work to prepare minds, to strengthen commitment, to organise sectors, to ensure success.

ILLEGALITY

Congress recognises furthermore that while it has no right to impose obligations on anyone, yet it believes that it is necessary to declare that as far as matters of breaking laws are concerned; (or to put the matter better to recover things) the moral value of those that work for such goals is in no way diminished (because, by reason of their altruistic motivations through which such actions are formed this is the only interest that there is – in acts and works of propaganda and of revolutionary revolt). It is quite clear that the right to life comes above all else.

WHAT WE ARE

Lastly congress declares that it is: *Communist*, seeking the suppression of the capitalist regime based on individual property, and the common collectivisation of every means of production and every form of wealth. *Revolutionary*, looking for social transformation from a comprehensive movement; prepared by educational work that is devoid of tricks or compromises; one that draws strength from a powerful organisation, one that is facilitated by methodical preparation as circumstances may demand; accomplished by active minorities in contact with the disinherited masses, and having the capacity – through clear-sightedness, energy and example – of drawing the latter towards the red road of revolt. *Anarchist*, so there can be no question of conquering a power that must be broken; or of taking over the state that must be supressed; rather what is needed is the abolition of moral, economic and political servitude, so that with social freedom, with liberation from the political authority which oppresses and from the economic tyranny that starves, every individual will develop – physically, in morality, and in intellect – in vigour, knowledge and well-being.[269]

The ACF gained some influence as the effective publisher of the weekly *Le Libertaire*.[270] It became a key journal for the revolutionary left, with an average print run of some 10,000. It drew support from many younger union activists. While it defended the autonomy of the CGT – in the face of state subsidies for *bourses* and against dependence on the Socialist Party – it also fought 'neutralism', the idea that unions should have no radical political inspiration: here then, there was a repudiation of the idea that in working for revolutionary change syndicalism was entirely sufficient unto itself.

The ACF provided a political base for some woman activists, something of an innovation among anarchists. Although capable organisers and speakers they had seldom assumed prominent roles; male union officials were common even in trades largely employing women. Some of these women activists were wives and partners of male militants, some had employment in the textile sector, and some worked with a women's committee [comité feminine], involving Jeanne Morand, Madeleine Pelletier, Nelly Roussel and others from a variety of radical networks, working to oppose militarism and war, and preparing tracts entitled 'Women revolt', 'Appeal to women', and 'Appeal to the mothers, sisters and partners of recruits'. The ACF took up positions defending the rights of women to join unions, and against women-only unions.[271]

The Politics and Strength of the CGT before the First World War

The strength of the anarchist presence within the CGT is not very clear. Many anarchists were elected to CGT posts. Some 2,500 members of the CGT could co-ordinate their activity with other members of collectivist anarchist organisations. Perhaps as many as 100,000 CGT members may have given some support to anarchists.[272] The anarchist movement may have doubled in strength in the run up to 1914, but radical influence on the CGT was not predominant. Several important strikes were defeated.

The CGT's opposition to militarism is discussed below. On this front, at least, radicals were winning congress votes. Earlier, circumstances may have favoured the development of the CGT, in that the republican state may have been looking for allies in the labour movement. But when, in 1908, the state perceived that the CGT would not be subservient its hostility became plain, and the members of the CGT's national bureau were arrested. In 1912, primary school teachers voted to support the *Sou du Soldat*, a penny levy for the CGT members compulsorily recruited into the armed forces. The state responded by banning the teachers' union, citing its anti-patriotism and anti-militarism.[273]

The pre-war achievements of the CGT were modest. It was unable to win either the eight-hour day, or, for state employees such as postal workers, the right to strike. A call for a general strike to support them was an abject failure. Engine drivers had kept aloof from a wider rail workers' union where the unskilled predominated, but after a strike defeat in 1910, in view of the erosion of their terms and conditions, they threw in their lot with other rail employees. Prime Minister Aristide Briand, himself an ex-socialist and a former advocate of the strike weapon, was responsible for the arrest of the leaders of the 1910 rail strike; to break the strike he had the army call up strikers as reservists for a three-month period. The widespread use of sabotage – particularly against communications equipment – was evidence that an intransigent current would not meekly sit on its hands. Briand invoked fears for the nation's ability to defend the frontiers to justify repressive action. Socialist members of the legislature were unable or unwilling to stop him. The French socialist party was nearing 60,000 strong, according to one speaker at a CGT conference.[274] A year later it has been credited with 100,000 members, while the German Social-Democratic Party had a million members.[275]

Experience of repressive laws, police spies, and other forms of action directed by the state against strikers and anti-militarist campaigners worked to convince radical activists of the utility of some form of revolutionary organisation beyond the ranks of French socialism. The run-up to the First World War was the period in which the ACF came together, following on from an earlier Revolutionary Communist Federation. It advocated radical policies in the CGT and opposition to militarism. The new federation was convinced of the need for a cohesive organisation, but it had to confront an ongoing, individualist-anarchist current.

In the years running up to 1914 the CGT faced a range of problems. It confronted modernisation in industry, and modern management techniques. Syndicalists feared the development of the Taylor system with its 'time and motion' studies, designed not just to make workers work harder, but also to eliminate workers' understanding and mastery of the entire work process: 'Workers will not be allowed to think. Thinking, any necessary cerebral effort, will be done for them, in the time and motion office. As for them, they only have to execute rapidly and unremittingly one of the number of motions into which operations are broken down.' The original Mr Renault was introducing this system into the car industry, but not without resistance and strikes, which involve four thousand workers. *La Bataille Syndicaliste* warned: 'And Taylor says that his method is truly a weapon in the war against workers' syndicalism. He's right! Don't let it be planted in this country.'

The CGT may have been in decline by 1914, with some parts of it moving towards some form of accommodation with the state; it was certainly not advancing. Membership figures vary: one source just over a million in members in various syndicates in 1912,[276] and some 600,000 CGT members,[277] and over 800,000 before August 1914. One contemporary observed: 'The CGT, in its activities from 1909 to 1914, abandoned none of its principles and none of its demands ... and grew in membership. But everybody realised that its vitality had failed since 1908 ...'[278]

At leadership level, the CGT appears to have been unsure of its course in the run up to 1914. Monatte attempted to respond by publishing a militant, bi-monthly review with news and analysis of developments. *Vie Ouvrière*[279] had a small circulation of around 2,000. (The weekly *Voix du Peuple*,[280] the official CGT newspaper, had a circulation of 6,000).[281] *Vie Ouvrière* published serious, critical reports and analysis, on the labour movement in France and abroad: on chauvinism in the German labour movement, on the dangers of Taylorism and on the influence of Catholicism among railway workers. On one occasion, it criticised the food industries' syndicate for failing to warn consumers of adulterated foods.

Bertoni revisited Paris in 1914. *Les Temps nouveaux* wondered if he spoke to anyone other than those already converted to anarchist ideals. He talked on several subjects. He noted that there were some socialist judges and police in odd parts of Switzerland – but everything was carried on in much the same way as anywhere else. He told how one local police chief – a socialist – told an Italian anarchist: I sympathise with your ideas and won't act on instructions to expel you, provided you do not attend meetings, do not sell pamphlets, do not receive anarchist papers, etc., – in all other ways you are entirely free. Bertoni said that Social-Democratic socialism respected legal order and restricted strikes, it was no longer any danger to capitalism or the Swiss state – they understood each other. The bourgeoisie had killed off socialism by offering it positions, and would try to buy off anarchism too.[282]

In a second lecture he presented a case for workplace organisation which would respect ideals and enhance local and individual initiative. His argument that syndicates – 'unless they have a strong anarchist presence within them, above all develop a corporate [trade] spirit, and end up with results that are among the worst'[283] – worked to stimulate a round of polemical exchanges on the capacity (or incapacity) of syndicalism alone to promote change. Bertoni was promoting a focus on three themes: a separation between workplace organisation on the one hand and party politics and the state; management of unions, as far as possible, through horizontal structures and through direct action; lastly the promotion of a conscious social morality, so that workers promoted not so much, or not just, their own trade interests, but rather a wider social agenda.[284]

Kropotkin noted the distinct reformist or Catholic linkages of unions in Germany. James Guillaume – probably with the French CGT in mind – opposed Bertoni and others who argued for the necessity of some other ideas-based body that might act as a catalyst and supplement radical syndicalism; he accused Bertoni of being anti-syndicalist.[285] *Les Temps nouveaux* commented that it was wrong to see in any criticism of aspects of radical syndicalism an opposition to radical syndicalism itself.[286]

After the outbreak of war in August 1914, union membership numbers fell precipitously in France. By 1916 the CGT had only 50,000 members. International comparisons often suggest that the French movement was weak. 'Barely 10% of workers were unionised and syndicalists were an unrepresentative minority within that minority. Bigger unions (miners, railwaymen, textile workers) scorned syndicalist tactics …'[287] French unions had a smaller membership than counterparts in Britain and Germany, but heavy industry had less weight in France.

Returning to the controversy over the apoliticism or political neutrality of the CGT, Alfred Rosmer, a contemporary of Pierre Monatte claimed, 'this alleged neutralism never existed'. He argued that the Amiens Charter was 'political', and directed against both socialists (who compromised the interests of the labour movement by putting 'politics' first), and against labourism (which prioritised bread and butter matters). In Rosmer's view, conflict persisted because the CGT was revolutionary while the Socialist party was reformist.[288] For Rosmer, the CGT was defined by its militancy, anti-militarism and its opposition to the compromises of French socialism.

For Georges Sorel, syndicalism was defined through the historic task it had adopted, promoting workers' capacity to work for transformative change.[289] However, G. D. H. Cole, writing in 1913, noted that if some did argue for transformation – as in la *Mine aux Mineurs* (Mines managed by miners) – nevertheless 'in the actual life of the CGT, and at its congresses, it takes a very small place'. The essence of syndicalism was class-struggle but 'the opposition to the state is fundamental as long as the state remains irretrievably bourgeois; but the opposition to all authority is not a consequence of syndicalism'.[290] Cole also wrote of syndicalists' views of reforms and revolution that:

> Unless the strike has a revolutionary aim extending beyond mere Reformism, it is the end of idealism, and can at any rate be no substitute for Parliamentary Action. If, on the other hand, it is purely revolutionary, and secures for the worker no temporary advantages, it is equally useless; for in that case it would be impossible not only to organise a majority of the workers in the *syndicates*, but also to persuade the unorganised to go on strike. The CGT depends on winning partial advantages for its power to lead as a conscious minority.[291]

Some currents of CGT opinion sought to prioritise 'bread and butter' unionism and immediate gains, others placed somewhat greater emphasis on looking forward, seeing revolutionary syndicalism as a path to revolution, a path that rejected the compromised politics of the parliamentary socialists. Before 1914, there were many small local, church and company unions outside the CGT network, and rival confederations were beginning to form, but as yet the CGT did not have a serious rival at the national level. Parts of the CGT saw unity as an end in itself. Such 'unity' might coral internal conflict within a particular union centre, with 'unity' holding the ring for ongoing tensions between various layers of workers' organisations. Within the CGT there were some cautious elements gathering. The CGT had a fragile unity, it had within it a diverse range of priorities and politics; some were sympathetic to anarchism, revolutionary syndicalism and dissidence, others had more everyday priorities. The CGT leadership had a degree of autonomy because no tendency was dominant.

Radical syndicalism appeared stronger before 1914, and more feeble after 1920, by which time revolutionary syndicalists were losing key positions in the CGT. But such facts do not tell the whole story. Some aspects of change would be fundamental and qualitative, as we shall see below, but in numerical terms the numbers of syndicalist militants with distinctively libertarian or anarchist views were not so different before and after 1914. The radical nature of the resolutions passed by CGT congresses did not imply that such resolutions were actively supported by the national leadership or by the most powerful unions. A voting majority at a congress did not signify that a resolute mass was convinced and ready to act in line with such resolutions. Radical syndicalists appeared more influential in some phases. Unity and solidarity came with success in action, so numbers grew as the tide rose; but at other times the movement became disheartened. In such times, tensions were more likely to cause internal conflict. CGT leaders responded to changing levels of confidence and morale.

11

SYNDICALISM AND ANARCHISM IN ITALY AFTER 1907

The Italian labour movement was an international entity. Italian workers facing unemployment frequently sought jobs abroad. Agricultural workers took seasonal jobs in neighbouring countries. It was mainly Italian labourers who constructed the important Swiss tunnels under the Alps. They faced very poor conditions both at work and in their accommodation and frequent strikes resulted. Strikers were frequently treated harshly and expelled. Radical French-Swiss syndicalists, close to the CGT, took particular pains to support Italian comrades. Less radical layers of the Swiss labour movement looked down on Italians – and despised them for working for lower wages. The Swiss government feared that syndicalism might 'infect' placid sections of the labour movement, if the Swiss and Italians made common cause. Luigi Bertoni, a long-term libertarian activist and publisher living in Geneva was threatened with expulsion; a defence campaign was mounted and he obtained a precarious licence to remain in Switzerland.[292]

Latin American government frequently blamed immigrant Italian (and Spanish) agitators for strikes and targeted foreigners for expulsion. Conversely there were also labour activists who sought to escape arrest in Italy, and sought refuge abroad. In 1912, some 170 active labour organisers were imprisoned and another sixty had fled abroad.[293] A two-way traffic facilitated some degree of international consciousness.

In Italy itself, anarchists who supported organisation developed their associations a little over the first decade of the twentieth century, while Malatesta lived mostly in exile. Regional federations proliferated and had greater strength and vigour than national organisations. For the most part, they supported some form of syndicalism.* Anti-organisation and individualistic currents also retained influence, both at home and in migrant

---

* The focus here is on forms of revolutionary syndicalism close to anarchism, but, as Carl

communities abroad, especially in the USA, where Galleani had a following.

On occasion Malatesta characterised disputes over organisation as disputes over words, in that both those for and against 'organisation' co-ordinated activity to promote their ideas. In Amsterdam, in 1907 he would conclude: 'Enough with quarrels over words, let us turn to action. It is time for all of us to work together to exercise an effective influence on social events.' An Anarchist International was also needed.[294] For Malatesta, organisation promoted accountability: if an organisation decided that one person would liaise with others then there was some accountability, otherwise choices might be made only by insiders and friends. Better that a journal's editor was responsible to some organisation rather than being self-appointed, perhaps indulging personal preferences. The lack of editorial accountability would be telling when disputes arose over policy. For example, in Britain in 1915, the anti-war policy finally adopted by Thomas Keell, the editor of *Freedom*, was disputed. Keell was not accountable to an organisation; his choice was personal rather than one discussed within a wider federation. Kropotkin and his friends saw *Freedom* as their paper and challenged that position.

Conflict in the labour movement

In Italy, as in Germany, the organisation of the Socialist Party (PSI) preceded the organisation of a strong national union centre; in both countries there was a reaction against 'political' and 'economic' reformism, with critics moving towards syndicalism or anarchism. In France in contrast, CGT unity preceded the unity of the French section of the Social-Democratic International. The labour movement in each country took on a shape reflecting its distinct history.

The PSI welcomed *political* strikes in support of the extension of the franchise. But the idea of a general strike, for a general radical agenda, held little appeal. In April 1901, their organ *Avanti!* declared: 'The idea of a general strike within an economic struggle is an idea which belongs only to the methods, and the perspectives of anarchism.'[295] For some Socialists small changes might come gradually and gently; for others, a revolution might yet arrive but it was not to be created so much by popular will, effort, or imagination, but rather more effortlessly, like rain from above, as a result of the inherent contradictions of the capitalist system.

Armando Borghi wrote that there emanated from Berlin the view that this was an era of evolution rather than revolution, that Socialism could be won through elections, that the era of the barricade and the revolt had passed

Levy stresses, ('Currents of Italian syndicalism before 1926', *International Review of Social History*), there were several streams of syndicalism, some of them not at all radical.

by. He saw such ideas as so many muzzles.²⁹⁶ He saw socialist personalities – the likes of Filippo Turati, Leonida Bissolati, Camillo Prampolini, and Claudio Treves – as men of good faith, although in his view their ideas were harmful.²⁹⁷ Italian socialism was also influenced by the ideas of Georges Sorel, and by the example of the CGT in France.

Socialists of all sorts were confronted by a state ready to use violence. In 1904, there were bloody confrontations in Sicily and Sardinia, and a general strike in Milan. The PSI and the General Labour Confederation (*Confederazione Generale del Lavoro*, CGL) became close allies. The formation of the CGL in 1906, was also the moment that another parting of ways began to take shape. Syndicalist currents which had cohabited in the PSI and CGL began to diverge. Radical syndicalists rejected the top-down relations that characterised the CGL, relations which collided with traditions of local organisation. Questions of unity were under discussion, and Borghi satirised top-down unity as: 'unity with confederal [i.e. CGL] leaders and with the Giolitti-like politics of the Socialist parliamentarians. In that system, the masses were disciplined to obey the leaders rather than the leaders obeying the masses.'²⁹⁸

The local labour centre, *Camera del Lavora* was often the focal point that facilitated syndicalist organisation. One strong point was Parma, where the *Camera* was led by Alceste De Ambris, and it was there that a National Direct Action Committee was set up, encouraged by a rising level of struggle. Later, when an Italian Syndicalist Union (USI) formed Parma would also become a base for an active rural organisation. A local general strike was attempted, but had little success. Dissident syndicalists suspended their membership of the CGL, citing the current placid orientation of that body and inviting workers to join them in a congress to decide future priorities. The CGL leaders were criticised for abandoning rail workers to government repression, for reasons of electoral expediency. CGL leaders were also accused of disregarding statutes, linking the future of the confederation with a political party, constricting local initiative and centralising power. By such action, it was argued, it had forfeited its right to represent proletarian interests. Workers' organisation, it was argued, should bring together those who would fight for the end of the boss/wage-earner system, over and beyond the interests of theories or political parties, a phrase that has echoes of the 'Charter of Amiens'. While the French union confederation integrated local bodies – *bourses du travail* – into a national CGT structure, the Italian CGL often failed to maintain harmonious relations with local *Camere del Lavora*.

In 1908, the PSI began to expel syndicalist dissidents. The general strike was rejected by the PSI as 'a dangerous weapon in present circumstances'.[299] Many workers began to organise outside the CGL – in Bologna, Milan, Piombino and Sestri Ponente, in construction, in metal industries and on the railway. There were ongoing debates as to whether supporters of direct action should leave the CGL. At a congress in Bologna, in May 1909, a large majority of dissident syndicalists voted for the CGL. Anarchists were influential in Ancona, Bologna, Carrara, Elba, Emilia-Romagna, La Spezia, Liguria, Puglia and Tuscany, but some of them still preferred to work in the CGL.[300]

In 1909 protests broke out over the execution of Francisco Ferrer. Cavalry was used to intimidate demonstrations, one of which brought together 35,000 protestors. A Ferrer school was organised in Turin; it was to play a significant part in expanding libertarian influence there. Anti-clericalists noted the sexual crimes of 'celibate' clergy – going so far as abusing five-year olds and giving them syphilis.

Economic conditions worsened in 1910, and conflicts increased. 'In Italy, as in other countries, there was a feeling that open battle was close – given that political circumstances were so precarious – and one could not easily foresee in which direction events might unfold.'[301] Many poor Italians emigrated. Indeed, people formed one of Italy's major exports, and remittances from them would help keep the country afloat.

In December 1910, a second direct action congress was held in Bologna networking some 150,000 workers. The CGL was criticised on many fronts: for its corrupt and reformist politicking, for working for social peace rather than class struggle, for looking after corporate rather than class interests. The congress was divided over priorities: should it work to renew and rejuvenate the CGL or was it best to found a new confederation? Economic downturn strengthened a wave of dissent. In subsequent events the Piombino *Camera del Lavora*, in a vicious conflict with employers, found itself abandoned by the metal workers' union (the FIOM). Other strikes and conflicts promoted tensions and provoked a condemnation of the leaders of the CGL and PSI. A report on the congress stated:

> In Italy, the syndicalist movement has a distinct character [...]; those who had formulated its economic programme were deserters from the political movement of the Socialist Party; the latter had all the mentality of the party member, it was almost impossible [to make] them understand that they had no rights within unions or over them, or in the working class; the union, the homogenous organ of the producer, must be able to satisfy both workers' necessities, and its own needs, by itself.

Dissident labour chose direct action rather than mediation, to confront emerging industrial trusts. Support for direct action rose in the face of an aggressive stance from management. The weakness and ineffectiveness of the reformist socialism was becoming apparent in the eyes of radicals. The Parma *Camera* acted as an organisational hub for the syndicalist current, publishing *L'Internazionale*, and entering into contact with the CGT, IWW and FORA.[302]

The USI

In May 1912, the CGL centre declared that CGL membership was incompatible with support for direct action committees. One could not have two conflicting spirits in one CGL body. The Italian Syndicalist Union, or USI, was founded in November in Modena.

A summary of discussion noted that attempts to build unity through and within the CGL had failed. The partisans of parliamentary politics, in unions and parties, had set up a narrow partisan network, one that was disrespectful and exclusive, one that rejected syndicalist direct-action priorities. The best organised workers were being excluded from the CGL, through sectarian abuse and procedural pretexts. CGL unionism was seen as political and reformist, centralised and bureaucratic. It was enamoured with seeking outside financial support. It engendered an organisation devoid of initiative, egotistical, corporatist, divided, uncertain of its own strength, believing in the illusion that it could obtain, through playing games with parties, things that it had failed to obtain through its own strength. The CGL belittled the power and impact of the general strike: for them it had only a symbolic demonstrative value and did not assert counter-power.

There were 42,114 votes for setting up in a new centre, as against 28,856 for boring-from-within to change the CGL (there were also 6,253 abstentions). A motion was agreed opposing war by all means and calling for support for anti-war demonstrations. The new centre looked forward to building industrial unions – a Metals Union was to be based in Milan, with Filippo Corridoni as its co-ordinator; a Construction and Furnishings Union was to be based in Bologna, co-ordinated by Ettore Cuzzani and an Agricultural Union co-ordinated by Amilcare De Ambris in Modena.[303]

Two traditions came together in the new union: firstly radicals – many of them former socialists – critical of the reformist course of the Socialist Party (PSI) and sympathetic to syndicalism as a means of building power for the labour movement, and secondly, anarchists and syndicalists who had little to do with the PSI. Armando Borghi had spent some time in exile in Paris. He brought back to Italy some of the thinking of Monatte and

Pelloutier. Membership was initially around 80,000. The emergence of the USI made plain the divisions that had grown within the organised labour movement. *Camere del lavora* came under syndicalist control in Carrara, Cerignola, Parma, Piombino and Sestri Ponente. In places, such as Bologna, two local union centres confronted each other – one revolutionary, the other reformist. New Syndicalist unions locals were formed in Florence and Milan.

The new USI did not attract every radical syndicalist. The railway workers' union did not become a permanent constituent part of the new union, despite the radical and syndicalist sympathies of a large part of its membership.[304] (The 'Translated News' column of *Industrial Worker*, 17 April 1913, commented that a decision to join the USI might have prejudiced the unity of the railworkers' union, so it remained autonomous, outside the CGL and USI.) Furthermore, some radicals continued to prefer to focus on working for their local labour movement centres rather than prioritising integrated national USI structures.

The USI did not receive unqualified support from all anarchists either. Fabbri for one, although he later accepted the inevitability of a split between radicals and reformists, initially regretted the division of the union movement. He perceived a polarisation between economic and political struggles; while all workers should work together in (one) union, diverse political organisations were both inevitable and necessary. He also wrote that it would be an error to say that parties should disappear and be absorbed by syndicates.[305]

The USI was organised on horizontal lines, with low union dues and without a large body of paid officials. It attempted to develop big industrial unions and had some strength among metal workers. Its rival, the CGL, had between 300,000 and 370,000 members,[306] and there was also a Catholic union federation with about 100,000 members. The USI's bastions were in Bologna, Carrara, Modena, Parma, Piombino and Sestri Ponente and in the provinces of Piedmont, Liguria, Tuscany, the Marches and Emilia-Romagna. It was, like the French CGT, anti-parliamentarian rather than anarchist.[307] The USI emphasised that it stood for workers' unity and that *unity in action* was the foundation for any future proletarian advance. Conflict over 'unity' was a case of one person's meat being another person's poison; organisational unity might entail the suffocation of activity and debate. Just what was entailed by 'unity' varied from organisation to organisation, perhaps depending on an evaluation of what was possible, desirable or timely. The USI had only a short interlude to prepare itself before it faced new trials and wars.

Anti-authoritarian and anti-patriotic priorities were reasserted at anarchist conferences in 1911-12, in the face of war and Italian intervention in Libya against Ottoman Turkey. (An Italian section of the Anti-Militarist International League had been formed in 1907). Anti-militarist propaganda was produced and a newspaper – *Rompete le file!* (Break Ranks!) – was published. Some copies were distributed in army barracks. Young socialists highlighted the abuses suffered by soldiers and sought to raise money – *Il Soldo al Soldato* (The Soldier's Penny) – an echo perhaps of the syndicalist French CGT union federation's campaign for a *Sou du soldat*, which may have come to the attention of Italian subversives via the Genoa-published journal, *La Pace* (Peace). Libertarians supported this campaign. In an article published in December 1912, Armando Borghi wrote that recently it had been not so much anarchists as young socialist who had campaigned against militarism, and their action had earned them their excommunication by the pontiffs of official socialism. Recently the Young Socialists' Federation had split: part of it staying with the Socialist Party, the other part joining with anti-parliamentary syndicalists. The revolutionary syndicalists frequently passed congress motions against militarism – although they had so far not backed these up with sufficient activity. There were grounds for hoping that this was being remedied.[308]

In the autumn of 1911, as Italian troops invaded Libya, Malatesta wrote: 'For Italy's honour we hope that the Italian people will come to their senses and will be able to impose on government a withdrawal from Africa; or if not, we hope that the Arabs win and throw them out.'[309] One soldier, Augusto Masetti, fired on his colonel, crying 'Long live anarchism'. Armando Borghi published a positive appreciation of Masetti's action in *L'Agitatore* and was forced into exile to avoid imprisonment. Malatesta argued that the cause of 'civilisation' was not promoted by theft and invasion by Italian troops, and in these circumstances, he could only side with people being attacked. While some socialists, including Leonida Bissolati and Arturo Labriola, supported the war, the larger part of the working class and its organisations opposed it. Support for Masetti was not confined to Italy – protests, anti-militarist propaganda and fundraising activities spread across the Italian diaspora.

Malatesta left London to return to Italy – that year saw more Italian workers going on strike than ever before. He had hopes and expectations. He wrote to Fabbri in May that his priority was to promote the development of anarchists, working within the workers' movements respecting 'our', i.e. anarchist priorities, and promoting the setting up of local groups.[310] In June, he seemed to echo a theme from *The Miners' Next Step*.* He wrote that one

---

* An extract from *The Miners' Next Step* is included below, pages 166-67

of the gravest dangers was that leaders of workers' movements (anarchists included) might focus too much on propaganda or organisation for its own sake, and that such work might become routine, a trade. In another letter, he wrote that the movement was in a scandalous state. Active methodical preparations were needed as opportunities would surely soon present themselves.[311] He supported militancy even if at first only small steps could be taken; small victories and concessions might be useful:

> … it is only if they are obtained in this fashion, that is to say seized with menaces and through action, that partial improvements are really a blessing, because thus, rather than consolidating a regime by making it more tolerable, they work to encourage the consciousness and strength of the masses, training them in struggle and pushing them towards greater ambitions …

Those who constituted the Social-Democratic party – once it took the electoral and parliamentary path – abased themselves, from one transaction to another, and had become a conservative force, often becoming the best defenders of the bourgeoisie. Some anarchists were seduced into supporting this strategy. Many activists were demoralised when such hopes proved false. It was time to reaffirm ideals, adjust tactics and, in everyday social life, to win over the conscience of the masses. He concluded:

> … what matters is the future: we need to set to work with energy, enthusiasm, and the spirit of sacrifice that were once so characteristic of anarchists. We need to reaffirm our ideals and tactics; exciting awareness in the masses. We need to make our activity felt in all aspects of social life. We need to relate all of our activity to the objective which we intend: a revolution for anarchism and communism.[312]

Determination, *Voluntà* was crucial. Socialism would not fall from a tree like a ripe fruit, it would be created and shaped by deliberate, human effort. Theoretical obstacles and fears that revolution was impossible – all this would evaporate when the time was right. A bloc might come together against militarism and imperialism, against capitalism, the church and the monarchy. It was right to question and doubt everything, to be open to new realities, but such openness should not obstruct a readiness to act.[313]

In August, he wrote that in his opinion the Italian proletariat was on the march towards revolution.[314] In his view, revolutions matured, they involved the capacity for mass organisation to respond to immediate necessities – keeping society moving, keeping people fed, defeating the state and preventing counter-revolution. The state felt endangered, and kept him under constant surveillance.

In the USI, the question of a general strike and its function was considered in March 1913. Armando Borghi raised the possibility of a general strike having one of three profiles: firstly a democratic general strike, operating within a legal ambit seeking concessions from the state of a political nature; secondly a politically defensive general strike, seeking to respond to an attack by the authorities, defending previously acquired rights; thirdly an aggressive and syndicalist general strike, seeking to expand and seize new rights from a bourgeois state and a capitalist economy, perhaps a trial for an expropriating and revolutionary general strike.[315] Borghi emphasised a radical form of workerism, but if he had his differences with Malatesta, they were over means, and not over ends or goals.[316] Seldom did these writers allow much attention to be given to the particular interests of women in this period, although a monthly paper for women, *Donna Libertaria*, for '*propaganda educativa & libertaria femminile*', began publishing in Forli around 1913.

12

INTERNATIONAL ENDEAVOURS AND PERSPECTIVES

Anarchists planned to organise a follow-up congress to the Amsterdam congress of 1907, but without success. A congress due to open on 30 August 1914 was cancelled when war broke out.[317]

A preparatory meeting had been organised in 1913 in Geneva. Alexander Schapiro was nominated as organising secretary and preparatory issues of a *Bulletin du congrès anarchiste international* were published. The initiative for an International Anarchist congress had come from the Anarchist Federation of Germany in July 1913; Russian émigré conferences had supported the idea, as also had organisations in Bulgaria, France, Italy, London, the Netherlands, Russia, Switzerland, the UK and the USA. In Hanover, a congress of the *Anarchistischen Föderation Deutschlands* met on 31 May and 1 June; it discussed the idea of a programme. One report in the journal *Kampf* (Struggle) commented: 'it would be a mistake to believe that one could bring all anarchist tendencies into one hut.' Paul Schreyer called for better co-operation between anarchists and syndicalists.[318]

A series of preparatory meetings took place between exiled Russian libertarians, who gave strong support to anti-militarist activities. The division between anarcho-syndicalists and advocates of force was still strong, with the former having a greater presence in exile rather than in Russia itself. Kropotkin was somewhat marginalised.[319] A Czech Anarchist Federation had decided to send two members; it had held a congress in April 1914, where thirty groups were represented by fifteen delegates.[320] Also in April, a congress of Dutch anarchists met in Amsterdam and chose J. H. Holwerka and Domela Nieuwenhuis as its London delegates. Ricardo Flores Magón wrote to ask that the subject of the revolution in Mexico should be discussed.[321] Representatives were expected from 21 countries. Everything was ready for the event but the outbreak of the First World War put an end to the project.³²²

Several attempts were made to set up anarchist federations, but this organisational work had limited success. Organisational work was left without secure foundations in the absence of a regular pattern of regional, national and international anarchist congresses. The press filled that gap a little, but often editors were not responsible or accountable. Journals often depended on support and financial contributions, coming in part from abroad; such subventions helped papers survive or revive on occasion, especially when they faced harder times from domestic repression. The relative fragility and poverty of anarchist and syndicalist organisation contrasted with the wealth and stability of the German labour movement. If Social-Democratic influence prevailed within the institutions of the international labour and socialist movement, this was due in large part to the wealth of German organisations.

Syndicalism before the First World War – critical perspectives

Malatesta was critical of 'syndicalism' as a political project. In his perspective the labour movement needed the widest possible unity. Malatesta probed the potential impact of general strikes; asserting that they would not solve problems 'automatically'.³²³ Revolution was needed, and it had a wider agenda to resolve, not least confronting and overcoming the armed forces of the state. His priority was not the USI, rather he wanted to facilitate the organisation of active and conscious anarchist minorities, however small they might be. Such perspectives were also debated overseas. In Brazil, an Italian émigré, Luigi (Gigi) Damiani, set out limitations found in some workplace organisations:

> In the union, there's room for everybody: who[ever] pays the dues and strikes when ordered, is always a good fellow, no matter if he is a nationalist or Catholic. In the union, idealistic propaganda is an offence, a violation of the rights of the stomach – the freedom of those that couldn't care less about the abolition of the state and of capitalist property. Everything that doesn't refer to eight hours and to ten cents increases is rejected.³²⁴

… so, another sort of organisation was needed beyond the workplace union. In November 1913 Malatesta wrote that as things were, and given that anarchists wanted a profound social revolution, 'we cannot expect the immediate and general achievement of our ideas, but only the creation of circumstances more favourable for our action and propaganda …'³²⁵ In December he wrote in *Voluntà*, the anarchist journal of Ancona: 'Historical experience shows us that progress, and all revolutions, are always, at first, the work of active and conscious minorities, however small these may be, and the masses have then accepted and defended these achievements. Of course, we cannot liberate the masses against themselves, [or] without their consent.'[326] Propaganda – if it helped clarify strategies – would facilitate opportunities being taken promptly, whenever opportunities arose. The principal objective was to organise an active minority, avoiding ideological divisions; educating, arguing and campaigning for insurrection and the union of [various] forces. The enemy was not just the bourgeoisie, but the state that defended economic privilege. While it would be a vain hope to expect that the army as a whole would join the movement for change, propaganda should target soldiers to help ordinary soldiers throw off military discipline.[327]

In February 1914, Malatesta wrote that the workers' movement on its own would not be able to abolish wage-labour, or foster new social relations. Something else was also needed: the deliberate and conscious action of minorities that managed to acquire influence, and that might give a sense of direction to movements. A general strike needed to develop into a general insurrection that redirected the economy, it needed to achieve more than merely changing the personnel of a political regime. The key task was to unite revolutionaries and attack the institutions of the state, beginning with the army.[328]

Malatesta continued to express a preference for broader and neutral unions, rather than smaller, more homogenous anarchist unions. Otherwise anarchist unions might come to resemble anarchist organisations, and it would become that much more difficult to keep in contact with those outside the anarchist 'party'. Malatesta's views on the politics of the USI were set out in *Voluntà*, in its issue of 20 July 1913. He advocated a strategy of boring-from-within, he did not mention the British Industrial Syndicalist Education League, but perhaps he had in mind an approach something like theirs. In his view, it was difficult to define one syndicalism, as different theories and ideas were frequently lumped together. Some syndicalists could only be distinguished from anarchist-communists with great difficulty. Some syndicalists, though they talked of opposing government, seemed to be akin to Social-Democrats: except that in a revolution, a syndicalist government might arise out of trades' or industrial organisations, rather than territorial constituencies; other syndicalists had fewer preconceived ideas about the future. He preferred to view syndicalism as a movement. It was, at one and the same time both essential and limited – and in any case, it was a fact. Much of the old [First] International had been a quasi-syndicalist movement. He wanted to avoid its errors. He feared some degeneration in current social movements:

> In the organisation of syndicates there is a fundamental contradiction between the ideas they advertise in programmes and the ways they recruit. Syndicates are open to all wage workers without distinction as to religious belief, or social or political opinions. It is said that they should be apolitical and non-confessional, with which we perfectly agree.
>
> Since syndicates wish to bring together all proletarians to draw them into struggle against the bosses and since among proletarians there are all [sorts of] opinions – political, religious philosophical, etc – unity is possible only on the terrain of common interest. The criteria of recruitment cannot be one of opinion but of social position. But, on the other hand, syndicalists place in their programmes declarations that despite all verbal scheming constitute political-social opinions as to how the future is to be conceived, opinions, that, were they to taken seriously, would in fact exclude from syndicates not only those who have other conceptions of social futures, but also, and this is the worst thing, the greater part of wage-earners who, being more inert and lacking in consciousness, most need to experience their first education in struggle and resistance, in workers' associations.

Malatesta went on to write that:

At the Modena Congress that gave birth to the USI, De Ambris, the designated speaker on the problem of proletarian unity said:

> When there is talk of unity among the organised forces of workers, one runs the risk of falling victim to a grand equivocation, if one does not define the meaning of this phrase. Evidently there can be no real unity except between those who, at least, have an identical goal to achieve. When our most ardent proponents of unity refuse to accept, or hear of unity with Catholic organisations, this is just as true, because it is clear that the aims of a confessional Catholic organisation are not ours.
>
> But if this is true, one must be thoroughly honest with ourselves, and we must ask if the goals of the CGL have something in common with those that we advance. Despite the scandal that my proposition may provoke, I say frankly, no. What separates us from reformists is not only a question of methods: because if methods are different, that

is because they are intended to achieve results that are different from ours.

We look for integral, complete, autonomous development of the workers' union [syndicate], [looking] forward to it becoming the principal constitutive element for, and the directing organ of the free and equal producers' new society for which we are struggling. The reformists for their part want the union to be only an instrument for partial and illusory improvements which, moreover, the working class may obtain, not through their own strength, but through the generosity of the boss class, or through state intervention. They wish to accomplish social transformation through the state and for the state, through a series of legislative measures, and through a growing extension of the power of the state which would end up as a substitute for private capitalism ....

Can one find any point of contact between this statist, authoritarian conception of a social future and the syndicalist anti-authoritarian and libertarian conception? No! ...

So, as I have said already, our understanding of social transformation, is not just different, but is opposed to that of the reformists. There is then nothing in common between them and us – neither method nor goals. For us to unite with them would be nothing but hypocrisy or mindlessness, as either one or other of us would be sacrificing their own conception of the future society; or it might produce mutual paralysis; unity would redouble our impotence rather than our strengths.

Congress approved these ideas and for the most part, insofar as they express goals to be obtained, we approve them too. But how can this be reconciled with apoliticism, that is to say with the neutrality of syndicates, a principle that was also approved by congress?

If these goals really are those of all members of the USI and if their conscious acceptance was a condition of admission, then the USI would be only an organisation of revolutionaries, more or less libertarian. One might rejoice, but then one would still feel the need for another organisation, one that really was neutral, that was just anti-management, that might bring together all workers, being a terrain for all sorts of ideas, open to all for the propaganda.

If, on the other hand, the USI intends to accept all workers with the only condition being that they do not 'go to the shop across the street', then it would be founded on lies. The mass of members would be composed of unconscious dues-payers, and the official programme of the USI would depend on the real or fictional majority from one moment to another.

A union, [one] that is revolutionary initially, because founded on revolution and composed of the most pugnacious minority of the most developed areas, would become ever more moderate or reactionary, as it developed and expanded. When the programme of an organisation is more advanced than that of its members and when recruitment is conducted without a strict acceptance of a programme one of two things happens:

— Either the initial core, as it develops its programme, becomes ever more revolutionary, or on the other hand a mass of ever more conservative elements grows and then the divergence between the vanguard and the mass of members grows to the point of incompatibility, and the organisation breaks up (as was the case of the First International).

— Or the leaders, so as not to lose their influence on the mass, adapt and allow themselves to be tamed, and so the organisation loses completely its educational and revolutionary value, to become a factor of social conservation (this is what happened in the larger workers' organisations of England and the USA and continuously threatens syndicalist organisations).

From the above one can conclude that those who say that 'syndicalism suffices unto itself' and that the existence of a workers' movement is enough to produce a social revolution are in error.

Malatesta thought that there was little prospect that syndicalists would develop class consciousness 'automatically', even if they were in struggle. Long term interests might be sacrificed. Even within the labour movement there were tendencies working for sectional privilege. To protect their own particular jobs some workers might seek increased state military expenditure. Class solidarity might be neglected for one reason or another: because of corporate interests or antipathy towards foreigners. The development and progress of apprentices might be obstructed. Apprentices and women might be deprived of work itself.

In view of such tensions within labour movements he preferred the tactics of the British syndicalists who worked in neutral unions that were open to all. He accepted that syndicalists would do whatever they thought best, but the task of anarchists was to work in all unions to plant anarchist ideas.[329] Malatesta's reference to recruitment of union members made some sense, but perhaps his argument missed the spot: the USI had evolved out of real frustration and the failure of the CGL to support action, and those who joined the USI *had chosen* something beyond the CGL; there had been discussion over some years. Much the same might be said for the CNT, FVdG, IWW and elsewhere. There was a widespread movement of discontent, which had led towards the formation of new and distinct organisations. Similar dynamics were at work within the labour centres of Argentina, Britain and France – within the FORA, TUC and CGT. Whatever the politics that might have been highlighted in official documents at a national level there were conflicting dynamics or stresses at play beneath this surface.

Malatesta urged anarchists to work in unions to promote solidarity. They should strive to prevent the development of layers of union functionaries and managers, with interests distinct from, or opposed to those of the mass of union members. Administration should be simplified as far as possible. Administrative activities should be unpaid. If union officials were paid, it should be that at the rate of an average worker. Anarchists should be in the front rank when it came to a fight, but when it came to negotiations with the bosses or authorities they should not take the lead. They should strive to ensure that workers' organisations were active bodies, with general assemblies and frequent discussions. They should work against strike insurance schemes when such things buried the élan of strikers. They should not be preoccupied with co-operatives, co-ops might just be a means of avoiding struggle. Union members should not be passive dues-payers. Money should be used for propaganda, to promote solidarity. Organisations that feared the loss of their wealth might well end up paralysed. His tactics were not geared toward building rich or massive organisation, structures that were stable but inert:

> ... we do not believe in their usefulness, in the real strength of gigantic organisations, whose very grandeur, in its excess impedes all movement, and in which too much money develops conservative shop-keeping instincts. What matters, is the spirit of struggle, the spirit of solidarity and the spirit of the collective. If, following persecutions and struggles a union is dislocated, this matters not, if members are conscientious, and their aspirations remain: when the storm has passed, it can be rebuilt. A strong organisation which does not budge for fear of being dismembered is a dead weight, and obstacle to progress.

Where there was a choice of organisation – such as between the CGL and USI – anarchists should choose the one that best facilitated their activities, and they should not expect change all at once. A purely economic struggle would not resolve social problems. The struggle against the government was a political struggle; the masses would not come to anarchism all at once. Some sort of gradual development was to be expected. Economic struggles were the best available means, and:

> Without doubt it is important, when means are being prepared, not to lose sight of goals, but there is also the need not to neglect in an abstract contemplation of goals, the real means to achieve them.[330]

It is interesting that radicals from different backgrounds and traditions – such as Pannokoek, Gorter and Connolly – were thinking at much the same time about the small-minded and deleterious effects of monolithic union organisations. All three, though they confronted labour organisations of differing provenance, had analogous worries. Malatesta had commented, in 1902, that in the USA:

> Today, and right from the outset, the American labour movement seems to have been made more for the benefit of its leaders than for workers. Starting with the [union] president who enjoys a ministerial salary and wields considerable political influence, and right down to the merest branch secretary, there is a whole hierarchy of employees who live off the movement and, having lost the habit of working and developed a taste for being regarded as important personages, fear nothing so much as they fear having to return to the mines and toil like common working men. This is the main reason why the entire movement boils down to monotonous round, inside a vicious circle.[331]

The views of Pannokoek and Gorter drew on experience in Germany. They were concerned with excessive discipline and the absence of a spirit of initiative. Connolly had noted the success of syndicalists in France and Italy. He became concerned with the growth of new amalgamated unions. In 1914, reflecting on recent defeats, he noted:

> As the General Executive cannot take action pending a meeting of delegates, and as the delegates at that meeting have to report back to their bodies, and these bodies again to meet, discuss, and then report back to the General Executive, which must meet, hear their reports, and then, perhaps, order a ballot vote of the entire membership, after which another meeting must be held to tabulate the result of the vote and transmit it to the local branches, which must meet again to receive it, the chances are, of course, a million to one that the body of workers in

distress will be starved into subjection, bankrupted, or disrupted, before the leviathan organisation will allow their brothers on the spot to lift a finger or drop a tool in their aid. Readers may, perhaps, think that I am exaggerating the danger. But who will think so that remembers the vindictive fine imposed by the NUR [National Union of Railwaymen] upon its members in the North of England for taking swift action on behalf of a persecuted comrade instead of going through all this red tape while he was suffering. [...]

Tactics That Will Win

The amalgamations and federations that are being built up today are, without exception, being used in the old spirit of the worst type of sectionalism; each local Union or branch finds in the greater organisation of which it is a part a shield and excuse for refusing to respond to the call of brothers and sisters in distress, for the handling of tainted goods, for the working of scab boats. A main reason for this shameful distortion of the Greater Unionism from its true purpose is to be found in the campaign against 'sporadic strikes'. [...]

The sudden strike, and the sudden threat to strike suddenly, has won more for labour than all the great labour conflicts in history. In the Boer War the long line of communications was the weak point of the British army; in a labour war the ground to be covered by the goods of the capitalist is his line of communication. The larger it is the better for the attacking forces of labour. But these forces must be free to attack or refuse to attack, just as their local knowledge guides them. But, it will be argued, their action might imperil the whole organisation. Exactly so, and their inaction might imperil that working-class spirit which is more important than any organisation. Between the horns of that dilemma what can be done? In my opinion, we must recognise that the only solution of that problem is the choice of officers, local or national, from the standpoint of their responsiveness to the call for solidarity, and, having got such officials, to retain them only as long as they can show results in the amelioration of the condition of their members and the development of their union as a weapon of class warfare.

Advance or Retreat

If we develop on those lines, then the creation of a great industrial union, such as I have rudely sketched in my opening reminiscence, or the creation of those much more clumsy federations and amalgamations now being formed, will be of immense revolutionary value to the working class; if, on the contrary, we allow officialism of the old, narrow sectional kind to infuse their spirit into the new organisations, and to strangle these with rules suited only to a somnolent working class, then the Greater Unionism will but serve to load us with great fetters ...[332]

Unions responded to the business centralisation and capital organised in cartels with new national industrial amalgamations. Such centralisation empowered the national officials of unions. James Connolly reflected on this process in the following terms:

The much-condemned small Unions of the past had at least this to recommend them, viz., that they were susceptible to pressure from the sudden fraternal impulses of their small membership. If their members worked side by side with scabs, or received tainted goods from places where scabs were employed, the shame was all their own, and proved frequently too great to be borne. When it did so, we had the sympathetic strike and the fraternisation of the working class. But when the workers handling tainted goods, or working vessels loaded by scabs, are members of a nation-wide organisation, with branches in all great centres or ports, the sense of the personal responsibility is taken off the shoulders of each member and local officials, and the spirit of solidarity destroyed. The local official can conscientiously order the local member to remain at work with the scab, or to handle the tainted goods, 'pending action by the General Executive'.

The London-based *Freedom* had come to analogous conclusions some years earlier, criticising the boring-from-within strategy preferred by Tom Mann:

In deciding for the retention of the present organisations, Mann has quite evidently failed to get to grips with the root of the problem he is facing. The curse of Trade Unionism in this country is the centralisation of executive power with its resultant multiplication of officials. The corresponding stagnation and death of local life and spirit is the inevitable consequence. This centralisation would be enormously extended and developed by Mann's scheme ... We must decentralise and as far as possible destroy executive power. Let the workers themselves bear the burden and responsibility of decisive action.[333]

A concern that larger national union structures fostered the power of officialdom, rather than workers' power was to be found elsewhere too. In France, new CGT structures facilitated a 'verticalisation of syndicalist leadership'. In 1910, Marc Pierrot, writing in *Temps nouveaux* had called for anarchist groups to work in unions to spread propaganda and support revolt, work for change, because unions were not sufficient unto themselves.[334] James Guillaume seemed to endorse a different view, seeing the CGT as the continuation of the First International and defending a nuanced interpretation of the relevance of Bakunin's thinking.[335]

In Italy, the USI was from its inception in confrontation with the reformist union movement. Perhaps for this reason relations between leaders such as Borghi and Malatesta were not as tense as in France between 'anarchists' and 'syndicalists'. Borghi asked Malatesta what should be the focal point of proletarian activity – today destructive, tomorrow reconstructive – should it be a nexus of political ideas or a union class nexus?[336] Further developments in the re-grouping of syndicalists are discussed below.

Militarism, nationalism, racism

One of the lines that demarcated anarchism and syndicalism from Social-Democracy, was its resolute opposition to all forms of militarism. Such campaigning was not supported by the Social-Democratic parties of the Second International. Domela Nieuwenhuis, a Dutch socialist, later a libertarian, criticised the overall drift of the Second International:

> When I proposed a strike against militarism to the Brussels congress in 1891, there was much opposition and the proposal was declared to be utopian and fantastic. So much for the progress of socialism over twenty years! Unfortunately, there was retrograde progress.[337]

Britain and the USA had only small professional armies. Elsewhere, anti-militarism was shaped by masses of recruits being forcibly recruited into conscript armies. Recruits, most of whom had never had a chance to vote, might be shipped off to fight in colonial and imperial wars, thousands of miles from home – in places they had never heard of, facing peoples whose languages and cultures seemed incomprehensible to them. Young metropolitan men might be forced to confront peoples called 'savage' and 'heathen', cast by racist ideologies as unfit to enjoy the human rights afforded to 'more advanced' and 'civilised' peoples.

Libertarians based in colonised societies were often more aware of issues of racism and imperialism than their counterparts in the metropolis. The

Peruvian liberal turned libertarian, Manuel González Prada, wrote in November 1906 that internationalism and patriotism were irreconcilable. 'We have no homeland [*patria*], if we appreciate as equals every nation; we are not patriots, if we choose not to prefer one of our own fellow citizens over and above someone from Lapland, France or China.' In his view, the pretension of some French and German socialists, that patriotism and internationalism might be reconciled was not logical; the idea that popular freedom and military service could be reconciled was wrong.[338] In 1907, 2,200 workers were killed by the Chilean army in a massacre in Iquique (an area rich in nitrates recently incorporated into Chile).* Some thousands of workers took refuge in Peru. Some months later González Prada endorsed the principle of sabotage.[339] In 1912, there was a rural slaughter in the Chicama valley in Peru. Delfín Lévano wrote in *La Protesta* that the massacre revealed the full horror of the militarist plague – the work of the President and his henchmen.

'*Down with compulsory military service. The army is a school of crime.*' Anti-military demonstrations in Santiago (Chile) began in 1900.

Many metropolitan libertarians promoted anti-militarism spurred by a hatred for the role of the armed forces breaking strikes. There was also some awareness of armed forces' role fostering imperialism and opposition to colonial adventures. The opposition of Malatesta to Italy's invasion of Libya, and the mass revolt of workers in Barcelona, have already been mentioned. Some French anarchists also condemned the state for its murderous policy

* Such massacres had class and racist dimensions: ordered by state elites against outsiders.

in North Africa. The French state had penal battalions in Africa where propagandists who subverted army conscripts were badly treated.[340]

There was, within parts of the labour movement, racism and an absence of sympathy for colonised peoples. On occasion, racist ideas also intruded into the libertarian press. Thomas Fauset MacDonald, for example, was allowed to publish, in *Freedom* and in *Mother Earth*, an article on the Australian and New Zealand labour movements, which implicitly defended a white Australian labour ideology, inveighing against cheap coloured labour, blacklegs brought in by capital to swamp (white) workers' organisation; 'alien workers (Chinese and Japanese), who were in reality slaves, having neither social privileges extended to them, nor could they in their helpless ignorance form even the simplest institution of self-defence'.[341]

In his memoirs, Tom Mann[342] shows an awareness of the unequal pay and living conditions of African people as he visited South Africa. In another text, he notes skilled white workers behaving 'towards the black man as a most superior and lordly personage[s]'. However, Mann did not advocate abandoning existing unions – formed of white workers – or forming new non-racial unions. He comments 'it remains the fact that in the days of dense economic ignorance the best of the workmen joined them ['white' unions] and through them and by means of them *they waged the class war*, guided generally by instinct and without the inspiration afforded by a clearly conceived ideal. Still they fought, and allowing for their environment, they fought exceedingly well.' He did not advise starting again: 'A few here are bitterly attacking all existing unions and unionists, but are not evidencing any capacity to organize the mass not affected by existing unionists.'[343] In Mann's view the white workers were waging the *class war*, and, one must presume, the black workers were not, however quickly they were dying. Evidently something was lacking here. The South African *Voice of Labour*, a journal first sponsored by the General Workers' Union 'charged that Mann had failed to attack racial segregation ... He had indeed largely avoided this issue ...'[344] Perhaps Mann was more concerned to build 'the labour movement' and resisted 'sectional priorities' that would have prioritised the interests of non-whites. From another viewpoint, a mindset focusing on building bigger, more powerful, white industrial unions was itself a sectional mindset, failing to address the non-white majority.

Alternatives did exist: a heterogenous South African International Socialist League was developing and there were the beginnings of African and Asian workers' unions being organised; struggles were underway to organise across the racial divide – with 'no bounds of craft, no exclusions of colour ...' – making a struggle for the recognition of the Black worker the very heart of official policy.³⁴⁵ This was an organisation shaped by IWW and kindred sensibilities. It believed that 'once organised, these workers can bust-up any tyrannical law. Unorganised, these laws are iron bands. *Organise industrially*, they become worth no more than the paper rags they are written on.'³⁴⁶

Liverpool transport strike, 1911

In Britain, in 1911, Fred Bower wrote a leaflet, *Don't Shoot*, an *Open Letter to British Soldiers* when a strike broke out on the Liverpool Docks.

> Men! Comrades! Brothers! You are in the army. So are we. You in the army of destruction. We in the industrial, or army of construction. We work at mine, mill, forge, factory, or dock, producing and transporting all the goods, clothing, and stuffs, which make it possible for people to live. You are working men's sons. When we go on strike to better our lot, which is the lot also of your fathers, mothers, brothers, and sisters, you are called upon by your officers to murder us. Don't do it!
>
> You know how it happens. Always has happened. We stand out as long as we can. Then one of our (and your) irresponsible brothers, goaded by the sight and thought of his and his loved ones' misery and hunger, commits a crime on property. Immediately you are ordered to murder us, as you did at Mitchelstown, at Featherstone, at Belfast. Don't you know that when you are out of the colours, and become a 'civvy' again, that you, like us, may be on strike, and you, like us, [will] be liable to be murdered by other soldiers.
>
> Boys, don't do it! 'Thou shalt not kill', says the book. Don't forget that! It does not say, 'unless you have a uniform on.' No! Murder is murder, whether committed in the heat of anger on one who has wronged a loved one, or by pipe-clayed tommies with a rifle.

Boys, don't do it! Act the man! Act the brother! Act the human being! Property can be replaced! Human life, never! The idle rich class, who own and order you about, own and order us about also. They and their friends own the land and means of life of Britain. You don't! We don't! When we kick, they order you to murder us. When you kick, you get court-martialled and cells. Your fight is our fight. Instead of fighting against each other, we should be fighting with each other. Out of our loins, our lives, our homes, you came. Don't disgrace your parents, your class, by being the willing tools any longer of the master class.

You, like us, are of the slave class. When we rise, you rise; when we fall, even by your bullets, ye fall also. England with its fertile valleys and dells, its mineral resources, its sea harvests, is the heritage of ages to us. You no doubt joined the army out of poverty. We work long hours for small wages at hard work, because of our poverty. And both your poverty and ours arises from the fact that Britain with its resources belongs to only a few people. These few, owning Britain, own our jobs. Owning our jobs, they own our very lives. Comrades, have we called in vain? Think things out and refuse any longer to murder your kindred. Help us to win back Britain for the British, and the world for the workers![347]

This ending – 'Britain for the British' – suggests an insensitivity towards racism. Bower was aware of Irish struggles but seemed unaware of the non-European communities then beginning to emerge in port cities like Liverpool. (He referred to the use of force against strikers: three Irish Land League rent strikers had been shot and killed by the police in 1887. In Featherstone, West Yorkshire, in 1893, soldiers had shot and killed two striking miners. In 1907, the police and the army protected imported scab labour used to break a Belfast dock workers' strike; three thousand men in uniform broke into homes in the Falls road area, and two workers were shot.)

Jonathan Hyslop has outlined a British Imperial *White Labourism*, a nexus of paternalist perspectives with racist roots, defined by a defence of superior wages and conditions against cheap Asiatic or African labour. 'The idea of the welfare state as belonging to a "white" nation was there at the start. The imperial working class of the pre-First World War era was unable to separate its hostility to its own exploitation from its aspiration to incorporation in the dominant racial structure.'[348] Bower's 'Britain for the British' appears to connect with this ideology.

Mainstream British, French and Spanish trade-unionist centres spread to colonies but for some time failed to consider indigenous peoples as equals, or to organise with them. Libertarian organisations in the Americas frequently organised immigrants – both recent immigrants without citizenship, and those with longer regional antecedents. In France, some libertarians noted the double standards that 'progressive' civilisation promoted and that colonialists sought to put in place in Algeria: demands for separate development in education; the application of law for individual property for themselves as against laws that regulated the collective property of indigenous people; opposition to the emigration of Arabs to metropolitan France to seek better paid work, thus ensuring that there should be a dependent labour force paid derisory wages. These remarks appeared in 1914 in an issue of *Les Temps nouveaux*. The same issue also noted an announcement in the *Atlanta Journal*: 'We offer 125 francs to whoever returns to us Walter Banks, a negro, a partial mulatto, aged 25 to 28, five foot four inches tall, thick lips, large eyes. This amount will be paid to the person who returns this negro to Estes Brothers, Gaz., Georgia …'[349]

Sometimes indigenous peoples were admired for having fair and communal lifestyles. B. S. Carrión profiled indigenous peoples in 1912, in an article in *La Protesta*, a Peruvian journal that promoted libertarian syndicalist ideas for over a decade. He suggested that there was a distinct culture of communal labour, the barter of produce, and that the Indian was naturally pacific, hating abusive authority and military conscription.[350] A debate began in *La Protesta* – as to whether universal modern and scientific (European) ideas should prevail? Or should anarchists resituate themselves and adjust perspectives and priorities?

Labour movements and anti-militarism

An Anti-Militarist International was founded in Amsterdam in 1904 involving some influential CGT figures (Miguel Almereyda, Émile Janvion and Georges Yvetot). (Not all anti-militarists were identified with a libertarian organisation. There were overlapping sympathies between many pacifists and libertarians, But, there were also divergences, insofar as many libertarians rejected pacifism.)

The International gathered some support in France and held a conference in Saint-Étienne, in July 1905. In October, a large poster headed 'Appeal to Recruits' was pasted up in Paris and other French cities: 'If you are ordered to discharge your weapons against your poor brothers … You will shoot the decorated mercenaries who dare to give you such orders. …When you are send you to the borders … you will not march. … Every war is criminal.' Prosecutions followed – 26 of the poster's signatories were sentenced to fines and terms of imprisonment of up to four years. Further posters followed, with similar responses from the state, and the organisation was disrupted. Anti-militarism had some support in the CGT.

> Workers, maybe tomorrow we will be facing the fait accompli of war having been declared. For five years now, a French colonialist party, for which [Théophile] Delcassé acted as the servant has been preparing the conquest of Morocco. Capitalist and imperialist Germany has intervened seeking its own share of booty. In June 1905 war was avoided only by the departure of Delcassé. Ever since, war might have broken out over the least incident. The press knows about these things ... and keeps quiet. Why? Because one wants to oblige people to go on the march, on the pretext of national honour, inevitable because defensive. But the people do not want war! If called on to express an opinion, it would unanimously affirm its desire for peace. The working class has no interest in war. It alone would pay all the costs, paying for all its work with blood! So, it is up to them to say that it wants peace at any price!
>
> Workers! ... In Germany, as in France, there is a formal communion of ideas on this point: the proletariat of both these countries refuses to make war. So, by our simultaneous and common action, let us force our respective governments to take into account our wishes: We want peace. Let us refuse to make war!
> THE CONFEDERAL COMMITTEE.

The question of trade-union responses to war proved to be very controversial within the international structures of the Labour movement. In 1905, Karl Legien, the ISNTUC bureau secretary, excluded from the ISNTUC conference agenda any discussion of anti-militarism and the general strike. In retaliation, the CGT boycotted its meetings and for a time withdrew dues. In the final chapter to his short book *L'Action Syndicaliste*, Victor Griffuelhes explained these conflicts:

> In the trade-union international the uniqueness (*originalité*) of French syndicalism is remarkable. Through its rapid march, it has advanced so far beyond most union movements of other countries that others can neither follow nor understand it. From this there flows the inevitable antagonism which brings out the opposition between French working class organised on new lines and the various working classes of other nations organised on older lines.
>
> The difference that has broken out recently between French syndicalism

and the ISNTUC bureau is the best proof of this. It is obvious that the CGT and the ISNTUC bureau are not agreed as to the practice and *goal* of the regular conferences held among the secretaries of national labour organisations.

German trade-unionism, as it chairs the ISNTUC – and following it other countries – has, as regards trade-union action, a conception which is quite consistent in making labour organisations a vassal of political parties. French syndicalism, on the contrary, without being opposed to parties, which it does not need to recognise, attaches to syndicalist action an *incontestable preponderance*.[351]

Griffuelhes noted that the Dublin ISNTUC meeting of 1903 had lasted only three hours – and that included time dedicated to translations – such a brief event did not merit the time and money it demanded. This brevity prevented anti-militarist matters being addressed, and when the agenda of the next meeting was being prepared the ISNTUC bureau refused to add such anti-militarism to the agenda. A letter to the CGT on these arrangements was sent to the wrong address and the result was that France was not represented at the 1905 ISNTUC meeting in Amsterdam. That meeting resolved that 'all theoretical questions and those relating to the *tendencies and tactics* of the labour movement of various lands should be excluded from discussion.'[352]

Victor Griffuelhes, a key CGT official, travelled to Berlin in January 1906, hoping to co-ordinate anti-war demonstrations in the face of the crisis in Morocco – he received no co-operation – August Bebel, the veteran socialist leader, refused to give him an audience. It was in the light of this, and following the refusal of both branches of the German labour movement to join protests with those of the CGT against the horrendous prospects of war, that the CGT Amiens congress of September 1906 approved a suspension of relations with the ISNTUC bureau, citing the refusal of that body to add to the agenda of international meetings the matters of the anti-militarism, the eight-hour day, and the general strike.

Griffuelhes wrote that the CGT will not take part in ISNTUC conferences the utility of which appears to be very debatable. 'It refuses to recognise the legitimacy of a German resolution which forever prohibits discussions which are essential aspects of the domain of labour, which, it proclaims, must only be touched on by political congresses, in which French labour does not want to a part.' In his view, this line aimed at forcing through respect for the authority of political congresses.

In August 1907, the CGT sent a letter out to other national labour centres, just before the next ISNTUC meeting in Kristiania (Oslo), citing Legien's practice – fixing the agenda and excluding from it the matters raised by the CGT – as an infringement on national labour autonomy, making unproductive an international conference of that body. The CGT refused to accept any limitation on the field of labour action, to do so would make conferences of little or no interest. The ISNTUC meeting held in 1907 in Kristiania also refused to consider either the question of the general strike or questions of militarism – resolving that such matters should be remitted to an international congress of Socialist *parties*. The congress was boycotted by the CGT.

Griffuelhes noted that the question of relations with the Socialist party was discussed in Kristiania – so that it seemed that some political matters might be addressed, but that the matters of the anti-militarism, the eight-hour day, and the general strike were perversely kept off the agenda. The agenda was fixed as a matter of political preference, and not because certain politics were outside Labour's remit – and the ISNTUC did not have the honesty to admit what it was doing. Griffuelhes commented that the resolutions passed invited the CGT to change its tactics even though the ISNTUC said that such tactics could not be discussed or placed on the ISNTUC agenda! Perhaps it was no coincidence that shortly afterwards the CGT's *La Voix du Peuple* published an article by Ernst Rieger, a member of a small radical German union federation – the FVdG – on the bankrupt methods of the 'free' *Generalkommission* trade union method, something that may have infuriated the latter.[353]

Griffuelhes was perhaps mistaken in his hopes. He sought to obtain a discussion of the CGT's new forms of action and its radical agenda. CGT leaders wanted a wider audience discussing labour politics, a congress involving many union members, not just a meeting over an hour or two, for a small number of officials. He hoped to see some respect for the politics adopted by the CGT in France, even if that politics was not shared elsewhere. He wanted a confrontation and a discussion between viewpoints and looked forward to some revision of direction and policy. In all these aims he, and the radicals in the CGT, were frustrated. Moreover, after a boycott of the ISNTUC, the CGT reengaged with it.

There were war scares over Morocco in 1908 and 1911, followed by conflicts in the Balkans, but the CGT was never able to move the ISNTUC from its apolitical stance. The German trade union leaders' refusal to discuss political matters was to have repercussions in 1914, as will be seen below.

The ISNTUC admitted only one labour centre for each land and excluded other bodies. It chose to de-recognise one radical Dutch labour network –

the *Nationaal Arbeids Secretariaat* – and took in a Social-Democratic rival instead. The IWW was refused admittance. The ISNTUC remained under German Social-Democratic non-confrontational and reformist leadership and 'the ISNTUC's work clearly mirrored Legien's own preoccupations at home'. Legien was looking for peaceful development, not social upheaval.[354] If the German unions were preoccupied with winning government recognition and building a subordinate power within capitalism and the Kaiser-state it did not have the same goals as the CGT, if, that is, the CGT was at root committed to something beyond capitalism. Things were not quite clear – there was some shading of emphasis and some lack of clarity – but fundamentally there was a large part of the CGT committed to revolutionary aspirations, and crucially able to work and organise for those aspirations in France; whereas in Germany, there was little or no such space, and in tandem there was a large majority of the German movement that paid only lip service to socialism. It was perhaps not as Griffuelhes thought, a matter of the CGT advancing too rapidly, but rather that the CGT and the German 'free' *Generalkommission* unions were – as far as their leaders were concerned – advancing towards different and conflicting goals. The CGT might have recognised that its new forms and older forms and goals were not compatible. It did not make that determination or make a break with the ISNTUC, but it did continue to reaffirm the anti-militarist policies that it had passed at its Amiens congress:

> CGT Congress ... affirms that anti-militarist and anti-patriotic propaganda must become ever more intense and more audacious. In every strike, the army sides with the bosses; in every European conflict, in every war between nations or over colonies, the working class is duped and sacrificed for the boss class of bourgeois parasites. Therefore, Congress approves and sanctions all anti-militarist and anti-patriotic propaganda ...

The conclusion of the motion passed at the Marseilles congress of 1908 (and reaffirmed at the next congress in Toulouse in 1910) was: 'Congress declares it must undertake the education of workers from an international viewpoint so that in the event of war between the powers, workers respond to a declaration of war with the declaration of a general strike.'[355] Commissions were to be organised to prepare for the organisation of the general strike. At the Toulouse congress, in 1910, it was noted that 33 had been organised in 150 *bourses* and unions, and some of these existed only on paper. However, anti-militarist propaganda was spreading and becoming livelier.[356]

The CGT published a *Manuel du Soldat* (Soldiers' Manual) as part of its campaign. It denounced the state as a government of assassins, whose army was used to intimidate, subdue or kill striking workers and rebellious peasants. The first of many editions of the manual was published in 1902 – some 200,000 copies were printed. The author, Georges Yvetot, recalled the army's reactionary role in 1830, 1848 and 1871. The army was denounced: it was a policeman, a strike breaker, it sided with capital and exploiters. The army lent its murderous strength to bosses, to beat and intimidate labour. Soldiers, unless they refused to obey orders, became servants of shame or mere assassins. Military service was a 'servitude and disgrace, for as soon as he puts on his uniform, the man of the people despite himself, betrays his own. The proletarian soldier is the "man of the people" set up to defend the rich and powerful, armed and equipped against his brothers.' The army was a school of crime, vice, laziness and hypocrisy; it was hateful, harmful and corrupt. It should be subverted: 'Turn the school of crime into a school of revolt.'

> ... They say that the homeland (*Patrie*) is the country of our birth, where we live, where we work, where we take a part in communal life. We should love our country. But would we cease to love her, if we seek happiness by coming to an understanding with those who live elsewhere, on the other side of rivers and seas? Do we cease to love her, because we dare to love those who live around her – in other countries, where language, custom or climate is different? ...
>
> That word – *Patrie* – is the motto for every infamy, every cruelty, ever corruption, every deceit. On account of that word we are locked up [conscripted] for three years, [we are] made into slaves, or perhaps into assassins, or [we] become victims of brutal non-commissioned officers. Taxes crush us, for *la Patrie*; our money is extorted for *la Patrie*; and its army – for twelve or fourteen hours, day after day – we have to do as we are told, labouring like a beast for a starvation wage. ...
>
> No! Militarism is a means of enslavement. The barracks make us into obedient machines ... What is the legacy of the barracks: moral cowardice, a pattern of [fear and] trembling and subservience. Men, when they leave the forces, show up having become traitors to the working class: as scabs or policemen and the army has another role as the nation's gendarme. In strikes, when workers, are driven out of work by the avarice of the employer and rightly think that their place is on the streets, it is soldiers who are sent in with the fixed bayonets and loaded rifles; it is they who

gallop and charge down the streets. And it is not just with the rifle that the army runs to assist capital. When strikes occur the soldier may even take the place of the worker. The national army, the army formed from people's youth, serves the bosses and lines up against the people. The army with all its capacity to murder, is loaned out to the bosses ...[357]

In 1907, the 17th regiment of the army mutinied and refused to fire on a protest movement of small peasant wine growers. (Subsequently the regiment was ordered off to the Gafsa region of Tunisia, an inhospitable fever-prone area – a place where they might be expected to die. ('It is true – the odd victim more or less – matters not to the sinister Clemenceau.')[358] The refusal of the regiment to commit murder was celebrated in the song, *Glory to the 17th*:

Your anger was right, to refuse was your very duty,
shoot not father, mother, for those who are in authority,
Soldiers your conscience is clear, we French don't kill one another,
Refuse to make your bayonets red, that's the best way to tread.
We salute the soldiers of the 17th, the brave poilus,
we salute your great work, we love and admire you,
had you fired on us, you'd have killed the republic too.

This was one of several songs, which along with dramatic sketches, disseminated anti-militarist ideas. CGT militants hated the army for its record of killings: for example, one death in Nantes in 1907, five in Narbonne (with many more wounded), one in Raon-l'Etape in 1908, and nine more in Draveil and Villeneuve-Saint-Georges (with some 200 wounded, also in 1908). Most galling was that much of this repression was organised by radical or 'socialist' ministers who had previously condemned such policies. Workers, wrote Yvetot, should fight for themselves and for the 'provinces' they had lost: life and liberty; rather than for Alsace and Lorraine in the cause of a bogus nationalism.[359] Such campaigning had some impact and tens of thousands refused conscription or deserted.

The libertarian press noted that class conditions were replicated in the armed forces. The sons of working people could expect harsh treatment and bad conditions, and the deprivation of all human rights; the sons of the upper classes could expect all sorts of privileges and liberties. The CGT paper, *Voix du Peuple*, carried some reports of deaths in the military, attributing assassinations to named officers and NCOs. CGT propaganda stressed that patriotism was a cruel hoax, and that class mattered more than nationality; recent deaths in the army were attributed to the same class hatred that had been shown in the past, as in May 1871, with the massacres perpetrated by the army attacking the Paris Commune.[360] On occasion comments suggested that the army was responsible for racist killings in North Africa. 'Several young soldiers selected by the government (it lacks sufficient mercenaries), for butchering in Morocco, have bravely preferred to desert rather than make a journey into dishonour – to pillage, kill and massacre inoffensive peoples. Bravo the deserters!'[361]

Civilisation in Morocco

This CGT militancy was disparaged by some socialists who thought that it damaged the socialist movement in the eyes of potential allies. Some CGT organisations did not share radical perspectives, arguing that it was illegitimate for the CGT to promote an anti-patriotism that was outside its remit, beyond its core function as an economic organisation. This line echoed that of the German labour movement with its separation between politics and economics, with politics being the preserve of the Social-Democratic Party (SPD). But this view was rejected by those who believed that soldiers should refuse to take arms against their other workers. The CGT called for public demonstrations for peace and published a leaflet entitled 'War on War', reiterating that workers had no homeland (*patrie*) and calling for a general strike as a response to any declaration of war.[362] If war came, workers should respond to a declaration of war by calling for a revolutionary general strike.

The CGT also initiated some practical work to help recruits. It collected a soldier's penny (*Sou du soldat*), it dispersed pocket money to recruits, attempts were made to keep recruits in contact with their original workplace syndicates and to forge links with syndicalists in whatever place they might be garrisoned.

In Switzerland Luigi Bertoni had an anti-militarist pamphlet published in French and Italian: *Travailleur, ne sois pas soldat! / Abbasso l'esercito!* (Workers: Don't become Soldiers! / Down with the Army!) – calling for a military walk out or strike. Bertoni attended the Rome Anarchist congress of 1907 and argued that without anti-militarism Syndicalism would be all in vain.[363]

Germany had, on the whole, a much weaker anti-militarist tradition, with only small currents in the labour movement opposing militarism. Engels believed that the German labour movement should fight Russian Tsarism and their French allies: '*In the interest of the European revolution, they are obliged to defend all the positions that have been won.*' In any case, he appeared to think that the army would change its nature: 'Today we have one soldier in five, in a few years' time we shall have one in three, by 1900 the army, hitherto the most outstandingly Prussian element in Germany, will have a *socialist* majority. That is coming about as if by fate.'[364] Bebel too defined himself as a patriotic German, ready to shoulder his rifle in the face of Russian barbarism. These Social-Democrats, and the bulk of their party, saw German and Socialist interests as intertwined in a 'proletarian patriotism', such they would fight in wars under the Kaiser. German Social-Democrats did demand that recruits should not be abused, but they did not seek to oppose army service. Military service was consistently refused by some Christian pacifists.

German libertarians worked to promote anti-militarism. Arnold Roller published *A Soldier's Handbook*, disguised in a form as a breviary, to facilitate it being smuggled into Germany.

> Do Germans kill Blacks in their African colonies because the German homeland is in danger? It is matter of plunder, of plunder pure and simple …*
>
> If we were to accept that Germany had real political freedoms, such

---

* The German army had waged a genocidal war in South-West Africa (now Namibia) in 1904.

as [might exist in] France or Switzerland; would such political freedoms really be so valuable then, that proletarians – by hundreds of thousands – should sacrifice their lives?

A smaller, milder dose of oppression and persecution is, in truth, not to be bought or maintained at the price of a hundred-thousand proletarian corpses ...

When the officer returns from war in one piece he then awaits rewards, promotion, a better pension; if he comes back wounded he has a medal, a full pension and a trouble-free life. If he is killed his family is richly looked after by the state. But when you, a soldier, are wounded in conflict or return crippled or unfit for work, you are forced to go a-begging or your wife and children will starve in misery, because no state will look after you. And if death claims you in battle your wife and children will soon follow you there, because they will be left undisturbed to starve.

To be free, one must have the capacity to be able to enjoy life and this is what proletarians do not have, not even in Switzerland, in the classic country of freedom.[365]

15,000 copies of this handbook were seized in February 1907 according to one report.[366] Pierre Bourey wrote a report published in *Les Temps nouveaux* on 9 March 1907. He recounted how Karl Sauter, one-time editor of the *Revolutionär* (the journal of the Anarchist Federation) and Arthur Malyscha, both from Berlin, were arrested on 7 February, along with Paul Schauf from Crefeld. The second was released. 1,200 copies of the *breviary* were discovered in the homes of the other two. Both men were still imprisoned, and enquiries and searches were directed against their known associates, hoping (vainly) to find other copies. *Vorwärts*, [the SPD paper] which for some time had refrained from attacking us [Anarchists] had recommenced its malicious insults – it wrote that the *breviary* was published with money provided by the police. 'Social-Democrats who are too scared to fight with any energy against militarism, become very brave when it comes to discrediting those who have dedicated themselves, body and soul, to this, a struggle that in Germany is calamitous and painful. [But] They will not manage to discourage our militants.' Karl Sauter was sentenced to a year in prison, Paul Schauf to three months.[367] Two other editions of the breviary were published later, one with a new title *Soldaten Freund* (The Soldier's Friend).[368]

At the Amsterdam Congress of 1907 Pierre Ramus had asked:

[W]hat is its meaning, what influence does German Social-Democracy have in parliament, where does it make manifest its anti-militarism? Where, in all the wide world, is it expressed – this Social-Democratic anti-militarism?

Social-Democracy is developing in its parliamentary activity a perfectly conservative element of militarism, everyone who reads and understands the speeches of Bebel[369] (Noske says nothing different to him) – and his international colleagues has to take that into account. They combat the 'abuses' of militarism, while it is, in itself, a unique danger ... Let us summarise: Social-Democratic anti-militarism is the hypocrisy of ambitious politicians, for them, making a reality of it, means not the abolition of militarism but rather a change in its forms and functions ...

Social-Democrats in many countries did demand that the armies be re-organised on a militia basis. On the face of it a citizen or militia army might appear as a popular force, but the question arose, what was the purpose of such a force? In Switzerland, the militia army was used to break strikes, and on several occasions fired on and killed workers. Military courts imposed penalties and imprisonment on recalcitrant soldiers.* Persons who refused Swiss military service were imprisoned for months at a time. In Germany Rudolf Oestreich, was sentenced to three years' imprisonment for treason, after writing anti-militarist texts for *Der Freie Arbeiter*, and having previously refused military service.

In Barcelona in 1903, a translation of Yvetot's work was published as the *Manual del Soldado*, the fifth in a series published as a *Biblioteca de la Huelga General* (Library of the General Strike). In *Temps nouveaux*, 23-29 April 1904, it was announced that the *Nouveau Manuel du Soldat* would soon be translated and published in Montevideo.[370] Such evidence suggests that a network of activists was working to spread anti-militarist propaganda.

An Anti-Militarist Congress convened by Domela Nieuwenhuis met in Amsterdam in June 1904, dedicating itself 'For militarism, not a person, not a penny'. It involved participants from the Austro-Hungarian empire, Britain, France, Italy, the Netherlands, Portugal, Spain and Switzerland. Several well-known figures attended: Émile Armand, Émile Janvion, Siegfried Nacht, Paul Robin, Georges Thonar and Georges Yvetot among others. A second smaller congress met in Amsterdam in 1907, coinciding

---

* In 1902, a general strike broke out in Geneva after tram workers were sacked. 3,500 soldiers were summoned and the city was placed under siege; 321 refused orders and 18 were imprisoned. Gianpiero Bottinelli, *Louis Bertoni, une figure de l'anarchisme ouvrier à Genève*, Geneva: Entremonde, 2012, p. 34.

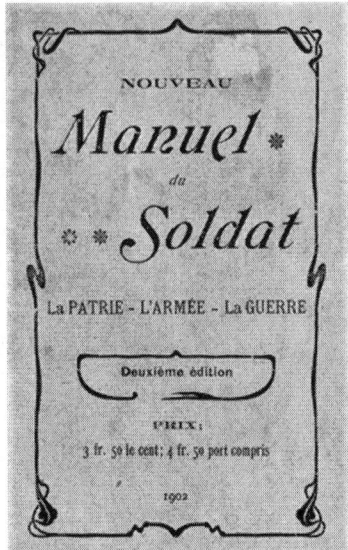

The Manuel du Soldat *(Soldiers' Manual) first published by the CGT in 1902*

with the Anarchist congress. An Anti-Militarist International League with national organisations was formed but it was fragile and ephemeral. The French republic equated anti-militarism with being anti-patriotic, and sentenced activists to terms of three or four years' imprisonment. Activists were kept under police surveillance and measures were put in place to have them incarcerated in the event of war (under the *Carnets B* system).

In France, in 1910, the socialist leader Jean Jaurès wrote a book, *L'Armee nouvelle*, calling for a new model, an army that was primarily 'defensive'. An article in *Les Temps nouveaux* condemned it as a lengthy hymn to warlike patriotism. Jaurès was using persuasion to drive people to support militarism,[371] while the government used force in its attempts to destroy anti-militarism.

Although armies were widely hated, patriotism was widespread too, and the determination to act to prevent wars was lacking in the labour movement as a whole. Among the strongest Social-Democratic movements there was an expectation that they would soon become the leading force in the state, and so they looked to support the armed forces of those states, in the vain expectation that these forces would serve labour interests. In the USA, Earl Ford and William Z. Foster commented in a text from 1913:

> The international Socialist Party stands committed to this patriotic policy. This, of course, involves militarism, and socialists the world over are militarists. August Bebel, the German Socialist leader, in his book, *Nicht*

Stehendes Heer, sondern Volkswehr (A people's army, not a standing army) urged that, in order to better defend Germany, every able-bodied male should be a soldier from earliest boyhood to old age. He says school and work boys should be drilled during their spare time, Sundays, evenings, etc. Jaurès, the noted French socialist leader, advocates that the sons of labour union officials be placed in command of the companies of boy soldiers he would organize to defend France. The militarism of various other socialist leaders, such as Ramsey McDonald of England, and Pablo Iglesias of Spain, is notorious.

The syndicalist is a radical anti-patriot. He is a true internationalist, knowing no country. He opposes patriotism because it creates feelings of nationalism among the workers of the various countries and prevents co-operation between them, and also, because of the militarism it inevitably breeds. He views all forms of militarism with a deadly hatred, because he knows from bitter experience that the chief function of modern armies is to break strikes, and that wars of any kind are fatal to the labour movement. He depends solely on his labour unions for protection from foreign and domestic foes alike and proposes to put an end to war between the nations by having the workers in the belligerent countries go on a general strike and thus make it impossible to conduct wars.[372]

13

SYNDICALISM IN 1913-14

Conflicting perspectives and priorities emerged more clearly when radical syndicalists proposed an international meeting and looked towards a new form of international co-operation. In April 1913, the IWW's *Industrial Worker* commented on the project for an International Syndicalist Congress. It indicated its general support while displaying a certain pridefulness, remarking that there were three reasons why the IWW position would demand attention:

> First, because the IWW presents, in its industrialism, an even more advanced form of organization than that of the syndicalists, this by reason of the higher degree of capitalist development in America; Second, because the IWW by its activities during the past year, has been the foremost labor organization in the world in spreading the idea of revolutionary direct action; Third, because the IWW was refused representation at the last congress of the present International [the ISNTUC/IFTU*], while the essentially capitalistic American Federation of Labor was granted a delegate despite the fact that the AFL is constantly waging an anti-Asiatic fight and is the antithesis of internationalism in every essential feature.[373]

This comment followed:

> The present International, while it is the best that has thus far been afforded, is not a working-class organization by any means. The bulk of the delegates have never been employed as wage workers. no extended discussion of the general strike is allowed. The attitude on militarism is that of the compromiser rather than the revolutionist. In many respects the International has adopted the reformist attitude that is so characteristic

---

* The ISNTUC changed its designation to International Federation of Trade Unions in September 1913.

of any socialist movement that inclines toward parliamentarianism. Its American delegates could not be classed as revolutionists by allowing the utmost charity in the interpretation of the word. As a growing menace to capitalism the present International is a farce.

In the regular 'Translated News' column of the same edition, reactions from various journals and organisations were reported: *Die Einigkeit* (the journal of the localists of the FVdG) was supportive; so too was *Syndicalisten* (Swedish Workers' Centre); so too *L'Internazionale* (USI). Cornelissen, whose name appeared at the foot of this column, commented:

La Vie Ouvrière, the fortnightly syndicalist review, criticizes the proposal of the Dutch comrades to create 'an International link between the organizations which favour direct action,' a proposal which the appeal but slightly hints at. The editor, P. Monatte, thinks that a second international would be as impotent as the existing organizations under the socialist tutelage. He would have the English syndicalists follow out the line of their propaganda within the old unions and have these same unions accept the idea of a real labour congress.

Monatte can easily say this, but to continue to give new life to the old unions can only be done by the syndicalists if they have a clear conception of aim and tactics. Monatte knows quite well that in France and elsewhere the revolutionary syndicalists are far from being unanimous as to principal questions and tactics; federations of industries or trades; nationalizations of mines and railways; insurance of workers, and generally the attitude to take towards labor legislation, etc. For the French as well as for the other syndicalists it would be of the greatest usefulness to discuss those problems among the International working-class delegates, and to hear the comrades of other countries tell their experiences.

The 'Translated News' column of *Industrial Worker* of 17 April 1913, commented that the ISNTUC had just organised a meeting of official union secretaries, but showed no enthusiasm for organising a wider assembly where many more workers' delegates might come together. Most of those who attended – 24 of the 28 – were based in offices in Germany.

Two weeks later, on 1 May 1913, an unsigned 'Translated News' column commented: 'we shall succeed more easily to oblige the conservative unions by direct action from our part, than by opposing them in the small conferences of secretaries of [ISNTUC] national centres.' On the 10 July, the column admitted mixed reactions and some opposition in France, but said:

'In all other countries the proposal of an international congress has been received with sympathy.'

The International Syndicalist Congress 1913

A proposal for an international syndicalist congress had been under discussion for several years. Already in 1910, J. Couture had noted the idea of an International Confederation of Revolutionary Syndicalists; the idea was not new then – but he suggested it be implemented if support could be found.[374] A journalist, Aristide Pratelle, raised the issue again in *Temps nouveaux* a few months later. He wrote that he had thought that such an idea was one that should have merited widespread support, even among CGT officials; he now called for it to be pursued through unofficial channels.[375] Eventually revolutionary syndicalists met in congress in 1913 despite opposition from the leaders of CGT. Many of those who did participate had looked to the CGT as some sort of model, but now rejected the CGT's thinking that it was better to work within the ISNTUC.

London was chosen as the congress location, perhaps recognising the recent activity of the British movement.[376] The most important delegations represented there were the German 'Localist' free unions, (the FVdG), the Italian Syndicalist Union (USI), the Dutch syndicalist National Labour Secretariat (NAS) union organisation, the Swedish Workers' Centre (SAC) and the British Industrial Syndicalist Education League. The single woman present – Evelyn Lilyan – represented London syndicalists. Other delegates and observers were present from France, from particular CGT unions, from the Spanish Labour Confederation (CNT), from rival Argentinean Federations,* and from the IWW. Thirty-eight delegates represented some sixty-five bodies from twelve countries. James Larkin was expected to attend at some point but was unable to get away from Dublin. In addition, there were translators and observers including Alexander Schapiro and Cornelissen, and Alfred Rosmer – attending as a reporter for *La Vie Ouvrière*.

Although a number of French syndicalists were present, representing local unions, the absence of an official CGT delegation gave the event something of a lop-sided character – somewhat akin to a Hamlet without the prince.[377] CGT leaders had declared their suspicion that the conference would do little and might harden divisions and encourage schisms.[378] For the leading members of the CGT participation in the ISNTUC helped maintain CGT 'unity'. A decision to break with the ISNTUC and support

---

* Antonio Bernardo represented the FORA; its rival, the Argentinian Regional Workers' Confederation (CORA), was represented by De Ambris. The FORA had adopted libertarian communism as its goal; the latter had encompassed some former socialist unions and was closer to the French CGT model of apolitical syndicalism.

syndicalists in other countries might have contributed to a split of the union movement in France itself. Choices were maybe being made as to priorities – organisational unity as against unity-in-action. Monatte had defended the CGT's prioritisation of working within the ISNTUC. He argued that even if they were in the minority in the ISNTUC, the CGT could open debates on their concerns within the biggest labour forum then in existence – this was 'the great goal that the CGT was determined to pursue'.

For the radicals in the CGT, the ISNTUC affiliation only facilitated the CGT's subordination to a Social-Democratic agenda. The existence of radical syndicalist bodies as alternatives to reformist-ISNTUC affiliates indicated the potential fragility of these hegemonic, national union bodies as single, unique centres. For many of the syndicalists who assembled in London, schism was an accomplished fact. They came together looking for something else and something more than could be obtained within the ISNTUC – not just resolutions from above, edited and prepared by union bosses, and meetings of full-time officials, but a forum linked in with grassroots activism.

The conference had a broad agenda including issues of anti-militarism, religion and the desirability of international language. (Translation was no easy matter, and Guy Bowman accused Cornelissen of biased translating.) The conference heard reports from delegations. Some comments on the subject of the CGT provoked controversy: the revolutionary identity and anti-militarism of the CGT was asserted by some delegates but others accused it of being soft on reformism.[379] The conference hailed solidarity and unity in the class struggle against capital and the state and preferred autonomous economic organisation and direct rather than parliamentary action. It looked to a future where industrial unions might administer production and distribution.

> Congress recognises that the working class of every country suffers under the capitalist and statist slave system; it declares itself for class struggle, for international solidarity and for the independent organisation of working classes, based on free association. The aims of this organisation are the immediate material and intellectual improvement of working classes and in the future the abolition of this system.[380]

Opposition to the compromised unionism of the Second International was widespread but there were varied views as to whether it was timely to found a new union international. The congress highlighted the development of an independently organised radical syndicalism that had abandoned attempts to reform older unions. Cornelissen was again made responsible for producing international information bulletins, but it was judged that this was not the best time to create a full-fledged new international. Alfred Rosmer defended the CGT tactics of changing or reforming the existing trade-union international, seeking to convert its unions to syndicalism.[381] In turn the Norwegian syndicalist Albert Jensen derided the latter's viewpoint:

> [I]t is not from the top downwards that this transformation takes place, but the opposite, from the bottom upwards by the continuous revolutionizing of the masses. The CGT as an organization has no influence in this direction; it is not the CGT which wins the international masses for syndicalism ... it is due to the advance of the revolutionary militants in their respective countries that these ideas get to be known and make victorious progress, and not at all due to the CGT, much less to its remaining in the old International.[382]

De Ambris of the USI saw the congress as a false start; he condemned Northern/Germanic influences and rejected Amsterdam as a proper location for a syndicalist bureau. He questioned the wisdom of launching a new international representing barely half a million workers, in competition with the ISNTUC representing several million. (The CNT was banned in 1913, but soon had half a million members, after it was unbanned, in 1914). Other participants saw it as a success.

The Argentinean FORA suggested that 600,000 members for a new international might soon be found in Latin America.[383] They viewed De Ambris as a reformist. They were not surprised when, just a month later, he was elected as a parliamentary deputy.[384] Comments in the official German trade-union press – that the London congress was a complete fiasco – adumbrated the hostile position of the German centralised trade unions (and most likely of ISNTUC/IFTU and other Social-Democratic leaders too).[385] A Syndicalist Information Bureau was set up publishing seventeen issues of a *Bulletin International du Mouvement Syndicaliste*, before the war interrupted its work. All these efforts helped pave the way for the subsequent development of a Syndicalist International after the war. Jensen commented:

> The child is no world power, simply because it *has been born*, but it can become one if we all strongly will it, for all the conditions exist for its growth. If we will it, we shall conquer, although after many a bitter struggle.[386]

The Approaching War

The First World War ushered in a new period, one shaped by militarism and nationalism. Social-Democratic and Labour organisations flowed along with this tide and for the most part worked with nationalist leaders to support the war effort. This came as no surprise to anarchists and radical syndicalists, but for those who had believed that Social-Democracy was a progressive force, this turn forced a reassessment of perspectives. Libertarian and labour movements were disrupted and reshaped first by war, and then by revolution. Why did the Labour movement fail to prevent war? And what were the effects of this war in the short term and after?

Premonitions of War

There were premonitions of war in the run-up to 1914: a series of disputes between France and Germany, and wars in the Balkans in 1912-13. In 1911, a visit by a CGT delegation to Berlin had caused a furore when Yvetot made an anti-military speech to a labour meeting; he had to be smuggled out of Germany.

Le Mouvement anarchiste, carried a series of articles on anti-militarism in various lands. The October 1912 edition carried reports and unsigned comment noting that anarchists in Germany were carrying out anti-militarist propaganda; that an adaption of our [French] *Nouvel Manuel du Soldat* had been introduced into army barracks disguised with imperial arms and colours. This essential work was also supported by syndicalist independent of Social-Democratic tutelage. Several comrades had been prosecuted, including Dr Friedeberg. 'And, in consequence of this persevering anti-militarist activity, that Social-Democracy has been compelled to recognise and modify somewhat its attitude.' (An article in the next issue adopted a more guarded approach noting that only anarchists were fighting militarism.)[387] Tom Mann wrote in a text on Britain, that: '... we syndicalists [trade unionists?] are resolved and prepared to declare a general strike in the eventuality that war threatens us',[388] (a statement largely if not wholly devoid of realism). A statement on Russia in the same edition noted that although much of the Russian people hated war, public anti-militarist propaganda was impossible and anarchist were persecuted.

Monatte's journal *Vie Ouvrière* re-published a text asserting that German socialism was imperialistic.[389] This text sparked reactions in the Social-Democratic press in Germany and France.[390] Max Nettlau was critical of the contributions to this debate of Andler, Guillaume and Cherkesov* – 'if one

---

* Or Tcherkesov, Tcherkezichvili; first name Varlaam.

thing is certain', he wrote, 'it is that a propaganda of national hate such as has been offered by these [three] can only have bad effects.'[391] Perhaps if there had been a more realistic assessment of the strength of opposition to war – or the lack of it – in Britain, France and Germany, the developments that took place in the summer of 1914 might not have come as such a surprise.[392]

The CGT proposed an anti-war demonstration in October 1912, in response to the war being fought in the Balkans. German and Austrian trade union leaders rejected invitations to join the CGT in staging protests, replying that such matters were for political parties and not for them. The CGT facilitated anti-war mass meetings in Paris – with speakers from Germany and the UK.

The organised anarchist movement – the *Fédération révolutionnaire communiste* later reformed as the Anarchist-Communist federation (ACF) – convened meetings across France. It also made plans for further action to disrupt communication systems and railways and sabotage mobilisation.[393] In November 1912, it took part in an anti-war demonstration near Paris, at the Pré-Saint-Gervais with French socialists. Declarations that the federation would sabotage mobilisation led to the arrest of many of its members. The ACF had agreed policies in case of war, of sabotage and neutralising state officials. It published a leaflet 'Do not go to the slaughterhouse ...'[394]

Henry Combes, an ACF activist speaking in Paris at the extraordinary CGT congress of November 1912, said: 'We should not trust in our governments' humanitarian feelings, they have none.' In his view, anti-war meetings should serve not so much to make an impression on Prime Minister Poincaré, but rather to prepare an insurrection in response to orders to mobilise. 'It should not be thought that we are afraid of war', he emphasised, 'It should be recognised that an outbreak of war would find us ready to make revolution and accomplish social transformation.'[395] That congress was attended by 750 delegates representing 1,452 syndicates. The ACF also developed a political priority – later named as 'revolutionary defeatism'. When asked at a meeting in November 1912 - *What would you do if the Germans do not sabotage their own mobilisation?* – two ACF speakers replied that they did not care what their official nationality might be – French or German. Proletarians had to face up to, and work to stop war regardless of any territorial invasion, workers should sabotage mobilisation and the war effort. Building workers in the Paris region, influenced by ACF members supported the printing of 100,000 copies of an anti-war leaflet.[396]

In December 1912, the CGT had sponsored a 24-hour general strike for peace, mobilising 600,000 workers – the first trial of a general strike since 1909.[397] CGT leader Léon Jouhaux said: 'if war is declared we will refuse to go to the frontier'. The *Voix du peuple*, the organ of the CGT confederation, wrote that this demonstration against war was beautiful. It was very significant for any government: 'Above all, it makes known that the working class has within it a dangerous revolutionary minority.' Émile Pouget was despondent: the main lesson learnt he wrote, was that mobilisation for peace had not been generalised. He thought, 'if the government committed the criminal folly of decreeing mobilisation for war ... such a mobilisation would be even less general than Monday's strike.'[398] The *Libertaire* said war was impossible: 'We won't have war. The people does not want it – and the government has been warned ... never up to now has a protest strike brought together so many strikers, for the moment this will do. In such conditions, no government would risk engaging with the hazards of war' (21 December). In his view, it was obvious that an active minority should be capable – on the day war is declared, or on the following day – of drawing the masses with it towards a social revolution. (22 December 1912).

The state reacted by seizing CGT cards and leaflets. Louis Lecoin, and other activists were arrested and sentenced to prison terms of two to four years. A few ACF activist fled abroad. Spies and informers were set to work targeting ACF speakers and other anti-militarists.[399] Thousands of copies of one ACF anti-war pamphlet were seized. The distribution of *La Battaile syndicaliste** and *Le Libertaire* was impeded and the financial viability of the former was undermined.

Another more practical, inflammatory text by Henry Combes was successfully circulated. It contained political and technical advice – not to wait for orders from anyone, with notes on sabotage, including the manufacture of explosives. It suggested that passive waiting behind barricades was no longer a viable tactic – it would be better to go on the offensive. It advised working with mass organisations, avoiding isolation. 2,000 copies of *En cas de guerre* (In the Event of War), an ACF manual of insurrection were printed. 1,500 copies were distributed among anarchists and another 500 were earmarked for CGT members.[400] Combes wrote a letter to the authorities from a refuge in London, challenging them to seek his extradition. He accused the French Republic of being the government most prone to killing off freedom; the ending of his letter inverted the flowery politeness that was customary: 'I present to you, Sir, those feelings of disgust which are inspired by such people as yourself.'[401] State officials did not pardon this contempt; Combes lived the rest of his life in exile, mostly in England.

The CGT seemed to be somewhat demoralised in 1913. Griffuelhes wrote

---

* The journal of the CGT with a circulation around 10,000.

an article on 'Powerlessness' published in *La Bataille Syndicaliste*, 23-24 January 1913:

> Experience suggests that people capable of intelligently managing responsibilities are rare, very rare. The same holds in all areas as in the working-class milieu: intelligence is lacking, initiative is rare. Let comrades reflect on this! There reigns in the union world a deplorable state of spirits, a profound ignorance of the necessity for action; extreme confusion exerts itself on spirits; the union mentality has lost its strength and its vigour ... Let us work to strengthen the working class, to cure it, to make it fit for serial assaults to prepare for [the much] desired social transformation ... Syndicalism is the power that forces progress.

If this article is anything to go by, the CGT and its leadership were not prepared for the challenges that would come. There was little in the way of an anti-war mobilisation in Germany. CGT policy opposed war, but that policy presupposed some common purpose and unity within the union and the possibility of collective action with workers' organisations in other countries.

A further general strike was proposed. CGT leaders opposed it, feeling that the limited support it had mobilised in December 1912 suggested it was time for caution. Leaders appeared to be talking sense when they urged caution: the CGT organisation was 'doing better' where confrontation was minimised. A CGT conference in July 1913 heard a condemnation of irresponsible people. Benoît Broutchoux, an ACF member, countered that the CGT needed to take charge of all sorts of action and not restrict its priorities to working for better pay and reduced working hours. However, radicals and Parisians were outvoted by more cautious provincial sectors. Anarchist critics accused CGT leaders of moving to the right – by this time radical libertarians were a minority within the CGT leadership. CGT general secretary, Jouhaux, was not prepared to back up words with action. He and other CGT officials, were concerned to make the goals of CGT campaigning more 'realistic'. In October, the Roubaix group of the ACF (FCAR) wrote that there were two currents in the CGT, one wanted to pursue direct action tactics, the other – officials – wanted to deprioritise a social agenda and focus on corporate and trade demands.[402]

Le Libertaire condemned prevaricators, writing 'we have to say and recognise that the CGT has done reactionary work. In the middle of a revolutionary situation, it gave in, and betrayed its tradition, [it allowed] the syndicalist movement to stray from its proper path.'⁴⁰³ Radicals who had looked previously to *Guerre Social* or *Bataille Syndicaliste* now looked to *Le Libertaire*. Pierre Monatte disputed this judgement as to the timeliness for a rising revolutionary movement: 'as for revolution – we did not feel it was close to us …' reality was in the way – we doubted the prospects for even a 24-hour protest. 'Those who wanted to look found weakness and lassitude in the syndicates striking them in the face … The CGT had not adjusted its aim in any way. It had not shifted an inch to deny the revolutionary goals of syndicalism. What it had rejected was headstrong insurrectionism.' It did not have the strength to stage mass demonstrations every fortnight.⁴⁰⁴ Perhaps then Monatte was half correct – this was not a revolutionary situation. But perhaps he was also half wrong – the CGT might have done more to support protests; revolutionary goals without revolutionary action became mere empty slogans. In any case 'the CGT' was not a monolith, there were inside the confederation various streams and currents and the CGT leadership was moving towards 'caution' rather than 'struggle'. Monatte also noted the infiltration of some bourgeois spirit – something not easy to measure – with many syndicate officials being attracted towards the freemasons (especially among teachers and postal workers). One writer in *Le Libertaire*, Broutchoux, was not at all impressed by mere revolutionary phrases issued in a manifesto from twenty-two CGT personalities.⁴⁰⁵ Some saw in this manifesto a crystallisation of a new group of leading officials.

In their opposition to militarism French revolutionary syndicalists faced problems – how were they to confront, overcome, or win over other elements of the left closer to the Second International and wedded to reforming military policy, or neutral and conservative workers wedded to catholic and conservative ideas? On a European wider-scale scene anarchism and radical syndicalism could anticipate little support, more likely no support at all from union organisations in German-speaking lands. *Vie Ouvrière* published an extensive critique of German socialist imperialism in February 1913. Such views were also circulated in *La Guerre Sociale* and *La Battaille syndicaliste*.

Anarchist-communists helped organise a large demonstration, in Pré-Saint-Gervais in May 1913. Some 150,000 persons came to hear 95 speech-makers. The ACF organised meetings, distributed leaflets (one had a print-run of 100,000), encouraged desertion and had members arrested. Building workers were particularly active within the CGT. Such work may have fostered opposition to war in general, but did it work to spread a will and determination to act to prevent war? Georges Dumoulin, writing in June 1918, thought otherwise, that it was not enough:

We thought it was enough to be horrified by the military and to hate barracks to ensure that war did not come. The proletariat lacked that hatred of things that it put up with, because it did not feel responsible for the war. The *union sacrée* was possible because for the masses of the exploited, capitalism was not recognised as responsible. Among us, that responsibility and culpability was not established with sufficient clarity. I heard poor sods saying: 'there has always been war, and there always will be.'[406]

Dumoulin noted that some workers only took the benefits that came with the CGT, but were not ready to act themselves. He concluded that the CGT should have made a greater impact on working people, and should have been able to react more quickly.[407]

In and around the year 1900 there were some 2,000 desertions and some 4,000 refusals to join the forces. These numbers increased year by year, towards 2,600 desertions and 80,000 draft-evaders. The army had *Biribi* punishment battalions tasked with disciplining dissidents and anti-militarists.[408] Libertarian journals publicised cases of deaths, abuse and maltreatment.

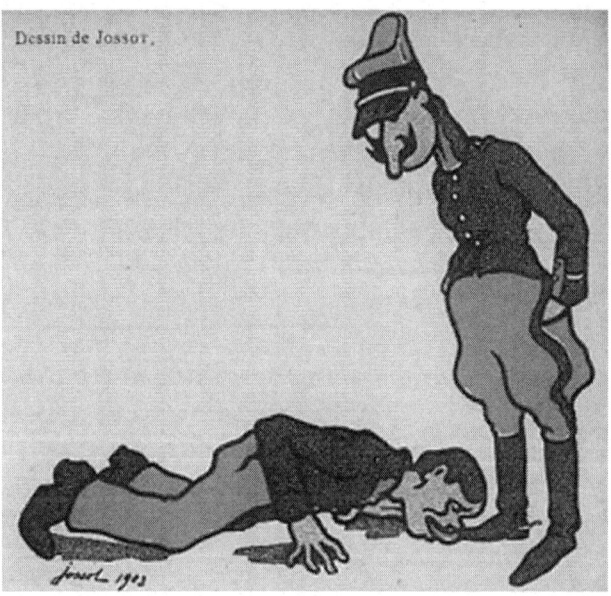

Army discipline, a French anti-militarist cartoon ny Henri-Gustave Jossot

George Darien's book on Biribi —
French military discipline, first published in 1890

Ancona and the Italian Red Week

In June 1914 mass protests erupted in Ancona, against militarism and the harsh treatment of young army recruits. Police forces opened fire and killed three people. A 'Red Week' of insurrection saw authorities evicted from their local offices. Strikes spread to several cities of central and northern Italy.[409] Sixteen people died. Anarchists influenced this movement, but did not dominate it. The CGL tried to quieten things down. In an article published in *Voluntà*, on 13 June 1914, Malatesta wrote:

> The CGL will not be obeyed. Already it has been announced that the *Camere del Lavora* of Milan and Bologna have revolted against these orders. The *Camera* of Ancona is autonomous. The USI will certainly not fail in its duty. The railway-workers have almost completely cut services, and lines have been tampered with so that the government will be unable to repair them in the little time that it has left. So, [I say] once again, this is no longer [just] a strike but a REVOLUTION. The movement has just begun, who should say that it should stop! Down with those who want us

to go back to sleep! Down with the traitors! Long live the revolution.[410] Outside Emilia, the Marches, Tuscany and Umbria the railways did run.

Three anti-militarist protestors killed in Ancona, June 1914

The movement remained largely urban. Radicals were able to resist the influence of CGL leaders in Ancona, Bologna and Milan, but elsewhere the CGL line won out, and the movement subsided. The subversive opponents of the monarchy did not come together. Alceste De Ambris, then leader of the USI, commented that everyone other than Malatesta was surprised by events.[411] Subversives found it difficult to communicate with friends in other parts of Italy.[412]

One week later, an article attributed to Malatesta condemned the CGL for coming to the aid of the regime, and for the pernicious betrayal of the Italian proletariat. Lessons should be learnt, he wrote. Many – whatever their 'school' or party – were ready to rebel; local strikes and general strikes needed to be broadened. Some things could not be foreseen. He repeated points he had made many times before: unlooked for opportunities might be taken if people were ready to act; preparation helped; practical matters should not be neglected, people needed to be fed.[413]

There followed a wave of repression. Rebellious railway-workers were targeted and a defence campaign was organised to support them. Malatesta, Fabbri and many others left Italy to avoid imprisonment. Malatesta returned to London in June 1914. Shots in Sarajevo – the shots that sparked the outbreak of the First World War – were fired on the same day that he arrived back.

Luigi Fabbri thought an Italian revolution might have developed had there been no war. The war, and its unhappy conclusion, promoted reaction and nationalism.[414]

Anarchists were coming together in national leagues and organisations but there had been little international organisation since the Amsterdam Congress. The cataclysm that erupted in 1914 erupted over somewhat disorganised and unprepared syndicalists and anarchists.

Part Two – War

14

AUGUST 1914

Despite some anticipation that a war was coming the fast pace of events took the radicals by surprise. For example, when *Les Temps nouveaux* noted the assassination of the Austrian Archduke in Sarajevo (4 July 1914) it did not comment that war was approaching closer, but rather that this royal had reaped his reward for sowing hatred. A notice for a Parisian meeting of the ACF on 18 July had the task of preparing for the September International Anarchist Congress and nominating delegates – war was not the main item on the agenda. On the 25 July, a front-page notice advertised a *Temps Nouveaux* group meeting to discuss the same congress. On 18 July in *l'Humanité*, Jaurès had written a front-page article *Les Furieux* [The Furies], saying that war would be prevented by a general strike that was concerted and bilateral, or not at all. Jean Grave commented on the 25th in *Les Temps nouveaux* that this was all very well. He also published a comment on an inside page, under a heading *Crocs et Griffes* (Tooth and Claw) that seemed to stress that this policy was merely there to save face:

> General Strikes against war are only a protest – moreover they must be simultaneous in both disputing parties – to promote arbitration. Cannons will utter the last word. In such a way, socialists will line up with the most ferocious defenders of the homeland. So, socialist deputies may become ministers without renouncing their party or risking their constituencies. Hitherto this was impossible. The Socialist Party is now ripe to exercise power.

But this seemed no more than a routine polemic on the credentials and intentions of political opponents. The *Les Temps nouveaux* issue of 1 August did report a demo on the evening of Monday 27 July – several tens of thousands demanding 'Down with War!' 'Long live Peace!' – but only on page 6, perhaps suggesting that it was a scare but not the real thing. Two days later Germany declared war on France.

Only on 8 August did the front page of *Les Temps nouveaux* take on a term of alarm. Its lead article announced – in bold type:

What we had refused to believe until the last moment is now an accomplished fact. War has been unleashed ...

The war, it said, had been prepared and willed by the military in Austria-Hungary and Germany. French republicans were guilty – they had made an alliance with Russia, the most autocratic and retrograde state. There was a recognition that the editors of *Les Temps nouveaux*, like other people, might be in the dark, but nevertheless, and notwithstanding that they were anarchists, they recognised that their French rulers had done all that was possible to prevent war. The editorial concluded:

But recriminations will not prevent blood being shed, that thousands and thousands of human beings will be killed by machine-guns, or that ruin, misery and despair will come into the homes of the most miserable. Every error is paid for, and it will be those who are least culpable who will pay first. Only one pale hope remains – a pretty feeble one – that if Europe is not to fall into ages of barbarism, the German people should refuse to be aggressors and proclaim a Republic.[415]

Les Temps nouveaux announced it would suspend publication until people regained their sanity. Jean Grave was surprised that the above comments passed censorship. He expected worse, and with no money likely to come in, suspended publication.[416]

No one expected a world war that would last so long, nor that it would spread across the world and kill millions. In Britain, volunteers filled the armed forces – elsewhere war meant mass male conscription. There was much talk of it being 'over by Christmas': what was expected was a short adventure in which real men would win glory.

The war spread to involve Brazil, Bulgaria, Cuba, Greece, Italy, Portugal, Romania, Turkey, and the USA. It lasted five years and trampled over wide areas of Europe, Africa and the Middle East. It involved the forcible recruitment of non-citizens as labourers, and appropriations of resources that caused disruption and mass starvation.

Very many anarchists opposed the war. Public meetings became impossible. Anti-war activists (e.g. Alexander Schapiro) and exiles (e.g. Rudolf Rocker) were incarcerated. The few libertarians and socialists who did attempt to stage anti-war demonstrations found little support. Some saw no hope and so lapsed into inactivity. Those who opposed the war were liable to be called into the armed forces and became subject to military law, facing imprisonment or execution if they refused conscription. Dissidents of all sorts fled to avoid military service. Willingly or not, many were conscripted.

Civilised Nationalism?

In Britain, France and Germany, patriotic talk of defending civilisation was used to justify the conflict. The French state used the discourse of 1789 – the spirit of the revolution – with images of a revolutionary republican army as the people in arms, a force of liberation against tyranny and feudalism. In France and Italy some anarchists and syndicalists adopted the logic of the lesser evil. Some talked of French liberty as against German autocracy. Age had an influence in respect of support for the war; some of the older generation saw 1914 as a repeat of 1870-71, a fight for 'French' radicalism and liberty against 'German' authoritarianism. Some of Marx's and Engels' thoughts on the Franco-Prussian war were re-published:

> The French deserve a good hiding. If the Prussians win, the centralisation of the STATE POWER will be beneficial for the centralisation of the German working class. German predominance would then shift the centre of gravity of the Western European workers' movement from France to Germany, and you only need to compare developments in the two countries from 1866 to the present day to realise that the German working class is *superior* to the French both in theory and organisation. Its predominance over the French on the international stage would also mean the predominance of *our* theory over Proudhon's, etc.[417]

Any search for civilization, pride or domination slipped easily into nationalism and could be used to justify war. Wherever labour was identified with the protection of 'advanced' welfare rights a certain paternalism and or racism might emerge more easily.

Most parties of the Socialist International supported their wartime governments, leaving Social-Democrats to fight each other on the battlefield. Left parties in Russia and Serbia refused to submit to jingoism, but elsewhere few socialists withstood the tide.

The German state invoked pride in national *Kultur*, something to be defended against Russian autocratic barbarism. Radicals were invited to join the defence of 'progress' against 'reaction'. Some SPD members said they felt 'liberated' when their party supported the war effort. One SPD deputy spoke enthusiastically of how the 'wooden theories' of party policy were abandoned. He could now join in the joyful singing of the national anthem.[418] Here and in many other countries, much of the labour movement floated along with the high-tide of patriotism. Kaiser Wilhelm offered the nationalist olive branch saying he did not recognise parties, only Germans, ready to defend the fatherland. German Social-Democracy was seduced by pride in national accomplishments. Germany was portrayed as a progressive nation, a productive, civilised nation, offering social security in contrast to a backward, reactionary culture in Russia.

Misinformation and propaganda played its part in cementing this patriotic fervour. In these times, the press was the key means of communication. Germans were told that French airplanes had bombed Nuremberg. The Social-Democratic party press failed to refute these lies. Few labour journalists emulated the FVdG, and were courageous enough to withstand the patriotic tide and provide a critical perspective. The FVdG and its newspaper *Einigheit* were both banned, so too was the anarchist journal *Der Freie Arbeiter*.

The choice made by the majority of the German Social-Democratic apparatus to collaborate with the war effort may also be explained in part by a desire for security and status. Thousands of officials and employees of the Social-Democratic movement had jobs to lose, if their structures were dissolved.[419] Trade union leaders – through the centralised union leadership, the *Generalkommission* – went to the government to ask on what conditions their organisation could continue; the *Generalkommission* was ready to forbid the use of strikes and to prevent financial contributions to strikers for the duration of the war. The centralised trade union's leaders and officials were to be exempted from the draft while their members were not. Labour, or military service, would become compulsory. Their government wanted stable industrial relations and offered toleration in exchange for support for the war effort. German Social-Democracy – much vaunted as the vanguard of the Socialist movement – chose to support the war and was rewarded by winning positions in subordinate state agencies from which they had been excluded hitherto. So too were French and British counterparts.

Internationalism in the Labour Movement

How could Labour oppose war when one of the largest components of the international labour movement displayed little or no commitment to internationalism? This was a key question in the era before the First World War. German Social-Democracy's commitment to internationalism was widely seen as bogus: it had never prepared to oppose its state or to act to prevent war. French syndicalism had – as has been seen – resolved and prepared to oppose war with campaigns and organising that had no equivalent in Germany.

Yet, the CGT did not face up to the question of how it might act if it was faced with a war, and *if the labour movement in another country went along with its nation in supporting that war*. Such a possibility could be envisaged but was not squarely confronted by leaders of the CGT. They were not prepared to go it alone, to act unilaterally, and to insist on opposition to mobilisation. If the CGT pledged to work with the German centralised Social-Democratic unions, it placed all its eggs – all its expectations that together they would prevent war – in one basket with a partner unfit and unready to achieve that policy.

In its international work the CGT chose to work with big union centres: the German union movement, the British TUC and the Italian CGL. Such a priority came before solidarity with the CNT in Spain, and the smaller syndicalist confederations in Italy and Germany. The CGT seemed to have adopted a strategy of boring from within, but the question that became moot, as this option was chosen, was *who* would adapt and change? Would the CGT move the centralised unions towards adopting a more active militancy, and specifically to act to prevent war, or would the quietism and nationalism of the centralised unions come to influence the policy of the CGT?

Was there any prospect that these larger bodies – the centralised unions of Germany, CGL, AFL, TUC, etc. – could be moved towards opposing war? The leadership of the German Social-Democratic movement – figures such as Bebel, Liebknecht and later Legien – had a history of ongoing antagonism to libertarian thinking in international socialist and labour congresses that could be traced back the 1870s. Given this tradition, given the financial weight of the German labour movement in international endeavours, and given that the German leaders obstructed popular labour organisations – both at home and abroad – it was unlikely that the CGT would ever have had any opportunity to challenge German Social-Democratic influence.

One can speculate as to what might have occurred, if the CGT had supported and prioritised relations with other radical syndicalists before 1914. A split with the ISNTUC/International Federation of Trade Unions (IFTU), might have become the occasion for a split in the CGT itself, and the formation of a new French trade union centre closer to the IFTU and to its Social-Democratic unions.

Splits came anyway, between pro- and anti-war labour bodies after 1914, but the CGT leaders were not to know that. What they could see, on an international scale, was widespread division even before 1914. On the one hand, there was division within the ranks of the ISNTUC, insofar as the Dutch labour was divided between two national centres, and one former affiliate had ceased to participate.* There had also been some controversy over the representation of the USA, with the CGT advocating recognition of the IWW rather than the AFL. Outside the ambit of the ISNTUC, a series of syndicalist centres organised – some of them of a size similar to the equivalent ISNTUC affiliate.

Perhaps the CGT might have developed a greater capacity to initiate an independent policy if it had broken earlier with the ISNTUC. Stronger links to a syndicalist international might have facilitated more resolute opposition to war. Opposition to the war might have been sharper even if conflict between anti-war and pro-war groupings had led to a secession of some of the membership, as happened in Italy within the USI. Syndicalist organisations might have more precarious organisational forms but they might have facilitated more lively action. All such thinking is speculation, but what can be said with certainty is that CGT's affiliation to the ISNTUC/IFTU left it isolated, with little or no capacity to change the opinions of that international's German leadership and failed to obtain the objective of shifting that leadership. The choice, it seemed, was between static organisational unity, and dynamic unity-in-action. 'Organization became the prime concern of the revisionists.'[420]

Within the libertarian camp opposition to war was strongest in Italy, and considerable in Germany, Spain, Sweden and the Netherlands. Most of the syndicalists who had met in London in 1913 opposed the war. In December 1914, Pierre Monatte concluded that he could no longer remain as a member of a leading committee of the CGT given the nationalist rhetoric adopted, and given the collaboration of the Confederal Committee with the government. He noted:

> I strongly fear that our central organisations, those in France and those in Germany, CGT and Socialist Party, Trade-Union International and Socialist International have shown their bankruptcy. They have shown that they were too weak to stop the war, after so many years of organising and propaganda. But one might also say to oneself – that perhaps the problem was there part and parcel among the masses who remained on the side-lines who failed to understand the responsibilities of internationalism. That last glimmer of hope was flickering behind the

---

* The Dutch Nationaal Arbeids Secretariaat (NAS) was reviving as the First World War approached; its journal *De Arbeid*, claimed a monthly circulation of 32,000.

talk of militants – from one land to another. It was in the centre, that the fire – that is to say the faith – was lacking.[421]

The leaders of the CGT were unready to adopt a unilateral line that it was better for France to be defeated rather than going to war; that anti-war rebellion was preferable to modern warfare; that so long as working people did not share in the wealth and direction of their nation, they had little or nothing to defend.

'If war breaks out – what we will do':
We will refuse to obey orders from bloodthirsty militarists!
French Anarchist Communist Federation poster, c. 1912

James Connolly concluded that the division between economic and political organisation – between trade-unions and parties – left Social-Democracy without any capacity to carry through measures that might have foiled mobilisation. Transport workers might have halted trains carrying soldiers to the front, if there had been a concerted anti-war movement binding all sorts of rebels together.[422] The mass force of labour might have slowed or prevented mobilisation.[423]

Such a mobilization would have needed organisational force, political will and structures that would serve a purpose – but all these were lacking. Only in France had there been some substantial and sustained work to oppose militarism. But even here anti-militarism was somewhat unclear as to priorities and action to be taken. The leadership of the CGT did not chose to act alone, but waited and eventually followed the line of the French Socialists, who supported a war of national defence. Libertarian ideas-based political organisations, and revolutionary syndicalists had fought for an active anti-war unity. Their anti-war preparation would find limited resonance within the CGT.

Historical hindsight was not available to the CGT and their counterparts elsewhere in 1914. They did not know that the coming war would last until 1918 and take the lives of millions. It was commonly assumed that wars would be short and sharp. The CGT and other labour movements may have hoped, and been seduced by the hope, that this would be a short war, and that things would soon return to normal. The American *International Socialist Review* was to speculate as to consequences, if the left had responded to the war with a series of anti-war insurrections. It admitted that thousands might have been killed. However, it argued that this was a sacrifice worth making, and that states faced with such determination would have eventually given in to this anti-war movement.

In 1916, James Connolly went into action. The Irish Citizen's Army had been formed earlier in part to defend striking workers; it was one of the most striking example of a counter-army. The labour movement Connolly influenced staged the Easter rising against Britain with Irish nationalist forces. Although defeated, the anti-British sentiment that he helped foster was perhaps a sufficient threat to the British state in Ireland that it thought it best not to introduce conscription there, as it did in the rest of the United Kingdom. A huge anti-war and pro-independence movement developed.

Labour at War

The military acquired emergency powers in each state that joined the conflict. Some workers were mobilised, but left in their jobs as 'militarised' workers under martial law, needing official approval to call a union meeting. Many militants went into exile and lost civil rights, both in their homelands and in their countries of exile. Enemy aliens were interned.

In France, patterns of loyalty and solidarity within the CGT were disrupted by the conflict. There were disputes over co-operation with the state and over arbitration of disputes, as well as over the war. Women and immigrants filled new jobs and the ethnic and gender balance of the labour force changed. Much of the protest movement against the war came from women, but syndicalists did not have a good record of organising among them. There were few female officials. The CGT made little effort to change or to rebalance its gender profile to better represent women. Women too were prominent among war-protestors. Women played a larger part in strikes (perhaps because they were less vulnerable to being compulsorily mobilised into the forces). Teachers and metal workers were prominent opponents of the war.

In Italy, CGL officials lost some authority as the war continued. Many strikes took place disregarding 'proper channels' for resolving industrial disputed. New internal commissions were formed in factories; they were designed to facilitate peaceful industrial relations. But the commissions developed in ways that had not been anticipated. All workers might participate: skilled and unskilled, union members or not; a matter of great importance insofar as a large majority of the workforce were not unionised. New organisational forms offered some opportunities for radicals; they facilitated some potential for conflict between active mass meetings of all workers and poorly accountable union leaders. Union officials often opposed the participation of non-members in workplace commissions.

Spain did not participate in the fighting but enjoyed a great expansion as its industries providing supplies for various armies. There was a great increase in the textile industry producing uniforms. Before the war the UGT had been the larger union, but things changed and by the end of 1917, after a period of revolt and repression that summer, the CNT was larger than the UGT. By 1919 CNT membership was approaching 800,000 (over 340,000 in Catalonia), while UGT membership lagged behind around the 200,000 mark. The CNT adopted libertarian communism as it goal, at its 'Comedia' congress in December 1919.

The war impacted in different ways in different places. Some markets dried up – for example many tobacco and cigar workers in Cuba were sacked because export markets disappeared. Exporters found new demand for resources. Many poor people faced hunger or starvation as local supplies were exported.

In Germany, the free trade unions aligned with the SPD worked for civil peace, renounced strike action, refused funds to strikers, and informed on troublemakers – with dire consequences for workers who found themselves mobilised and placed under military law. The labour leadership acquired privileges such as appointments to quasi-governmental bodies, and industrial conciliation bodies, from which they had previously been excluded. Such positions facilitated their role as subservient partners of industrial management in an increasingly planned system. New, modern forms of planned state capitalism were portrayed as being close to socialism.[424]

Wartime industrial relations fostered authoritarianism. Workers from Belgium, France and Polish/Baltic areas were recruited by force to serve the German economy. Pannekoek later wrote that freedom could not be won by paying dues and following leaders, but only by active responsible participation within a body of equals. Otto Rühle commented that the SPD was organised on authoritarian lines. Party secretaries were like NCOs, members of parliament were like officers and the party was characterised by a zombie-like obedience which was typical of centralism:

> The secure appointment, the heightened social position, the punctually paid salary, the well heated office, the quickly learnt routine in the carrying out of formal administrative business, engender a mentality which makes the labour official in no way distinguishable from the petty post-office, tax, community or state official as much in his position as in his domestic milieu. The official is for correct management of business, painstaking orderliness, smooth discharge of obligations; he hates disturbances, friction, conflicts. Nothing is so repugnant to him as chaos, therefore he opposes any sort of disorder; he combats the initiative and independence of the masses; he fears the revolution.[425]

The centralised unions of Germany organised some two and a half to three million workers shortly before the outbreak of the First World War, as compared to a number approaching four million in Britain, most striking was the degree of concentration in Germany, where the bulk of organised workers were members of fifty or so large unions. It is interesting to consider here some quasi-syndicalist British thinking as expressed in the unofficial *The Miners Next Step*. The official miners' organisation was and remained later largely decentralised, with workers having a loyalty primarily towards local organisations (lodges) or areas, rather than to a wider national structure.

The Miners Next Step, (Extract); The Bad Side of Leadership

1. Leadership implies power. Leadership implies power held by the Leader. Without power, the leader is inept. The possession of power inevitably leads to corruption. All leaders become corrupt, in spite of their own good intentions. No man was ever good enough, brave enough, or strong enough to have such power at his disposal, as real leadership implies.

2. Consider what it means, this power of initiative, this sense of responsibility, the self-respect, which comes from expressed manhood, is taken from the men, and consolidated in the leader. The sum of their initiative, their responsibility, their self-respect becomes his.

3.   The order and system – the order and system he maintains, is based upon the suppression of the men, from being independent thinkers into being 'the men' or 'the mob'. Every argument which could be advanced to justify leadership on this score, would apply equally well to the Czar of all the Russias and his policy of repression. In order to be effective, the leader must keep the men in order, or he forfeits the respect of the employers and 'the public', and thus becomes ineffective as a leader.

4.   He corrupts the aspirants to public usefulness. He is compelled, in order to maintain his power, to see to it that only those who are willing to act as his drill sergeants or coercive agents shall enjoy his patronage. In a word, he is compelled to become an autocrat and a foe to democracy.

5.   He prevents solidarity. Sheep cannot be said to have solidarity. In obedience to a shepherd, they will go up or down, backwards or forwards as they are driven by him and his dogs. But they have no solidarity, for that means unity and loyalty. Unity and loyalty, not to an individual, or the policy of an individual, but to an interest and a policy which is understood and worked by all. Finally, he prevents the legislative power of the workers. An industrial vote will affect the lives and happiness of workmen far more than a political vote. The power to vote whether there shall or shall not be a strike, or upon an industrial policy to be pursued by his union, will affect far more important issues to the workman's life, than the political vote can ever touch. Hence it should be more sought after, and its privileges jealously guarded. Think of the tremendous power going to waste because of leadership, of the inevitable stop-block he becomes on progress, because quite naturally, leaders examine every new proposal, and ask first how it will affect their position and power. It prevents large and comprehensive policies being initiated and carried out, which depend upon the understanding and watchfulness of the great majority. National strikes and policies can only be carried out, when the bulk of the people see their necessity, and themselves prepare and arrange them.[426]

Several critical writers recognised that union leaders had distinct interests, in conflict with the interests of ordinary workers. In the view of a growing number of English, Welsh and Scottish miners, union leadership was not promoting progress to socialism, and other structures were needed. Syndicalism in Britain did not develop a strong autonomous national structure, but in the development of lay shop stewards a measure of space developed in which shop-floor concerns might be articulated.

Similar dynamics were at work in Germany. Officials did not have everything their own way. New patterns of employment and resistance emerged. Unofficial workplace networks and shop-steward organisation developed hostile to the *Generalkommission* 'free' *Gewerkschaften*. Many activists shifted their allegiance towards the radical left. Doors opened for new workplace organisations – *Unionen* – akin to the IWW, CNT, or USI.

Within the *Gewerkschaften*, workplace representatives, *obleute* – shop stewards or trustees – won some recognition and space, coming to represent both skilled workers and the unskilled, newly recruited, often female. They helped focus criticism and opposition to the collaborationist trade union officials. They noted that officials were largely exempted from wartime service on the front line because of their services in the rear. Many of these *obleute* became opponents of the war and were expelled from the SPD, supporting the new-formed Independent Social-Democratic Party (USPD). Karl Korsch wrote in 1919: 'The few who saw this condition of increasing passivity as dangerous and fatal stood mostly outside the actual socialistic movement …'[427] Other left-wing groups, allies and friends of Rosa Luxemburg and distinct groups of leftists in Northern Germany, also came together as 'Spartacists', and later founded the German Communist Party (KPD).

The wider world

Neutral countries were also afflicted by a loss of civil rights. Switzerland provides an example: some 30,000 persons – including 11,000 Italians and 7,000 Germans – took refuge there to escape army service; the state forced them to work to support themselves. Early in 1918 they staged a strike over their conditions. They received some help from Swiss anarchists and other progressives but were treated as undesirables by conservatives.

The Swiss government began moves to restrict exiles' political activity, to deport troublemakers, and obstruct acceptance of any further deserters.[428] Luigi Bertoni tried to influence an unsympathetic Swiss government but had little success. Social tensions were increasing. A limited Swiss national general strike, led by socialists, was soon to break out. (It was defeated). In the last year of the world war Italian revolutionaries who used Switzerland as a refuge and organisational base had to keep their heads down in the face of government repression. Subsequently many of the revolutionaries who had been in exile left Switzerland for home.

In Latin America, the war years posed problems and opportunities. Labour was in demand as supplies were sought in neutral countries. Foodstuffs were very much in demand, and their supply sometimes left local consumption short. Prices rose. Protests were organised against the rising cost of living, in the war years and after.

The war – its prolonged horror, its massive impact, and the millions of deaths that it engendered – provoked some reassessment of the value of modern 'European civilisation'. Other models were viewed with greater sympathy. In many colonies authorities were blamed for the shortage of food and any resulting starvation. Soldiers and labourers – many of them forcibly recruited – returned home with a new awareness of the world, sometimes with a resentment that they had been used and discarded; they were equals at one moment, fighting for civilisation, at another told they were inferiors, and told to go home.

The war also stimulated new industries – the manufacture of vehicles and aircraft – changing the balance of several economies. The net effect of all of these changes was felt most strongly after 1917 and at the end of the war as the labour movement re-organised and attempted to confront new social and political issues. The impact of these changes, and the development of new states and new revolutions in the 1920s, form the subject of volume two in this series.

15

OPPOSITION TO THE WAR

Germany

In Germany, the outbreak of war lead to the suspension of the peacetime constitution. Generals in charge of various military districts had dictatorial powers in their areas under a 'Law of Siege'. The army was officered by aristocrats and by the sons of the bourgeoisie. Unions were not banned and for the most part they were quick to pledge support for the war. There were some openings for dissidents as opposition to the war won an ever-greater audience against the warmongers in socialist parties and the unions. Lay workplace organisers – shop-stewards, *obleute* and factory commission representatives – developed here and there, challenging trade union leaders who had been co-opted by and integrated into the German state. They sought to dispute the harsh effects of the war on organised workers, but not so much the overall direction of policy, or the leadership of the trade-unions and Social-Democratic Party. At first, they did not object to the war itself, or adopt a revolutionary perspective, although this changed in and after 1916.[429]

The earlier position of the *obleute* was perhaps not so far removed from the attitude of skilled engineers in the UK. A famous example of this being in November 1916 over Leonard Hargreaves, a worker who had been called up by the British Army in spite of the exemptions negotiated by the Amalgamated Society of Engineers. Unofficial strike action by some twelve thousand workers secured his release in three days. Although the form of direct action was one that syndicalists might have welcomed, the object of that action – to maintain differentials and privilege – was not so radical. The war sparked protests, and these protest movements might harbour revolutionaries and libertarians, but the political direction of these protests was seldom decided by revolutionaries and libertarians.

The FVdG was probably about 6,000 strong in 1914. (Altogether the organised labour movement encompassed some three million members in SPD, Catholic and Liberal union networks.) The FVdG held its 11th congress in May 1914 with 54 delegates representing 65 local unions. In the first weeks of the war twenty of its officials were arrested[430] and the organisation was banned. Nevertheless, it had some organisational continuity in at least eighteen cities.[431] It attempted to maintain its press, despite having successive titles banned. The police reported that FVdG syndicalist were active and found an audience. Several activists were placed in *Shuttzhaft* (protective custody), some were transferred from custody into army barracks. Internal FVdG circulars continued to be published until February 1917. Some thirty of its members were given long prison sentences. Its decentralised structure facilitated the survival of branches which continued some activity. Helge Döhring provides details of local union activity in several industries and areas. The Berlin organisation maintained a library and continued to meet, organising socials – for peace, or for children. There was a discussion on state socialism in 1916. Members in employment set aside money to support the unemployed. They had a presence in several enterprises. FVdG members supported strikes while the SPD/free unions distanced themselves from disputes.[432] There were many occasions when the SPD/free unions instigated the arrest of dissidents. They saw themselves as defenders of a 'national community' at war, and saw dissidents as enemies of the Fatherland – such attitudes anticipated Nazi politics.

Helge Döhring has related one official report on an anarchist who refused to serve – Wilhelm Wehner.

> In front of the assembled company he declared to his captain that he would not do this; he had had already said to him that he would not allow himself to be trained as a killer of men, and he would prefer that he should be arrested. He was then led back to his barracks by the corporals and shortly after, without permission, he left his unit and after six days was arrested in Schweinfurt. In the course of investigations, he was asked what his reply to the charges was, he again replied he had another worldview to other people, he was an anarchist, he did not recognise compulsion, [but] only freedom ....'[433]

Regional organisations in Berlin and the Ruhr subsequently provided a base for a new and more numerous generation of revolutionary syndicalism.[434] Other left groups were also banned.

France

When war did come, in the summer of 1914, no action was taken by the CGT. The preventative general strike agreed at the Marseilles congress in 1908, was not launched. In the short space of time between realising the danger of war and the mobilisation of the French army the CGT lacked capacity, strength, will and a resolute and determined leadership. At the national level, the CGT was unready and unwilling to act to launch a general strike. At any time, such a project was demanding and/or close to a call for revolution. On 13 June, *Les Temps nouveaux* had commented that while revolutionary tempers were aroused in Italy, in Ancona, in France they were dead or sleeping. (If this was the case, and if a general strike was impractical, perhaps the CGT might have called for some lesser form of protest that was less demanding but had at least some symbolic value?)

There were initially large anti-war demonstrations in many places, and one might speculate that a larger anti-war movement might have been forthcoming sooner, if the CGT had stuck to the policy agreed in its congress resolutions. Some 32,000 French war resisters evaded orders and/or refused to join the forces, but there were millions who did rally to the colours.

The national CGT, after a few crucial days of inaction, merely 'noted' rather feebly, that events had passed it by. Socialist and CGT leaders excused themselves, blaming the German movement and citing its support for the war. The war, it was said, was a defensive war, against German imperialism, against German invasion, but not against the German people. Jouhaux talked of French soldiers as a nation united. 'We' are soldiers of freedom winning 'freedom' for the oppressed;[435] speaking for the CGT, he spoke in the name of syndicates, in the name of all workers who have already joined their regiments and of those, like himself, who would be leaving tomorrow; he declared that 'we' would be going to the field of battle with the will to repel the invader, driven on by the hatred of imperialism.

Pierre Besnard, later a leader of a small Revolutionary Syndicalist CGT centre, commented that Jouhaux did not go off to war. He did not reproach Jouhaux for that, but did condemn him for speaking without a mandate in the name of workers who had not been consulted. In his view, the CGT capitulated and underwrote the war.[436]

In France and elsewhere the anti-war opposition needed access to the press and printers to get their views known. Some twenty years later Pierre Monatte wrote that the unanimity of the French press – the bourgeois and the left press – contributed greatly to the absence of protest against the outbreak of war.[437] Much of the anarchist press was owned by older individuals who were more sympathetic to the rhetoric of defending national freedoms.

Those anti-war papers that tried to publish were fined or banned. Many who opposed the war felt isolated. *Vie Ouvrière,* ran out of funds and ceased publication. Anti-war publications were censored, or had to be circulated clandestinely. Monatte wrote that it was a saddening spectacle to see CGT militants devoid of clear thinking, unable to analyse critically government assertions, swayed by the fever of national arrogance and forgetting those principles that had governed them hitherto.[438]

Switzerland, being neutral, provided some space for open debate. Luigi Bertoni wrote in *Le Réveil,* on 31 October 1914: 'Nothing is more painful than seeing certain representatives of the French proletariat reasoning like the most genuine of capitalists and nationalists.' Bertoni published writings by Jean Grave – who believed that France and its allies had right on their side – but he also published texts refuting this pro-war position.[439] He opposed the war and worked among Italian workers in Switzerland, to dissuade them from leaving to join up.

Certain historic figures in the anarchist movement came to support aspects of the war effort. The editor of *Temps nouveaux,* Jean Grave was invited to meet Pierre Martin, editor of *Le Libertaire,* but declined. Grave accused Martin of 'pedantry' and said he had little trust in his entourage. Martin's political line – opposing the war – was the opposite of that of Grave.[440] Some energy was spent on infighting among *Temps nouveaux* contributors for and against the war.

The ACF was disrupted and disorganised by the impact of the war. A handful of members reneged on prior commitments but many more – among them Péricat, Thullier, Jean-Baptiste Vallet, Broutchoux, Lepetit and Le Meillour – became key figures in a Syndicalist Defence Committee, a body described as the leading force in war resistance,[441] organising for the most part as a minority movement in the CGT and somewhat at odds with both moderate pacifists and with pro-government leaders of the CGT and Socialist Party. Péricat continued to have a leading role in opposition to the war and suffered imprisonment; while at large he had headed the *Comité d'action internationale* (Committee for International Action). Louis Lecoin, earlier a secretary in the ACF, had been sentenced to five years' imprisonment in November 1912, for publishing an antimilitarist poster. He was released in 1916. He was imprisoned again in 1917 after distributing a pamphlet *Imposons la paix!* (Let us impose peace); reports of his sentence were systematically censored; he was released in 1920.

In January 1915, Sébastien Faure had an appeal printed, *Aux socialistes, syndicalistes, révolutionnaires et anarchistes.* He called for a quick peace without conquests or humiliation. Those who regarded the defence of the French state as betrayal of the movement, worked with pacifists, anarchists and socialists to produce *Ce qu'il faut dire* (What needs to be said). Opposition to the war emerged only slowly and gradually. It was difficult to organise in the face of the threat of state repression.

Italy

Malatesta and his co-thinkers were resolutely opposed to the war. Pasquale Binazzi wrote in the *Il Libertario* paper: *Né un uomo, né un soldo per l'iniqua guerra*. (Not a man, not a penny for this unjust war).[442] There were numerous anti-war demonstrations in Italian cities.[443]

In September 1914, the USI expelled a pro-war minority which believed that by supporting republican France they were defending progress against German and Austrian reaction. This minority went on to form the Italian Labour Union (UIL) taking with them many members in Castrocaro, Milan and Parma, and the USI newspaper, *L'Internazionale*. The USI was deprived of much of its infrastructure and financial resources.[444] Its remaining zone of influence was in the North and along the coast, in mining areas, La Spezia, Piombino and Sestri Ponente.[445]

The USI created *Guerra di Classe* (Class War) as its new journal. Armando Borghi replaced De Ambris as the USI's national secretary. The job was no sinecure – in his eight years as secretary Borghi had five years of imprisonment and internment[*] and only three years of freedom. Rebels, radicals and subversives were forcibly located in remote locations, mail was censored and all social contact heavily restricted.[446]

The USI general council called for class solidarity to upset war-mongering, monarchist and bourgeois states. Italian Anarchists, meeting in a conference in Pisa in January 1915, resolved on:

> our uncompromising opposition to all war – other than for our own liberation and social emancipation – and our immutable internationalist and Anarchist beliefs, in opposition to all forms of compromise and collaboration with bourgeois and militarist classes of whatever nationality or race; we give a mandate to the comrades of the anarchist press present at this conference to fashion an accord with comrades from abroad to call an international meeting able to make concrete plans for activities to prevent the extension of the war, to impose its cessation and to reaffirm internationalist principles; furthermore, working to promote immediately anti-war activities; directing a manifesto towards the people

---

* Internment was a new form of *domicilio coatto*, adapted to war-time imperatives.

and proposing rallies, organising movements against unemployment and the high cost of living, and working towards the launching of, first, a general protest strike, and subsequently, insurrection.[447]

Italy joined the war in May 1915. A two-day protest general strike was met by police repression. Workers from the south of Italy were moved to the North to serve in war production. Nominally the Socialists and the CGL adopted a policy of *né aderire, né sabotare* (neither support, nor sabotage); in practice, the CGL and FIOM usually co-operated with employers and the military to maintain labour discipline. They obtained some concessions from the state, but at a price of 'painful collaboration'. Oppositionists, who condemned union leaders for class collaboration, suffered internment. The Socialist Party was somewhat divided. The future fascist leader Mussolini, had been a member of its national leadership team and an editor of its paper *Avanti!*, before being expelled from the party for his pro-war politics.

A minority of libertarians did support the war. A pro-intervention paper, *La Guerra Sociale*, was also published by individualist anarchists – they motivated their support for the war in terms of a preference for republican France, free and constitutional Britain, and Russia, against militarist Germany and Catholic Austria-Hungary.[448]

Anti-war perspectives were circulated quite widely through an underground press. Luigi Fabbri later argued against talk of defending 'civilisation':

> At the bottom of this there is often an incomplete understanding of anarchism, it is seen as being separated from actual everyday life, inapplicable, in practice, to the problems of real life, not responding to the everyday immediate necessity of defending liberty, the rights of the individual and of the proletariat. Hence the accusation addressed to those who, in life and in the struggle, wish to remain in accord with their principles and separated from reality, neglecting the pressing demands of human civilization, sacrificing them to an arid abstract formula. This is the accusation made by the partisans of intervention [the Sixteen] against us anarchists, as in the great conflict we remained on the great revolutionary terrain, a terrain of freedom and of the proletariat. Their error was a fundamental error of analysis. Anarchism is not only a far-off ideal for a future society, nor just a spiritual abstraction above human contingency, it is all of that, and more: a living and struggling practice, a method of conscious evolution, of preparation and revolution, a concept of movement and action, an ideal that is, continuously, being achieved.

In remaining faithful in practice to anarchist ideas, as far as we could, as we struggle, we contribute to solving the problems of liberty and of human civilisation. So, in contradicting this way, we go better, much more quickly, and much further.[449]

A clandestine anarchist conference was held August 1916, the largest such event since the national congress held in Rome in 1907, bringing together groups from Northern and central Italy and from Naples. Fabbri and Borghi worked to produce resolutions capable of winning widespread support, calling for organisation of all internationalist and socialist labour forces. An International Anarchist Action Committee was nominated[450] – it was to work to prepare further campaigns and to defend anti-war campaigners. Fabbri replied to the 'Manifesto of the Sixteen' – a statement prepared by Kropotkin and others in support of continuing the war. His reply, 'though it had to be disseminated clandestinely, was circulated quite widely'. It alarmed the authorities. Anarchists called for the recovery of their 'lost liberties'. An anarchist leaflet later demanded: 'Proletarians! Raise your axes now, your picks, your barricades, social revolution! Proletarian soldiers, desert! If you must fight, let it be against those who oppress you! Your enemy is not on the so-called border, but here. Proletarian women, rise up! Impede the departure of your loved ones!'[451] Anarchists worked hard to build a campaign in defence of Carlo Tresca – an Italian active with the IWW – who was convicted for building a miner's strike. They helped deserters to escape to Switzerland.[452] Clandestine meetings helped keep organisations alive. Luigi Galleani came up with the rhyme: *Contro la guerra, contro la pace, per la rivoluzione sociale.* ('Against war, against peace, for social revolution'). The USI adopted anti-war policies: not to support or participate the war effort; to condemn any collaboration with bourgeois institutions; to build class consciousness, and direct action through syndicates; and never to excuse politicians responsible for oppressing labour. Some unions campaigned for, and won, an eight-hour day.

Between December 1916 and April 1917 3,901 persons were arrested for participation in anti-war protests, and 48,282 resisted conscription. One large anti-war demonstration in Milan was focused on mobilising women protesters. It resulted in the arrests of twenty women and three men. A bread riot in Turin in August 1917 turned into a city-wide revolt. Machine guns and aircraft bombs were used by the state, resulting in some 60 deaths and over 800 arrests. Some 300 civilians were sent to punishment battalions in the armed forces. Forty members of the armed forces were hospitalised.[453] Another writer records 500 workers were killed and 2,000 wounded.

Anarchists called for a revolt, for soldiers to desert, women were urged to prevent their loved ones fighting, and workers to stop the production of weapons of war.[454]

USA

The Industrial Workers of the World had more time to see the effects of war and to consider their policy before the USA joined the war in April 1917. The IWW convention of 1916 denounced the war as a drive for conquest and exploitation:

> for the prevention of such, we proclaim the anti-militarist propaganda in time of peace, thus promoting class solidarity among the workers of the entire world, and, in time of war, the general strike in all industries. We extend assurances of both moral and material support to all the workers who suffer at the hands of the capitalist class for their adhesion to the principles, and call on all workers to unite themselves with us, that the reign of the exploiters may cease and this earth be made fair through the establishment of industrial democracy.'[455]

There was some popular opposition to recruitment when the USA declared war. In Eastern Oklahoma rebels hailed it as a 'Rich man's war but a poor man's fight'. In their view, this was a war for speculation, and profits would go to the likes of J.P. Morgan & Co. Alexander Berkman wrote a satirical 'War Dictionary', re-defining the terms: *Humanity*: Treason to Government; *Loyal Citizen*: Deaf, dumb and blind; *Patriotism*: Hating your neighbour; *Un-American*: Independent Opinion,[456] and campaigned for a No-Conscription League.

There were extended assaults on the liberties supposedly guaranteed under the constitution. The confrontation between the state and opponents of the war came to a head in and after April 1917. Editorials in *Solidarity* opposed the war and were used by the government to justify its decision to destroy the IWW. It was viewed as a threat, even though some IWW leaders were opposing any resolute anti-war action. Big business saw an opportunity too. Frank Little was lynched in Butte, Montana, in August 1917. Government repression achieved its objectives – disorganising the IWW, destroying its locals and imprisoning many of its key leaders.[457]

There were scores of deaths, hundreds of deportations, (including Luigi Galleani, Emma Goldman and Alexander Berkman) and thousands of imprisonments. Alien agitators were targeted for deportation and the IWW framed for destruction. Mexican anarchist, Ricardo Flores Magón was sentenced to twenty years in prison for his anti-war activities in the USA. (Firmin the son of Rudolf Rocker said that after Goldman and Berkman were deported, the American movement failed to find new inspiring leaders. An old generation died, but no new generation followed on and the movement died.)[458]

Libertarians' International Organisation against the War

In 1914 Malatesta condemned German imperialism, placing it alongside other imperialisms – Belgian, British and Spanish – and recalling atrocities in the Congo, India and Morocco; there was nothing to choose between them; revolution was the only hope. In Argentina, the FORA called the war a commercial enterprise of the bourgeoisie, run for their gain and bringing nothing but loss for working people. An editorial in the London anarchist paper, *Arbeter Fraint*, published on the outbreak of war by Rudolf Rocker, argued that '[t]he workers were the only class who could have prevented the horrible lapse into barbaric bloodshed'. For their failure to prevent war breaking out, 'the working classes of the nations at war will be scourged with whips and scorpions …'[459]

Kropotkin, however, declared his support for the allies, in October 1914:

> It is certain that the present war will be a great lesson to all nations. It will have taught them that war cannot be combated by pacifist dreams and all sorts of nonsense about war being so murderous now that it will be impossible in the future … The German invasion must be repulsed … All efforts must be directed that way.[460]

An international peace congress was convened in El Ferrol in April 1915. Some 47 delegates attended, hailing mainly from Spain or Portugal, mostly but not all libertarians. One Cuban arrived late. Some delegates represented organisations from Brazil and France; others wanting to travel from France, Italy (USI) and Britain were prevented from attending.[461] The congress called for strikes and agreed to prepare anti-war tracts to distribute to soldiers. It was agreed to revise the statutes of the old IWA to serve for a revived Labour International, recasting its aims as '[t[he economic and social emancipation of the workers is the primary objective which every movement must aim for'.[462] An extensive work of propaganda was initiated – the *Federación Regional Anarquista Catalana* had 40,000 copies of an anti-war manifesto printed.[463]

In October, a follow-up peace congress was organised in Rio de Janeiro, with two members of the El Ferrol congress present. When Brazil declared war on the Central Powers in October 1917, syndicalists and anarchists resisted conscription.

In November 1915, an anarchist inspired international action committee against war was formed, joining an anti-war tendency of the CGT, and the Zimmerwald minority in 1916, in declaring 'this war is not our war'.[464] Merrheim and Bourderon represented the anti-war CGT minority at the Zimmerwald conference in 1915 and signed its declaration. The paper of the USI criticised the ongoing refusal of socialists to collaborate with syndicalists like themselves; they looked for greater inclusiveness and warned that otherwise: 'our past will kill our future'.[465] Other syndicalists and anarchists might co-operate with socialists in opposing the war, but had less enthusiasm for longer term co-operation. Such differences would play themselves out once the war ended, as attempts were made to develop a syndicalist international. In April 1918, Armando Borghi reminded readers of the USI's journal that Marx had advocated that *all workers* should unite – not just partisans of electoralism and parliamentarianism.[466]

In 1915, a London international group including Alexander Berkman, Luigi Bertoni, Henry Combes, Carlo Frigerio, Emma Goldman, T. H. Keell, Harry Kelly, Malatesta, Domela Nieuwenhuis, Gerhard Rijnders, Alexander Schapiro, Paul Schreyer, and Bill Shatov declared:

> It is naïve and puerile ... to seek to establish the responsibilities of this or that government [for the outbreak of war]. No distinction can be made between offensive and defensive wars. ... Whatever their clothing, states are oppressors organised in the interest of the privileged minorities. Whatever their place and whatever their situation, the role of anarchists in this current tragedy, is to continue proclaiming that there is only one war of liberation: the war of the oppressed against the oppressors, of the exploited against the exploiters. Our role is to call on slaves to revolt against their masters.

In February 1916, fifteen notable anarchists, many of them contributors to *Les Temps nouveuax*, signed a manifesto which took the view that German imperialism was the greatest danger to liberty. The statement, published in *La Bataille* (formerly *La Bataille Syndicaliste*) argued that in the circumstances that then obtained, with German power waxing strong and with German troops in Belgium, northern France and Poland, it was impossible to call for a peace that would permit that power to remain in place:

> [T]alk of peace at this moment, would be playing the game of the Bülow's German ministerial party and its allies. For our part, we absolutely refuse

to share the illusions of some of our comrades concerning the peaceful intentions of those who now direct Germany's destiny.[467]

The signatories included: Christiaan Cornelissen, Henri Fuss-Amoré, Jean Grave, James Guillaume, Kropotkin, Charles Malato, Marc Pierrot, Paul Reclus, Varlaam Cherkesov, and others. They declared their opposition to capitulation to the German war machine. This was the misnamed 'Manifesto of the Sixteen' – misnamed as a place name was taken as a person, to make fifteen into sixteen. Kropotkin reasoned that Britain and France represented progress while Germany, both the state and German Social-Democracy, represented reaction, militarism and despotism.[468]

Malatesta responded to the 'Manifesto of the Sixteen', arguing that the war ought to have been prevented by revolution, or by the fear of revolution.[469] He wrote that the sixteen did not represent the movement. Cornelissen – something of a father figure to Dutch syndicalists – was repudiated by the NAS. There was a counter-argument noting that 'there is no difference between the thesis they support and that of the [political] parties holding power in each belligerent nation, the theme of "Sacred Union"'. There was not a vestige of anarchism in the choice of supporting this or that warring state. 'The only way to end war, to prevent all war, is an expropriating revolution; there is only one war in which we anarchists can give our lives, and that is in social [class] war.'[470] Malatesta called for a return to principles:

> I think that the oppressed are always in a state of legitimate self-defence, and have always the right to attack the oppressors. I admit, therefore, that there are wars that are necessary, holy wars: and these are wars of liberation, such as are generally 'civil wars' – i.e., revolutions. [...]
>
> If, when foreign soldiers invade the sacred soil of the Fatherland, the privileged class were to renounce their privileges, and would act so that the 'Fatherland' really became the common property of all the inhabitants, it would then be right that all should fight against the invaders. But if kings wish to remain kings, and the landlords wish to take care of their lands and of their houses, and if the merchants wish to take care of their goods, and even sell them at a higher price, then the workers, the socialists and anarchists, should leave them to their own devices, while being themselves on the look-out for an opportunity to get rid of the oppressors inside the country, as well as of those coming from outside.
>
> In all circumstances, it is the duty of the socialists, and especially of the anarchists, to do everything that can weaken the state and the capitalist class, and to take as the only guide to their conduct the interest

of Socialism; or, if they are materially powerless to act efficaciously for their own cause, at least to refuse any voluntary help to the cause of the enemy, and stand aside to save at least their principles – which means to save the future. [...]

In my opinion, the victory of Germany would certainly mean the triumph of militarism and of reaction; but the triumph of the Allies would mean a Russo-English (i.e., a knouto-capitalist) domination in Europe and in Asia, conscription and the development of the militarist spirit in England, and a clerical and perhaps monarchist reaction in France.

Besides, in my opinion, it is most probable that there will be no definite victory on either side. After a long war, an enormous loss of life and wealth, both sides being exhausted, some kind of peace will be patched up, leaving all questions open, thus preparing for a new war more murderous than the present.[471]

Kropotkin lost influence because of his ongoing support for the war. His stance affected the resilience and strength of the anarchist movement. Internal conflicts dissipated energy. He was repudiated by many Russian anarchists.

Organisations, Terms, Abbreviations

ACF: the Anarchist-Communist Federation (Fédération communiste anarchiste) founded July 1912, a successor to the French Revolutionary Communist Federation. Its weekly journal was *Le Libertaire*.

AFD: *Anarchistische Föderation Deutschlands* (German Anarchist Federation).

AFL: The American Federation of Labor – the dominant trade union centre in the USA.

AIT: see IWA

Bolsheviks: (Communists), the name refers literally to 'of the majority' as opposed to Menshevik meaning 'of the minority' – reflecting the winners and losers in party votes at the Russian Social Democratic Party Congress of 1903.

Bourses du travail (France) see *Camera del Lavoro*

Camera del Lavoro (Italy); and **Bourse du travail** (France): Local, multi-purpose union centres: job centres, social and labour offices, their dynamics, traditions, ideologies, and affiliations varied from place to place.

CGL (CGIL): *Confederazione Generale del Lavoro*, (The Italian General Labour Confederation).

CGT: General Confederation of Labour, the initials of national union centres in several countries including Mexico and Portugal, the largest of them being the *French* union, which, before the First World War, was influenced by libertarians. *In Portugal*, the once highly influential CGT became an underground syndicalist union that survived – in vestigial form – the fascist Salazar period. An *Argentinian* CGT was formed in 1930.

Commune: administrative area, rural village or urban community.

CNT: National Confederation of Labour; Spain.

CP: Communist Party.

Domicilio coatto: A form of open imprisonment – victims were directed to live in locations chosen by the state (sometimes remote islands), under police supervision.

FAUD: Freie Arbeiter-Union Deutschlands (Free German Workers Union), founded 1919, German Section of the IWA. In the 1920s their main organ was *Der Syndikalist*. website: www.fau.org

FdCA: Federazione dei comunisti anarchici (Italian Anarchist-Communist Federation), www.fdca.it; publish *Alternativa Libertaria*.

FIOM: Italian metal workers' union.

First International (IWA): international coalition of regional labour federations 1864 to 1877.

FORA: Argentinian Regional Workers' Federation. It set libertarian communism as its goal. In 1915 there emerged (1) the FORA-*V* (of the 5th congress), defending that goal. Press: *La Protesta* and (2) The FORA-*IX* (of the 9th congress) of radicals and syndicalists who refused to maintain libertarian communism as their union's explicit goal.

FVdG: Freie Vereinigung deutscher Gerwerkschaften, predecessor of the FAUD, German 'localist' union confederation.

IFTU: International Federation of Trade Unions, see ISNTUC.

IISG: International Institute of Social History, Amsterdam.

ILP: Independent Labour Party.

ISNTUC: The International Secretariat of National Trade Union Centres 1901-1913, re-named as the IFTU.

IWA or IWMA: International Workers' (Working Mens') Association, of two eras, (1) the First International, q.v.; (2) the Berlin or syndicalist IWA; journal: *Die Internationale*.

IWW: International Workers of the World.

Maximalists: (1) In Russia, an 'extreme' left tendency of the Socialist Revolutionary Party (SRs), some joined the Bolshevik in 1920. (2) In Italy, the most radical tendencies of the Socialist Party.

Nabat: (Tocsin), Ukrainian federation of anarchist-syndicalists and anarcho-communists.

NAS: *Nationaal Arbeids Secretariaat*, a labour centre in the Netherlands. It political complexion evolved, from Social-Democratic to syndicalist to communist and leftist.

Parti Ouvrier (POF): French Workers Party, inspired by Jules Guesde. (Guesdistes).

Possibilists: In the language of revolutionists, possibilists were reformists who looked to what was practical and possible; rather than revolution.

RACF: (Revolutionary Anarchist-Communist Federation), see ACF.

SAC: Swedish central workers' organisation, founded in 1910.

Second International: a grouping of left parties who prioritised parliamentary strategies and expelled those who denied that priority.

Socialist Revolutionaries: see SR's.

SPD: Social-Democratic Party (Germany), newspaper: *Vorwärts*.

SR's / Socialist Revolutionaries: Russian Populist Party with considerable peasant following.

Taylorism: A system of industrial management (time and motion) developed by F. W. Taylor, 'Scientific Management'.

TUC: Trades Union Congress, the British trade union centre.

UGT: General Workers Union – acronym widely used by Social-Democratic union centres in Spain and elsewhere.

Union Sacrée – Sacred Union – alliance to support war, a.k.a. 'King and Country'; 'Ein Reich, ein Volk, ein Fuehrer', etc.

Unionen: post-1917 German unions, influenced variously by IWW, syndicalist or revolutionary politics, offering an alternative to the 'Free' trade-unions (*Gewerkschaften*) allied to the SPD.

USI: Italian syndicalists union. Its organ was *L'Internazionale*, until 1914, then *Guerra di Classe*.

NOTES

1 Errico Malatesta, *Umanitá Nova*, 11.9.1920, Vernon Richards, Ed., *Malatesta: Life and Ideas*, London: Freedom Press, 1965, p. 43.
2 Errico Malatesta, *Umanità Nova*, 26 August 1922.
3 Errico Malatesta, *Umanità Nova*, 13 March, 1920, quoted in Manfredonia, 1994, p. 145; Giampietro Berti, *Errico Malatesta e il movimento anarchico italiano e internazionale 1872–1932*, Milan: Franco Angeli, 2003, p. 665.
4 Daniel Guérin, *Pour le Communisme Libertaire*, Paris: Spartacus, 2003, p. 115.
5 See for example Lawrence Davis & Ruth Kinna (Eds.), *Anarchism and Utopianism*, Manchester University Press, 2009.
6 Emphasis added, from Mikhail Bakunin, *Selected Texts 1868-1875*, London: Merlin/Anarres, 2016, p. 3.
7 Bakunin, *Selected Texts*, op. cit., p. 2.
8 Lead article, *Les Temps nouveaux*, 8-14 March 1902.
9 Sheila Rowbotham, *Dreamers of a New Day: Women who invented the Twentieth Century*, London: Verso, 2011.
10 Malatesta, in *Agitazione*, Ancona, 11 June 1897.
11 Errico Malatesta, (Vernon Richards, Ed.), *Malatesta*, op. cit., p. 29
12 e.g. A report by Rosmer: http://www.marxists.org/archive/rosmer/1949/yestoday.htm
13 *Umanità Nova*, 20 June, 1922, see Gaetano Manfredonia, Ed., *La Pensée de Malatesta*, Antony (France): Groupe Fresnes-Antony, 1996, p. 69.
14 Ibid., pp. 99-101; *Umanità Nova*, 25 May 1922.
15 Mikhail Bakunin, *Selected Texts 1868-1875*, op, cit., pp. 107ff.
16 Murray Bookchin, *The Ghost of Anarcho-Syndicalism*, http://dwardmac.pitzer.edu/Anarchist_Archives/bookchin/ghost2.html
17 From texts edited in 2007-8: Federação Anarquista do Rio de Janeiro, (Translated by Jonathan Payn), *Social Anarchism and Organisation*, Johannesburg: Zabalaza, 2012, https://zabalazabooks.net/2012/03/20/social-anarchism-and-organisation/
18 Past rural revolts, such as those of Zapata in Morelos, or Makhno in the Ukraine or of Andalusian anarchists, have posed questions about the possibility of social reorganisation in liberated areas escaping the domination of the state and capital, see also Gaston Dauval, 'Deux révoltes paysannes en Bolivie', *Interrogations*, No. 6, 1976, p. 44.
19 'To put it another way, anarchism was not a West European doctrine that diffused outwards, perfectly formed, to a passive "periphery". Rather, the movement emerged simultaneously and transnationally, created by interlinked activists on three continents ...' Steven Hirsch and Lucien van der Walt, Eds, *Anarchism and Syndicalism in the Colonial and Postcolonial World, 1870–1940*, Leiden: Brill, 2010, p. liv.
20 Other works, in addition to the one just cited, provide a broad international focus, e.g.: Lucien van der Walt and Michael Schmidt, *Black Flame: The Revolutionary Class Politics of Anarchism and Syndicalism*, Oakland & Edinburgh: AK Press, 2009; and Wayne Thorpe, *'The Workers Themselves': revolutionary syndicalism and international labour, 1913-1923*, Dordrecht: Kluwer, 1989. Many other works address national movements barely addressed here, e.g. on Brazil, Chile, Mexico, Portugal, etc.
21 Chilean governments sought for over eighty years to cover up the massacre of 2,200 workers in Iquique in 1907. Argentina's regimes sought to destroy publications that exposed killings (in Patagonia). From another perspective, the efforts of libertarian researchers, editors, librarians, web-managers, etc., have laid much of the ground work for a revival of libertarian historiography.
22 Gregory P. Maxsimov, in *Constructive Anarchism*, Chicago: Maxsimov Memorial

Publication Committee, 1952; he argues that the thinking of the libertarian movement can be traced back to the positions outlined by the First International.
23   Bakunin, *Selected Texts 1868-1875*, op. cit., p. 176.
24   According to one historian, this policy was rejected by the French group publishing *Le Libertaire*. Sébastien Faure, and co-thinkers accepted strikes but looked to spontaneous rather than organised protests. Georges Lefranc, *Le syndicalisme en France*, Paris: Presses Universitaire de France, (11th ed.), 1981, p. 21.
25   Rudolf Rocker, *Anarchisme et organisation*, Paris: Spartacus, 1985.
26   Between 1894 and 1913 the list of prominent victims of assassins, killed by anarchists and others included an Empress (Austria-Hungary), two Presidents (France and the USA), three Kings (Greece, Italy and Portugal), not to mention two near-misses – Belgium and Spain), and two Prime Ministers (both Spanish).
27   Rudolf Rocker, *La gioventù di un ribelle (1873-1895)*, Milan: Centro studi libertari/ Archivio G. Pinelli, 2014, p. 487.
28   Emphasis added, Robert Graham, *Anarchism: A Documentary History of Libertarian Ideas*, Montreal: Black Rose 2005, Vol. 1, pp. 160-61; 181-83.
29   Errico Malatesta, 'Against Monarchy: A Call to All Progressive People', http://dwardmac.pitzer.edu/Anarchist_Archives/malatesta/againstmonarchy.html
30   'Towards Anarchism' (Verso l'anarchia), *La Questione Sociale* (Paterson), 9 December 1899. https://theanarchistlibrary.org/library/errico-malatesta-towards-anarchism
31   There is a copious documentation on the geographical reach of *Tierra y Libertad* in Joan Zambrana, *El anarquismo organizado en los orígenes de la CNT (Tierra y Libertad 1910-1919)*, 1915, pp. 773-80; http://www.cedall.org/Documentacio/IHL/Tierra%20y%20Libertad%201910-1919.pdf
32   No 22, 1932; http://bibliotecaborghi.org/wp/wp-content/uploads/2016/10/n_22.pdf
33   Davide Turcato, 'Italian Anarchism as a Transnational Movement, 1885–1915', *International Review of Social History*, No. 52, 2007, pp. 407-44. On the impact of Jewish libertarian organisation, see: Rudolf Rocker, *Nella Tormenta, Anni d'esilio (1895-1918)*, Milan: Centro studi libertari/Archivio G. Pinelli, 2016, pp. 262-63.
34   Domela Nieuwenhuis was particularly influential in the Netherlands; Cornelissen, Landauer and Rocker were known internationally.
35   The title of the key journal of Dutch Anarchism, *Vrije Socialist*, (Free Socialist) recalls this transition.
36   Emphasis added, *Freedom*, (London), October 1895.
37   On the politics of this congress see: Davide Turcato, *Making Sense of Anarchism: Errico Malatesta's Experiments with Revolution, 1889-1900*, Edinburgh, AK Press, 2015.
38   Rudolf Rocker commented that it was not so much the resolutions insisting on the necessity of 'political' action that were so controversial; the sticking point in the conflict was on the *parliamentary form* of action that Social-Democrats advocated, and which anarchists rejected. *Nella Tormenta*, op. cit., pp. 41-2.
39   See, ibid, pp. 40ff for extensive commentary on these controversies.
40   Ariane Miéville, & Maurizio Antonioli, Eds, *Anarchisme & syndicalisme. Congrès Anarchiste International d'Amsterdam* (1907), Paris: Monde Libertaire, 1997, pp. 24-5ff, *Les Temps nouveaux*, 3 May 1913; Freedom, *The International Anarchist Congress held at the Plancius Hall, Amsterdam, on August 26th-31st, 1907*, London: "Freedom" Office, 1907, https://theanarchistlibrary.org/library/freedom-ed-the-international-anarchist-congress; see also Daniel Guérin, *Neither God nor Master*, Edinburgh: AK Press, 1997; references here are to the French edition, *Ni Dieu ni Maître*, (4 volumes), Paris: Maspero, 1970-76; Vol. III, pp. 23-30.
41   *Proceedings of the International Worker's Congress, London, July-August, 1896*, Glasgow & London, The Labour Leader, 1896, p. 95.

42 Edith Thomas, *Louise Michel*, Montreal: Black Rose Books, 1980, p. 344.
43 The section on France considers these developments.
44 *Proceedings of the International Worker's Congress*, op. cit, p. 66.
45 Ibid, p. 67; see also Rocker, *Nella Tormenta, Anni d'esilio*, op. cit., pp 52ff.
46 Quoting *Les Temps nouveaux*, 1900, supplement. http://www.pelloutier.net/dossiers/dossiers.php?id_dossier=149&idparent=144_ftn30;
47 *Temps nouveaux*, 7 (and 14) September 1901
48 Guillaume Davranche, 'Septembre 1900 : La fusion entre l'anarchisme et la gauche du socialisme échoue' *Alternative Libertaire*, 2010, http://www.alternativelibertaire.org/?septembre-1900-La-fusion-entre-l
49 On the background to these developments see Guillaume Davranche, 'Pelloutier, Pouget, Hamon, Lazare et le retour de l'anarchisme au socialisme (1893-1900), *Cahiers d'histoire. Revue d'histoire critique*, Paris, No. 110, 2009, pp. 139-161.
50 Emma Goldman, *Living My Life*, (two volumes), New York: Dover Publications, 1970, I, chapter 22.
51 http://www.alternativelibertaire.org/?Amour-libre-Depasser-le-couple; Jean Maitron, *Le mouvement anarchiste en France*, Vol. 1, Paris: Maspero, 1975, p. 348.
52 Émile Armand, *De la liberté sexuelle*, 1907; and *Amour libre et liberté sexuelle*, (Free Love and Sexual Freedom), 1925; Jean Marestan, alias Gaston Havard, *L'Éducation sexuelle*, 1910.
53 *Les Temps nouveaux*, 9 May 1914, quoting *La Protesta*.
54 S. Fanny Simon, 'Anarchism and Anarcho-Syndicalism in South America', in *Hispanic American Review*, Vol. 26, No. 1, February 1946, p. 40.
55 Hélène Finet, 'Ni dieu, Ni patron, Ni mari!, militantes anarchistes en Argentine (1890-1930)', in: Joël Delhom, et al.; *Viva La Social! Anarchistes et anarcho-syndicalistes en Amérique Latine (1860-1930)*, Paris: Nada editions, 2013, p. 30.
56 Emphasis added, *Voz de la Muher*, 31 January 1896, in ibid, p. 38.
57 Ibid, p. 39.
58 Ibid, p. 46.
59 Ruth Thompson, 'Argentine Syndicalism' in Marcel van der Linden, & Wayne Thorpe, Eds., *Revolutionary Syndicalism: An International perspective*, Aldershot: Scolar Press, 1990, p. 170.
60 Ibid., p. 171.
61 Eduardo Colombo, 'La FORA. Le finalisme révolutionnaire', Actes du Colloque International 'Pour un Autre Future'; *De l'Histoire du mouvement ouvrier révolutionnaire*, Paris: Éditions CNT, 2001, p. 103
62 Iaacov Oved, *El anarquismo y el movimiento obrero en Argentina*, Mexico City, Siglo XX1, p. 431
63 Eduardo Colombo, 'La FORA. Le finalisme révolutionnaire', op. cit., pp. 103-04.
64 Diego Abad de Santillán, *La F. O. R. A.: Ideología y trayectoria*, Buenos Aires: Libros de Anarres, 2005, pp. 145-6.
65 Iaacov Oved, *El anarquismo*, op. cit., p. 420.
66 See Eduardo Colombo, 'Anarchism in Argentina and Uruguay', in David E. Apter & James Joll, Eds, *Anarchism Today*, London: Macmillan, 1971, p. 185.
67 Diego Abad de Santillán, *La F. O. R. A.: Ideología y trayectoria*, op. cit., pp. 167-72.
68 Kirwin R. Shaffer, 'Cuba para todos: Anarchist Internationalism and the Cultural Politics of Cuban Independence, 1898–1925.' *Cuban Studies*, No. 31, 2000, pp. 45–75.
69 Ariel Mae Lambe, *Cuban Antifascism and the Spanish Civil War: Transnational Activism, Networks, and Solidarity in the 1930s*, Columbia University Press, 2014, p. 327
70 Joël Delhom, *El movimiento obrero anarquista en el Perú (1890-1930)*, 2001, http://dwardmac.pitzer.edu/Anarchist_Archives/worldwidemovements/peru/Movimiento.

html
71 Robert Graham, *Anarchism: A Documentary*, op. cit., Vol. 1, p. 322.
72 Quoted in Kirwin R. Shaffer, 'Contesting Internationalists: Transnational Anarchism, Anti-Imperialism and US Expansion in the Caribbean, 1890s-1920s', *Estudios Interdisciplinarios de América Latina y el Caribe*, Vol. 22:2; 2011, p. 18.
73 Ibid., p. 17.
74 Kirwin R. Shaffer, 'The Radical Muse: Women and Anarchism in Early-Twentieth-Century Cuba', *Cuban Studies*, Vol. 34, 2003, pp. 130-153, http://www.jstor.org/stable/24487880
75 Ibid., p. 150.
76 Kirwin Shaffer, 'Rebel Soul: Cultural politics and Cuban anarchism, 1890s-1920s', in Geoffroy de Laforcade and Kirwin Shaffer, Eds., *In Defiance of Boundaries: Anarchism in Latin American History*, Gainesville: University of Florida, 2015, pp. 155-58
77 Kirwin R. [Kirk] Shaffer, 'Tropical Libertarians: anarchist movements and networks in the Caribbean, Southern United States, and Mexico' in Hirsch, Steven & van der Walt, Lucien, Eds, *Anarchism and Syndicalism in the Colonial and Postcolonial World, 1870–1940*, Leiden: Brill, 2010, p. 282.
78 Kirwin R. Shaffer, 'Havana Hub: Cuban Anarchism, Radical Media and the Trans-Caribbean Anarchist Network, 1902-1915', *Caribbean Studies*, Vol. 37, No. 2, 2009, pp. 51ff.
79 Kirwin Shaffer, 'Rebel Soul', in Geoffroy de Laforcade and Kirwin Shaffer, Eds., *In Defiance of Boundaries*, op. cit., pp. 151-52.
80 Kirwin R. Shaffer, 'Contesting Internationalists: Transnational Anarchism, Anti-Imperialism and US Expansion in the Caribbean, 1890s-1920s', *Estudios Interdisciplinarios de América Latina y el Caribe*, Vol. 22:2, 2011, pp. 12-13.
81 Nunzio Pernicone, *Italian Anarchism: 1864-1892*, Oakland: AK Press, 2009, p. 291.
82 Nunzio Pernicone, *Italian Anarchism*, op. cit., p. 293.
83 Errico Malatesta, (Davide Turcato, Ed), *The Method of Freedom: An Errico Malatesta Reader*, Oakland: PM Press, 2015, pp. 296-8.
84 'Errori e rimedi', (Schiarimenti), in *L'Anarchia*, London, August 1896, see writings on www.liberliber.it
85 Luigi Fabbri, *Le mouvement anarchiste italien et la lutte contre le fascisme*, Paris: Monde Libertaire, 1994, p. 18.
86 Armando Borghi, *Mezzo secolo di anarchia (1898-1945)*, Catania: Edizioni Anarchismo, 1989, p. 43.
87 Errico Malatesta, (Davide Turcato, Ed), *The Method*, op. cit., p. 158.
88 Ibid., pp. 308-13.
89 In 1906 'Titi' wrote a series of essays entitled *Alle Donne, Emancipiamoci!* (To the Women: Let's Emancipate Ourselves!), for *La Questione Sociale*. See also: Jennifer Guglielmo, 'Transnational Feminism's Radical Past', *Journal of Women's History*, Vol. 22, No. 1, Spring 2010. http://www.smith.edu/history/documents/22.1.guglielmo.pdf
90 Armando Borghi, *Mezzo secolo*, op. cit., pp. 48-9.
91 Carl Levy, 'Currents of Italian syndicalism before 1926', *International Review of Social History*, Cambridge University Press, 2000.
92 Errico Malatesta, *The Method of Freedom*, op. cit., pp. 315-7.
93 Enzo Santerelli, 'L'anarchisme en Italie', *Le Mouvement sociale*, No. 83, 1973, Paris: Editions de l'atelier, pp. 142, 149.
94 Armando Borghi, *Mezzo secolo*, op. cit., p. 78.
95 Ibid, p. 81.
96 Adriana Dadà, *L'anarchismo in Italia fra movimento e partito: Storia e documenti dell'anarchismo italiana*, Milan: Teti Editore, 1984, p. 56.

97 Giampietro Berti, *Errico Malatesta e il movimento anarchico*, op. cit., pp. 467-70.
98 Luigi Fabbri, *L'organisation anarchiste, Rapport présenté au Congrès anarchiste italien de Rome (16-20 juin 1907) et au Congrès anarchiste international d'Amsterdam (24-31 août 1907)*; *Volonté anarchiste*, No. 7, Edition du Groupe Fresnes-Antony de la Fédération anarchiste, 1979, http://www.cga-rp.org/wp-content/uploads/2016/05/fl_organisation_anarchiste.pdf
99 Robert Graham, *Anarchism: A Documentary*, op. cit., Vol. 1, pp. 121-2; Paul Avrich, *Anarchist Voices*, Edinburgh & Oakland: AK Press 2005, p. 157.
100 Santerelli, 'L'anarchisme en Italie', op.cit., p. 144.
101 Rudolf Rocker, *La gioventù di un ribelle (1873-1895)*, op. cit., 2014, p. 449.
102 Jean Jaurès, *La Petite République*, 29 August & 1 September 1901.
103 Daniel Guérin, *Neither God nor Master*, Edinburgh: AK Press, 1997; *Ni Dieu ni Maître*, (4 volumes), Paris: Maspero, 1970-76. Volume III, p. 92 & 87.
104 'Anti-militarisme et Révolution', 11 November 1905.
105 A text from 1908; Georges Sorel, *Reflections on Violence*, Mineola NY: Dover, 2004, pp. 241-2; 116; 168-9.
106 Sharif Gemie, 'Anarchism and Feminism: a Historical Survey', in *Women's History Review*, No. 5, 1996, p. 433.
107 13 February 2004, see http://www.marievictoirelouis.net/document.php?id=148&auteurid=147
108 Sophia Zaïkowska, 'Le féminisme', in *La Vie anarchiste*, No. 12, 1 May 1913; quoted in: Luce Turquier, 'De la liberté en amour au début du XXe siècle – Réflexions et pratiques anarchistes sur le mariage, la liberté en amour et la liberté sexuelle'; http://refractions.plusloin.org/IMG/pdf/turquier.pdf
109 For a fuller discussion see Geoff Brown, *Sabotage: A Study in Industrial Conflict*, Nottingham: Spokesman, 1977, chapters 1 and 2.
110 Commission des Grèves et de la Grève Générale, Réponse de la CGT à Jaurès: 'Grève générale réformiste et grève générale révolutionnaire', 1901, http://monde-nouveau.net/spip.php?article471
111 CGT, *Grève générale réformiste et grève générale révolutionnaire*, Paris: 1903, p. 23. https://bataillesocialiste.wordpress.com/2011/10/20/greve-generale-reformiste-et-greve-generale-revolutionnaire-cgt-1903/
112 Both quotes from René Villard, *Le Syndicalisme Révolutionnaire*, Toulouse: Editions AIT, n.d. pp. 33-4.
113 Victor Griffuelhes, Le syndicalisme révolutionnaire, 1909, http://www.pelloutier.net/dossiers/dossiers.php?id_dossier=125
114 Jean Maitron, *Le mouvement anarchiste*, Vol. 1., op. cit., p. 306.
115 F.F. Ridley, *Revolutionary Syndicalism in France*, Cambridge University Press, 1970, pp. 72-3.
116 Circa 1900; Emma Goldman, (Alix Shulman, Ed.), *Red Emma Speaks*, London: Wildwood House, 1979, p. 75.
117 Hugues Lenoir, 'Georges Sorel et l'éducation', *Les Temps Maudit*, No. 27, October 2008, p. 92.
118 G.D.H. Cole, *The World of Labour: A Discussion of the present and future of Trade Unionism*, London: Bell & Sons, 1913, p. 76
119 Jean Maitron, *Le mouvement anarchiste*, Vol. 1, op. cit., pp. 313-15.
120 F.F. Ridley, *Revolutionary Syndicalism*, op. cit., p. 178.
121 Ibid., pp. 313-23, 318.
122 George Woodcock, *Anarchism*, Harmondsworth: Penguin, 1963, p. 301.
123 Emphasis added; from Emile Pouget, *L'action directe* (1910), Marseille: Le Flibustier, 2009, pp. 16-21 extracts.

124 Guérin, *Ni Dieu*, 1970, III, 89.
125 *Les Temps nouveaux*, No. 26, 27 & 28, October & November 1906, http://acontretemps.org/spip.php?article291
126 Jean Maitron, *Le mouvement anarchiste*, Vol. 1, op. cit., p. 322.
127 The practices of Georges Thonar, one of the delegates to the Amsterdam congress, to promote a Belgium Federation, were condemned as excessively centralist. A looser structure was created instead.
128 *Die Freie Generation. Dokumente der Weltanschauung des Anarchismus*, No. 2, August 1907.
129 *Les Temps nouveaux*, 25 May 1907.
130 See also: George Woodcock & Ivan Avakumovi, *The Anarchist Prince: A Biographical Study of Peter Kropotkin*, London: T. V. Boardman, 1950, p. 297.
131 *Les Temps Nouveaux*, 21 September 1907.
132 An extended report published in three issues of *Mother Earth*, 1907, pp. 275; 270ff, 320ff, 378ff. http://dwardmac.pitzer.edu/Anarchist_Archives/goldman/ME/mev2n1-12.pdf
133 *Les Temps Nouveaux*, 28 September 1907.
134 Emma Goldman's account of this discussion is in *Mother Earth*, October 1907, pp. 309f. http://dwardmac.pitzer.edu/Anarchist_Archives/goldman/ME/mev2n1-12.pdf
135 *Les Temps Nouveaux*, 28 September 1907.
136 Alexandre Skirda, *Facing the Enemy*, op. cit., pp. 83ff. notes reservations; that a minority should not be forced or obliged to comply.
137 Ariane Miéville, & Maurizio Antonioli, Eds., *Anarchisme & syndicalisme: Congrès Anarchiste*, op. cit., p. 177.
138 Ibid., p. 161.
139 In 1910, the NAS had 3,454 members, as against 40,660 in the NVV; at its peak, in 1920, the NAS had 51,570 members as against 247,748 in the NVV. Rudolf De Jong, 'Le Mouvement libertaire aux Pays-Bas', *Le Mouvement social*, (April – June 1973), p. 172.
140 The IWW took in Japanese workers, the AFL did not. European immigrants were soon granted US citizenship but not Japanese workers. They were also denied the right to own land. In 1919, during the Seattle general strike, barriers that existed before the strike were partially destroyed; but striking Japanese workers were not allowed equal representation on the strike committee. 'The Seattle General Strike', in Root & Branch, Ed., *Root & Branch: The Rise of the Workers' Movements*, Greenwich, Conn., 1975, p. 244.
141 Miéville, & Antonioli, *Anarchisme & syndicalisme*, op. cit., pp. 192-3.
142 Wayne Westergard-Thorpe, *Revolutionary syndicalist internationalism, 1913-1923: the origins of the International Working Men's Association*. (Thesis) 1979, pp 30ff. 1
143 On 26 September 1907 in *L'Humanité*.
144 Cornelissen mentioned Austria, Britain, Germany and the USA as places where the union movement was conservative and where a new revolutionary syndicalism might be needed. Miéville, & Antonioli, *Anarchisme & syndicalisme*, op. cit., pp. 85-86.
145 Not completely hegemonic: some unions did not join the CGT, and there were two competing federations in parts of the mining industry; perhaps Monatte was imagining the state of affairs he would have wished, rather than what existed.
146 A reference to the expulsion of Bakunin and Guillaume – at the behest of Marx and Engels – resolved at the unrepresentative congress held at The Hague in 1872 and subsequently rejected by the majority of First International federations.
147 The Workers' Party; its programme can be read on http://www.marxists.org/history/etol/revhist/otherdox/whatnext/po-prog.html
148 Miéville, & Antonioli, *Anarchisme & syndicalisme*, op. cit., pp. 178-187.
149 Errico Malatesta, *Articles politiques*, Paris: Union Générale d'éditions, 1979, pp. 168-69.

150 Miéville & Antonioli, 1997, pp. 193-99, see also the introduction in that volume by Miéville; Guérin, *Ni Dieu*, III, 1970, 31ff; and short extracts on the General Strike in *Malatesta*, Richards ed., 1965.
151 *Les Temps Nouveaux*, 5 October 1907.
152 *Freedom*, November 1907, Vol. 21, No. 223; quoted in Selva Varengo 'Il pensiero anarchico attraverso le pagine di *Freedom*', (Thesis), p. 98. https://air.unimi.it/bitstream/2434/208930/2/tesi%20Freedom.pdf
153 Miéville, & Antonioli, *Anarchisme & syndicalisme*, op. cit., p. 194.
154 Ibid., p. 199.
155 Arthur Lehning, Ed., Bakounine; *Les conflits dans l'Internationale: 1872*, Antony (France), Ed. Tops-H. Trinquier, 2003, pp. 139.
156 Miéville, & Antonioli, *Anarchisme & syndicalisme*, op. cit., pp. 205-09.
157 Maurizio Antonioli, *The International Anarchist Congress, Amsterdam, 1907*, Federazione dei Comunisti Anarchici, p. 19. http://dwardmac.pitzer.edu/Anarchist_Archives/sla-5.pdf
158 Errico Malatesta, (Davide Turcato, Ed), *The Method of*, op. cit., p. 339.
159 Errico, Malatesta, (Vernon Richards, Ed), *The Anarchist Revolution*, London: Freedom Press, 1995, p. 32, 26.
160 Alexandre Skirda, *Facing the Enemy: A History of Anarchist Organisation from Proudhon to May 1968*, Edinburgh & Oakland: AK Press, 2002, p. 81.
161 Miéville, & Antonioli, *Anarchisme & syndicalisme*, op. cit., p. 212.
162 Marcel van der Linden & Wayne Thorpe, Eds., *Revolutionary Syndicalism: An International perspective*, Aldershot: Scolar Press, 1990, p. 239. According to Maitron only twelve editions were issued. Jean Maitron, *Le mouvement anarchiste en France*, Vol. 2, Paris: Maspero, 1975.
163 See http://gallica.bnf.fr/ark:/12148/bpt6k55181521
164 Alexandre Skirda, *Facing the Enemy*, op. cit., 2002, p. 86. Fabbri wrote that the comrades were more worried about the internal movements in their own nation and did not take the international project seriously.
165 It was published over four issues of *Les Temps nouveaux*, 14, 21, 28 September and 5 October 1907;
166 In November 1905, Paul Avrich, *The Russian Anarchists*, Princeton University Press, 1967, p. 81.
167 Ibid., pp. 79-89.
168 *Les Temps Nouveaux* of 19 October 1907; the same report noted that the use of violent tactics in economic struggles was now being condemned by the several Social-Democratic organisations. It went on to note: 'add up the results of any one day and you would regularly find three or four death sentences.'
169 *Les Temps nouveaux*, 9 November.
170 Murray Bookchin introductory essay in Sam Dolgoff, Ed., *The Anarchist Collectives*, New York: Free Life Editions, 1974, pp. xxii-xxiii.
171 James Baer, 'The FACA and the FAI', in Geoffroy de Laforcade & Kirwin Shaffer, Eds., *In Defiance of Boundaries*, op. cit., p. 98.
172 Martha A. Acklesberg, *Free Women of Spain: Anarchism and the struggle for the Emancipation of Women*, Edinburgh & Oakland, Ca.: AK Press, 2005, p. 54.
173 See position adopted on women and work at 1st CNT congress, http://archivo.cnt.es/Documentos/congresosCNT/CONGRESO_CONSTITUCION_CNT.htm
174 Quoted in Gaston Leval, 'Constructive conceptions of libertarian socialism', in *Autogestion et Socialisme*, No. 18-19, January-April 1972, pp. 39-40.
175 Antoni Dalmau i Ribalta, 'Jesús Navarro Botella (1881-?)', *Hispania*, 2015, Vol. LXXV, No. 249, p. 130.

176 Emma Goldman, *Anarchism and other essays*, New York: Dover,1969, p. 165.
177 Antoni Dalmau i Ribalta, 'Jesús Navarro Botella (1881-?)', op. cit., p. 141.
178 *Solidaridad Obrera*, quoted in Walther L. Bernecker, *Colectividades y Revolución Social*, Barcelona: Editorial Critica, 1982, p. 79.
179 Hélène Finet, 'Hétérodoxie anarchiste en Argentine : analyse d'une déviance contre-démocratique', Nuevo Mundo Mundos Nuevos [Online], Workshops, http://nuevomundo.revues.org/56503; DOI: 10.4000/nuevomundo.56503
180 Steven J. Hirsch, 'Peruvian Anarcho-Syndicalism: Adapting Transnational Influences and Forging Counterhegemonic Practices, 1905–1930, in Steven Hirsch and Lucien van der Walt, Eds, *Anarchism and Syndicalism in the Colonial and Postcolonial World, 1870–1940*, Leiden: Brill, 2010, p. 231.
181 *International Socialist Review*, November 1916, http://www.weneverforget.org/hellraisers-journal-big-bill-haywood-on-the-a-f-of-l-the-i-w-w-and-class-struggle/
182 Joyce L. Kornbluh, *Rebel Voices An IWW Anthology*, London: Merlin Press, 2011, pp.12-13, 387.
183 Ibid., pp. 158ff.
184 https://libcom.org/files/justice.pdf
185 William A. Pelz, Ed., *The Eugene V. Debs Reader*, Chicago: Institute of Working Class History, 2000, p. 45.
186 David Poole, Ed., *Land and Liberty: Anarchist Influences in the Mexican Revolution*, Sanday: Cienfuegos Press, 1977, p. 88.
187 Meredith Tax writes that 14.5 million immigrants came to the USA between 1901 and 1920; in 1900 44% of miners in the USA were foreign born, Meredith Tax, *The Rising of the Women: Feminist Solidarity and Class Conflict*, 1880-1917, New York: Monthly Review Press, 1980, p. 27.
188 Stewart Bird, Dan Georgakas, & Deborah Shaffer: *Solidarity Forever: An Oral History of the Wobblies*, London: Lawrence & Wishart, 1985, p. 96.
189 See Sheridan Johns: *Raising the Red Flag: The International Socialist League and the Communist Party of South Africa 1914-32*, Bellville: Mayibuye, 1995, p. 32, 72, 106 and H.J. & R.E. Simons, *Class and Colour in South Africa, 1850-1950*, Harmonsdworth: Penguin, 1969, p. 215; Bird, et al, *Solidarity Forever*, op. cit., pp. 207-08 also notes the influence of particular IWW leaders in Italy, Norway, Spain and the UK.
190 Magónista ideology sought to defend the traditional interests and land rights of the indigenous peoples of Mexico; women were given greater respect than in other movements at the time; Magónistas understood that their fight was international, involving families and comrades in the USA, and migrant labour both in Mexico and further afield.
191 See: http://www.alternativelibertaire.org/spip.php?page=imprimir_articulo&id_article-3876
192 Lead article, *Les Temps nouveaux*, 7-13 May 1904.
193 From Engels, Introduction to Karl Marx's '*The Class Struggles in France 1848 to 1850*'; in W. O. Henderson, Ed, *Engels: Selected Writings*, Harmondsworth: Penguin, 1967, p. 289.
194 Helge Döhring, *Generalstreik: Abwehrstreik... Proteststreik... Massenstreik?* Lich (Hessen): Verlag AV, 2011, pp. 38-39.
195 Ibid., p. 33.
196 Ibid., p. 38.
197 Karl Kautsky, *The Social Revolution*, Chicago: Charles Kerr, 1902, pp. 186-87.
198 Gustav Landauer, *Revolution and Other Writings: A Political Reader,* (Ed. Gabriel Kuhn), London: Merlin Press, 2010, p. 220.
199 Rudolf Rocker, *La gioventù di un ribelle (1873-1895)*, op. cit., p. 413.

200 Ibid., p. 360.
201 Helge Döhring, *Generalstreik*, op. cit., p. 28.
202 Alfred Grosser, *Germany in Our Time: A Political History of the Postwar Years*, Harmondsworth: Penguin, 1974, p. 15. Wolfgang Mommsen argues that the perspective of the centralised trade unions' leadership was founded on desire for compromise with the employers, Wolfgang Mommsen & Hans Gerhard Husung, Eds, *The Development of Trade Unions in Germany and Great Britain 1880-1914*, London: Allen & Unwin, 1985, p. 384. Another historian notes that local strikes were characterised by: 'anything but clarion calls of revolution…' rather workers only wanted their due and their strikes were channelled by corporatism and regulations, in a pattern that strengthened a tendency towards reformism. Adelheid von Saldern, in David E. Barclay, & Eric. D. Weitz, *Between Reform and Revolution: German Socialism from 1840 to 1990*, Oxford: Berghahn, 2005, pp. 202-3.
203 Arnold Roller (Siegried Nacht), 'Der Generalstreik und die soziale Revolution' in Helge Döhring, *Generalstreik*, op. cit., p. 91.
204 Otto Rühle, *From the Bourgeois to the Proletarian Revolution*, London: Socialist Reproductions, n.d., p. 34.
205 Rosa Luxemburg, *The Mass Strike*, London: Merlin Press, n.d., Chapter 1; our emphasis.
206 Ibid., last chapter, and penultimate paragraph of Chapter 1.
207 J. Peter Nettl, *Rosa Luxemburg*, Oxford University Press, 1969, p. 203.
208 Carl Schorske, *German Social-Democracy: 1905-1917*, London: John Wiley, 1955, p. 39; Wolgang Abendroth, *A Short History of the European Working Class*, New York: Monthly Review Press, 1972, p. 58.
209 R.C. Ensor, Ed., *Modern Socialism as set forth by Socialists in their Speeches, Writings and Programmes*, London: Harper, 1910, p. 196.
210 *Les Temps nouveaux*, 27 October 1906.
211 *Les Temps nouveaux*, 9 February 1907.
212 Bakunin, (Michel Bakounine), *Oeuvres*, six volumes, Paris: P. V. Stock, 1895-1913. (Available online, e.g. http://fr.wikisource.org/wiki/Bakounine/%C5%92uvres); James Guillaume, *L'Internationale: documents et souvenirs 1864-78*, Paris: Societé nouvelle de librairie et d'éditions/P. V. Stock, (Four books: 1905, 1907, 1909 and 1910) Available online: http://fr.wikisource.org/wiki/Auteur:James_Guillaume.)
213 See Rosa Luxemburg, *The Mass Strike*, chapters 6-8; these chapters are not in Peter Hudis & Kevin B., Anderson, *The Rosa Luxemburg Reader*, New York: Monthly Review Press, 2004, but see p. 363 of that volume for her later perspectives.
214 Georges Sorel, *Reflections on Violence*, op. cit., pp. 241-2; 116; 168-9. It is interesting that Lenin's *State and Revolution*, disregards Sorel.
215 See *International Council Correspondence*, Vol. 2., No. 5, and Vol. 3. Nos. 11. & 12, in Karl Korsch, Paul Mattick, Anton Pannekoek, Otto Rühle & Helmut Wagner, *La contre-révolution bureaucratique*, Paris: Union Générale d'Editions, 1973, pp. 157, 243, 245.
216 The 'free' SPD unions being generally advocates of contrasting or opposite practices. Helge Döhring, *Syndikalismus in Deutschland, 1914-1918*, Lich (Hessen): Verlag AV, 2013, pp. 35-36.
217 Helge Döhring, *Generalstreik*, op. cit., pp. 32-33.
218 Pierre Ramus, *Generalstreik und direkte Aktion*, Berlin: Verlag- und Sortiments- Buchandlung, 1910, p. 20. See also : http://www.syndikalismusforschung.info/Ramus_(1910)_Generalstreik_&_direkte_Aktion.pdf
219 Ramus, *Generalstreik und direkte Aktion*, op. cit., p. 59.
220 *Die Aktion*, 4 October 1913.

221 Relations were not especially close between the FVdG and the German Anarchist Federation.
222 See Arnold Roller (Siegried Nacht), *Generalstreik*, op. cit., pp. 79ff.
223 See notes by Gaël Cheptou, in: Freddy Gomez, Gaël Cheptou et al, *Rudolf Rocker ou la liberté par en bas*, Saint-Georges d'Oléron (France): Les Editions Libertaires, 2014. (À contretemps), pp. 150-153.
224 Dieter Nelles & Hartmut Rübner, 'Avantgarde einer egalitären Bewegung', *Moving the Social*, No. 51, (2014), p. 194.
225 Gustav Landauer, *Revolution and Other Writings*, op. cit., pp. 215-6.
226 Ibid, p. 190; the longer quote is from Gustav Landauer, *For Socialism*, New York: Telos Press, 1978, (first published, 1911).
227 Rudolf Rocker, *Anarquismo y Organisación*, http://www.almeralia.com/autores.html
228 Quoted in Serge Bricanier, *Pannekoek and the Workers' Councils*, St Louis (Mo.): Telos Press, 1978, p. 135.
229 Hans Manfred Bock, *Syndikalismus und Linkskommunismus von 1918-1923*, Meisenheim am Clan: Verlag Anton Hain, 1969, p. 55.
230 Bricanier, *Pannekoek and*, op. cit., 1978, p. 132.
231 Carl Schorske, *German Social-Democracy*, op. cit., 1955, pp. 269-270, and 261; Bock, *Syndikalismus und*, op. cit., p 39.
232 Dick Geary, Ed., *Labour and Socialist movements in Europe before 1914*, Oxford: Berg, 1989, p. 110.
233 G.D.H. Cole, *The World of Labour*, op. cit., pp. 61, 169, 175, etc.
234 Hans Manfred Bock, *Syndikalismus und*, op. cit, pp. 32-33.
235 Ernst Toller, *I Was a German: The Autobiography of a Revolutionary*, New York: Paragon House, 1991, p. 187.
236 Landauer, *Revolution and Other Writings*, op. cit, pp. 222-29.
237 'Die Sozialdemokratie und der Krieg', *Der Sozialist*, 1 December 1912.
238 Fritz Kater, 'L'union libre des syndicats allemands et sa lutte dans le mouvement allemand', *La Voix du Peuple*, 20-26.04.1914.
239 Hugo Heinemann, *Die sozialistischen Errungenschaften der Kriegszeit*, Chemnitz: Landgraf & Co, 1915, p. 6; quoted by Eric Vilain, *Kropotkine et la Grande Guerre*, Éditions du Cercle d'études libertaires – Gaston-Leval, 2011, p. 88.
240 Rudolf Rocker, *Nationalism and Culture*, Montreal: Black Rose Books, 1998, p. 237.
241 J. Peter Nettl, *Rosa Luxemburg*, op. cit., p. 314.
242 Guillaume Davranche, *Trop jeune pour mourir: Ouvriers et révolutionnaires face à la guerre (1909-1914)*, Paris: Libertalia, L'Insomniaque, 2014, pp. 140-1, 436.
243 Marcel van der Linden & Wayne Thorpe, Eds., *Revolutionary Syndicalism*, op. cit., p. 3. This word 'subordination' echoes the call for politics to be subordinated to the great goal of economic liberation, as set out in the aims of the First International, in French texts agreed at the first IWA congress.
244 Guillaume Davranche, *Trop jeune*, op. cit., pp. 226-7.
245 *Les Temps nouveaux*, 18 August 1906.
246 *Les Temps nouveaux*, 3 November 1906.
247 Georges Lefranc, *Le syndicalisme en France*, Paris: Presses Universitaire de France, (11th ed.), 1981, pp. 32-33; Ariane Miéville, & Maurizio Antonioli, Eds., *Anarchisme & syndicalisme. Congrès Anarchiste International d'Amsterdam (1907)*, Paris: Monde Libertaire, 1997, p. 42.
248 *L'anarchie*, No. 255 February, 1910, from www.marxists.org/archive/serge/1910/02/anti-syndicalism.htm.
249 Maurizio Antonioli, *Bakounine entre syndicalisme révolutionnaire et anarchisme*, Paris: Noir et Rouge, 2014, p. 33.

250 Ibid., p. 41-42.
251 Ibid., pp. 51-52.
252 Ibid., p. 52.
253 Ibid., p. 55.
254 Guillaume Davranche, *Trop jeune*, op. cit., p. 422.
255 Pierre Monatte, *Souvenirs sur La Vie Ouvrière*, 1959, https://revolutionproletarienne.files.wordpress.com/2007/05/monatte59.pdf
256 Guillaume Davranche, *Trop jeune*, op. cit., p. 17.
257 Jean Maitron, *Le mouvement anarchiste*, Vol. 2, op. cit., p. 57.
258 Alexandre Skirda, *Facing the Enemy*, op. cit., p. 103.
259 Georges Fontenis, *Changer le monde: Histoire du mouvement communiste Libertaire*, Paris: Alternative Libertaire, 2000, p. 21. Earlier it had claimed to bring together 31 groups, see: Guillaume Davranche, *Trop jeune*, op. cit., p. 233.
260 'Diagnostic de l'état du mouvement anarchiste en 1911', *Les Temps nouveaux*, December 1911 http://monde-nouveau.net/spip.php?article521
261 Jean Grave, *Ce que nous voulons*, Paris: Les Temps nouveaux, 1914, p. 7.
262 Quoted by René Berthier in the postscript to Maurizio Antonioli, *Bakounine entre syndicalisme révolutionnaire et anarchisme*, Paris: Noir et Rouge, 2014, p. 109.
263 Guillaume Davranche, *Trop jeune*, op. cit., pp. 383-412.
264 *Le Mouvement anarchiste*, October 1912, No. 3, p. 70, http://archivesautonomies.org/IMG/pdf/anarchismes/avant-1914/lemouvementanarchiste/lemouvementanarchiste-n03.pdf
265 Ibid, p. 74.
266 Guillaume Davranche, *Trop jeune*, op. cit., pp. 270.
267 Francis Delaisi, *Les Temps nouveaux*, 23 August 1913.
268 Pierre Martin *Les Temps nouveaux*, 23 August 1913. There were several comments from various figures in this, and in the next edition.
269 Guillaume Davranche, *Trop jeune*, op. cit., pp. 527-28.
270 Ibid., p. 240; perhaps the first time that a journal was dependent on an organisation as owner and publisher (rather than one or more individuals).
271 Ibid, p. 336.
272 David Berry, *A History of the French Anarchist Movement, 1917-1945*, Westport: Greenwood Press, 2002, p. 20, 24n; Maitron, *Le mouvement anarchiste*, Vol. 2, op. cit., pp. 123-5; see also Woodcock, 1963, p. 297.
273 Pierre Monatte, *Souvenirs sur La Vie Ouvrière*, 1959.
274 Le CGT, *Le Proletariat contre la guerre et les trois ans*, Paris: Maisons des Fédérations, 1913. http://bataillesocialiste.files.wordpress.com/2008/07/guerre1913.pdf, p. 69.
275 Edward Mortimer, *The Rise of the French Communist Party 1920-1947*, London: Faber, p. 21.
276 F.F. Ridley, *Revolutionary Syndicalism*, op. cit., pp. 77-78.
277 Le CGT, *Le Proletariat contre la guerre et les trois ans*, Paris: Maisons des Fédérations, 1913, p. 69.
278 Max Nettlau, *A Short History of Anarchism*, London: Freedom Press, 1996, p. 275; Nuclei Libertari di Fabbrica di Milano, *Histoire de l'anarcho-syndicalisme italien*, Paris: Volonte Anarchiste, 1978; Jean-Marie Mayeur & Madeleine Rebérioux, *The Third Republic from its Origins to the Great War, 1871-1914*, Cambridge University Press, 1987, p. 305 says membership rose steeply to 350,000 in 1908 and stagnated afterwards.
279 Available online, see for example: http://www.la-presse-anarchiste.net/spip.php?rubrique332
280 Available online http://gallica.bnf.fr/ark:/12148/cb34429549x/date&rk=64378;0
281 F.F. Ridley, *Revolutionary Syndicalism*, op. cit., p. 183.

282 *Les Temps nouveaux*, 7 February 1914.
283 *Les Temps nouveaux*, 14, 28 February, 7 March, and 1 August 1914; Gianpiero Bottinelli, *Louis Bertoni, une figure de l'anarchisme ouvrier à Genève*, Geneva: Entremonde, 2012. p. 58.
284 Alexandre Elsig, *La ligue d'action du bâtiment (1929 – vers 1935): L'éphémère emprise de l'anarcho-syndicalisme sur les chantiers genevois*, Université de Fribourg, 2009, pp. 36-37.
285 Guillaume Davranche, *Trop jeune*, op. cit., pp. 458-59.
286 *Les Temps nouveaux*, 28 February 1914.
287 Dick Geary, Ed., *Labour and Socialist movements*, op cit., p. 87.
288 As expressed after 1918; see: *Revolutionary History*, Vol. 7, No. 4, pp. 72-3.
289 Larry Portis, *Georges Sorel*, London: Pluto Press, 1990, p. 76.
290 Cole, *The World of Labour*, op. cit., pp. 124-5.
291 Ibid., p. 94.
292 Bertoni was allowed to remain on a renewable three-month licence – a licence that was extended until his death in 1947. Gianpiero Bottinelli, *Louis Bertoni*, Geneva: Entremonde, 2012, p. 46.
293 Willy Gianinazzi, 'Le syndicalisme révolutionnaire en Italie (1904-1925)', *Mil neuf cent*, No. 24, 2006, p. 17.
294 Gaetano Manfredonia, Ed., *La Pensée de Malatesta*, op. cit., pp. 60-1, 66.
295 *Avanti!*, 12 April 1903, quoted in Maurizio Antonioli, *L'USI : le syndicalisme révolutionnaire italien*.
296 Armando Borghi, *Mezzo secolo*, op. cit., p. 83.
297 Ibid, p. 85.
298 Ibid, p. 96.
299 Quoted in Dick Geary, Ed., *Labour and Socialist movements*, op cit., p. 195. The USI – of which more below – was also affected by such tensions.
300 Giampietro Berti, *Errico Malatesta e il movimento anarchico*, op. cit., op. cit., p. 474-5.
301 Maurizio Antonioli, *L'USI*, http://www.monde-nouveau.net/IMG/pdf/USI-Antonioli_RTF.pdf
302 T. Masotti, 'Le Congrès des Syndicalistes italiens', *La Vie ouvrière*, 5 January 1911, quoted in Antonioli, *L'USI*, emphasis added.
303 Willy Gianinazzi, 'Le syndicalisme révolutionnaire', op. cit., p. 42.
304 Carl Levy writes that anarchists enjoyed a permanent leadership in that union. Carl Levy, *Gramsci and the Anarchists*, Oxford: Berg, 1999, p. 9.
305 Giampietro Berti, *Errico Malatesta e il movimento anarchico*, op. cit., op. cit., p. 417; Fabbri had similar views to Malatesta on role of the anarchist party.
306 The lower figure is in Berti, ibid., p. 484; the higher figure is from Carl Levy, in 'Italian Anarchism, 1870-1926' in David Goodway, Ed., *For Anarchism: History, Theory, and Practice*, London: Routledge, 1989, p. 54. Berti notes that CGL membership declined.
307 Armando Borghi, *Mezzo secolo*, op. cit., p. 136.
308 *Le Mouvement anarchiste*, December 1912, No. 5, p. 142, http://archivesautonomies.org/IMG/pdf/anarchismes/avant-1914/lemouvementanarchiste/lemouvementanarchiste-n05.pdf
309 'La guerra e gli anarchici', *La Guerra Tripolina*, April 1912.
310 Giampietro Berti, *Errico Malatesta e il movimento anarchico*, op. cit., op. cit., p. 490.
311 Ibid., pp. 489-91.
312 *Volontà*, 8 June 1913, from Manfredonia, *La Pensée de Malatesta*, op. cit., pp. 93-8.
313 Giampietro Berti, *Errico Malatesta e il movimento anarchico*, op. cit., op. cit., p. 498.
314 Ibid., p. 507.
315 Federico Torza, *Il Sindacalismo Rivoluzionario di Armando Borghi*, p. 29.

316　Ibid, p. 31.
317　The project was announced in 'De la Internacional Anarquista – el congreso de Londres', in *Tierra y Libertad,* No. 215, 27.5.1914, http://www.cedall.org/Documentacio/IHL/Tierra%20y%20Libertad%201910-1919.pdf (p. 757).
318　Luigi, 'Zum Kongress in Hannover', *Kampf,* (Hamburg), June 1914, No. 24; https://archivkarlroche.files.wordpress.com/2009/12/kampf-nr-24-juni-1914.pdf
319　Michaël Confino, 'Kropotkine en 1914 : la guerre et les congrès manqués des anarchistes russes', *Cahiers du monde russe et soviétique,* Vol. 23, No. 1, 1982, pp. 63-107. There appear to have been several Russian Secret Police spies working within various groups.
320　*Les Temps nouveaux,* 30 May 1914.
321　Guillaume Davranche, *Trop jeune,* op. cit., p. 477.
322　Rudolf Rocker. *Nella Tormenta,* op. cit., p. 466
323　Giampietro Berti, *Errico Malatesta e il movimento anarchico,* op. cit., pp. 503-4.
324　Luigi Damiani, 'Deviazioni e specializzazioni', *La Barricata,* 17 November 1912; quoted in Edilene Toledo and Luigi Biondi: 'Constructing Syndicalism and Anarchism Globally: The Transnational Making of the Syndicalist Movement in São Paulo, Brazil, 1895–1935' in Steven Hirsch and Lucien van der Walt, Eds, *Anarchism and Syndicalism in the Colonial and Postcolonial World, 1870–1940,* Leiden: Brill, 2010, pp. 378-9.
325　*Volontà,* 1 November 1913.
326　*Volontà,* 6 December 1913, in Giampietro Berti, *Errico Malatesta e il movimento anarchico,* op. cit., p. 500.
327　*Volontà,* 8 June 1913; 13 September 1913; and 6 December 1913; quoted in Berti, *Errico Malatesta e il,* op. cit., pp. 500-1.
328　Ibid, pp. 500-507.
329　Manfredonia, *La Pensée de Malatesta,* op. cit., pp. 119-125.
330　Ibid., pp. 127-130 (*Le Réveil,* 1 November 1919,); *Volontà,* 20 September 1913.
331　Errico Malatesta, (Davide Turcato, Ed), *The Method,* op. cit., p. 324.
332　Excerpts from *New Age,* 30 April 1914, in James Connolly, (P. Berresford Ellis, Ed.), *Selected Works,* Harmondsworth: Pelican, 1973, pp. 178-80.
333　*Freedom,* Vol. 24, No. 259, November 1910, p. 86.
334　Marc Pierrot, 'Les Syndicats et l'Anarchie', Paris, *Les Temps nouveaux,* 19 March 1910; http://monde-nouveau.net/spip.php?article500
335　Writings by Bakunin on the Alliance and on intimate close friends exerting influence contrasted with writings on democratic public structures in branches of the International. It was never entirely clear how such structures should co-operate.
336　A. Borghi, 'Polemica sindacalista', in *Volontà,* 21 February 1914; Maurizio Antonioli, *Bakounine entre,* op. cit., p. 52; Maurizio Antonioli, 'Bakunin sindacalista?', *A rivista anarchica,* No. 49, June 1976; http://www.arivista.org/index.php?nr=49&pag=49_09.htm
337　*Le militarisme et l'attitude des anarchistes et socialistes révolutionnaires devant la guerre,* Paris: Temps nouveaux, No. 17, 1901, p. 28
338　An article, 'The Soldiers' Rebellion', quoted in: Carlos M. Rama, & Ángel J. Cappelletti, *El anarquismo en América Latina,* Caracas: Biblioteca Ayacucho, 1990, p. 301.
339　Joël Delhom, 'Le mouvement ouvrier anarchiste au Pérou (1890-1930): essai de synthèse et d'analyse historiographique', in Joël Delhom, et al.; *Viva La Social! Anarchistes et anarcho-syndicalistes en Amérique Latine* (1860-1930), Paris: Nada editions, 2013, p. 229
340　Geary, *Labour and Socialist movements,* op cit., p. 95.
341　*Mother Earth,* November 1907, pp. 405ff. http://dwardmac.pitzer.edu/Anarchist_Archives/goldman/ME/mev2n1-12.pdf
342　Tom Mann, *Tom Mann's Memoirs,* London: Macgibbon & Kee, 1967.

343 Emphasis added, Tom Mann, "Diamond Mining in South Africa", *International Socialist Review*, Vol. XI, July 1910.
344 Jonathan Hyslop, *Notorious Syndicalist: J.T. Bain – A Scottish Rebel in Colonial South Africa*, Johannesburg: Jacana Media, 2004, p. 189.
345 Libertarian politics had germinated in the South African Social Democratic Federation, and developed in new organisations, including unions (e.g. the Industrial Workers of Africa). Such organisations were not homogenous and contained a mix of ideas. See Lucien van der Walt, 'Revolutionary Syndicalism, Communism and the National Question in South African Socialism, 1886–1928', in: Steven Hirsch & Lucien van der Walt, Eds, *Anarchism and Syndicalism in the Colonial and Postcolonial World, 1870–1940*, Leiden: Brill, 2010, p. 71, 36.
346 Ibid, p. 72, quoting: *International*, 19 October 1917, 'The Pass Laws: organise for their abolition', emphasis added.
347 Fred Bower, *Rolling Stonemason: An Autobiography*, Talgarth: Merlin Press, 2015, pp. 121-22.
348 Jonathan Hyslop, 'The Imperial Working Class Makes Itself "White": White Labourism in Britain, Australia, and South Africa Before the First World War', *Journal of Historical Sociology*, Vol. 12, No. 4, December 1999, p. 403; 418.
349 J. Scarceriaux commented slavery still exists in the USA; *Les Temps nouveaux*, 25 July 1914. (*The Atlanta Constitution*, 8 June 1914; https://www.newspapers.com/newspage/26820211/ [?])
350 Gerardo Leibner, '*La Protesta* y la andinización del anarquismo en el Perú, 1912-1915', *Estudios Interdisciplinarios de América Latina y el Caribe*, Vol. 5., No 1., Tel Aviv, 1984.
351 Emphasis added, Victor Griffuelhes, *L'Action Syndicaliste*, Paris: Librairie des sciences politiques et sociales, 1908, chapter 5, pp. 52ff.
352 Ibid., p. 57.
353 October 1908, cf. John Schwarzmantel, 'Nationalism and the French Working-Class. Movement 1905–1914', in Eric Cahm & Vladimir Claude Fišera, Eds., *Socialism and Nationalism*, Vol 2, Nottingham: Spokesman, 1979. pp. 65–80.
354 Susan Milner, 'The International Labour Movement and the Limits of Internationalism', *International Review of Social History*, XXXIII, 1988, pp. 6, 15.
355 CGT, *Le Proletariat contre la guerre et les trois ans*, Paris: Maisons des Fédérations, 1913 p. 12.
356 Guillaume Davranche, *Trop jeune*, op. cit., pp. 187-8.
357 Georges Yvetot, *Nouveau manuel du soldat*, (first published in 1902), quoted in Henri Dubief, *Les Anarchistes (1870-1940)*, Paris: Armand Colin, 1972. pp. 156-157. Extracts in: A. W. Zurbrugg, Ed, *Not Our War: Writings Against the First World War*, Talgarth: Merlin Press, 2014; http://www.katesharpleylibrary.net/66t21j
358 *Les Temps Nouveaux*, 6 July 1907.
359 The two provinces seized by Germany in 1871.
360 For example, *Voix du Peuple*, No. 532, 6 December 1910, p. 2.
361 *Le Mouvement anarchiste*, No. 2, September 1912, http://archivesautonomies.org/IMG/pdf/anarchismes/avant-1914/lemouvementanarchiste/lemouvementanarchiste-n02.pdf
362 CGT, *Le Proletariat*, op. cit., p. 18.
363 Gianpiero Bottinelli, *Louis Bertoni, une figure de l'anarchisme ouvrier à Genève*, Geneva: Entremonde, 2012, pp. 69-70.
364 Emphasis added, Friedrich Engels, 'Socialism in Germany', 1891-2, see: https://www.marxists.org/archive/marx/works/1892/01/socialism-germany.htm
365 February 1907. The first edition of the Handbook was printed in London. In an attempt to disguise it, editions were printed with Imperial icons on the cover and

purported to be printed by 'A Patriotic Publisher'. From: *Not Our War* [as above] and: Arnold Roller (Siegfried Nacht), *Soldaten Brevier*, in Ulrich Bröckling, Ed, *Nieder mit der Disziplin! Hoch die Rebellion – Anarchistische Soldatenagitation im Deutschen Kaiserreich*, Berlin: Harald Kater Verlag, 1988, and http://www.anarchismus.at/texte-antimilitarismus/7307-anarchistische-soldatenagitation-soldaten-brevier

366 Paul B. Miller, *From Revolutionaries to Citizens: Antimilitarism in France, 1870–1914*, Durham NC: Duke University Press, 2002, p. 83.
367 *Les Temps nouveaux*, 9 and 30 March 1907.
368 *Les Temps nouveaux*, 12 October 1907.
369 The veteran leader Social-Democratic party leader, August Bebel, advised German army recruits to keep a low profile in the army, so that their politics went unnoticed. He advised recruits to hold their tongue. Writers who insulted the army could expect prosecution.
370 http://gallica.bnf.fr/ark:/12148/bpt6k9909829.r=
371 Guillaume Davranche, *Trop jeune*, op. cit., p. 256.
372 Earl C. Ford & William Z Foster, *Syndicalism*, Chicago: W Z Foster, 1913, pp. 29-30.
373 Emphasis added; 3 April 1913, available online: https://www.marxists.org/history/usa/pubs/industrialworker/iw/v5n02-w210-apr-03-1913-IW.pdf
374 *Les Temps nouveaux*, 5 February 1910.
375 *Temps nouveaux*, 23 July 1910, also 17 Jan 1909.
376 Bob Holton, *British Syndicalism, 1900-1914*, London: Pluto Press, 1976, p. 212.
377 *New Statesman*, 11 October 1913.
378 Wayne Thorpe, *"The Workers Themselves" revolutionary syndicalism and international labour, 1913-1923*, Dordrecht: Kluwer, 1989, pp. 65, 248.
379 Ibid, pp. 74-5.
380 *Vie Ouvrière*, 20 October 1913.
381 Thorpe, *"The Workers Themselves"*, op. cit., p. 81.
382 Ibid, p. 73.
383 Ibid, p. 78.
384 Ibid, p. 82. He was an abstentionist, and did not take up work in parliament. The status of a parliamentary deputy provided him with some immunity from arrest.
385 Westergard-Thorpe, *Revolutionary syndicalist internationalism*, op. cit., p. 89.
386 Thorpe, *"The Workers Themselves"*, op. cit., p. 83.
387 *Le Mouvement anarchiste*, November 1912, No. 4, pp. 98-99, http://archivesautonomies.org/IMG/pdf/anarchismes/avant-1914/lemouvementanarchiste/lemouvementanarchiste-n04.pdf
388 *Le Mouvement anarchiste*, October 1912, No. 3, pp. 63ff, http://archivesautonomies.org/IMG/pdf/anarchismes/avant-1914/lemouvementanarchiste/lemouvementanarchiste-n03.pdf
389 Charles Andler, 'Le socialisme impérialiste dans l'allemange contemporaine'; first published in *Action Nationale*, November and December 1912; reprinted in: *Le socialisme imperialiste dans l'allemange contemporaine*, Paris, Bossard, 1918.
390 Salomon Grumbach wrote in *Neue Zeit* in February 1913 that Andler had 'discovered' socialist imperialism; Jean Longuet wrote a small brochure for the French Socialist party publisher in 1913: *Les socialistes allemands contre la guerre et le militarisme*.
391 *Les Temps nouveaux*, 3 May 1913; see also a reply on the 17 May.
392 One historian has commented: 'If there had been any illusions among French workers about the intentions of the German left in the event of war, they must have been few and far between'; John Schwarzmantel, 'Nationalism and the French Working-Class. Movement 1905–1914', in Eric Cahm & Vladimir Claude Fišera, Eds., *Socialism and Nationalism*, op. cit., p. 92.

393 Guillaume Davranche, 'Printemps 1911, Agadir: la guerre est déjà là', *Alternative libertaire*, Paris, February 2011, p. 203.
394 Jean Maitron, *Le mouvement anarchiste*, Vol. 1, op. cit., pp. 374-75.
395 Ibid., p. 294.
396 Ibid., p. 287.
397 Guillaume Davranche, *Trop jeune*, op. cit., p. 292.
398 *La Guerre sociale*, 18 December; Guillaume Davranche, '1912: La CGT en grève générale contre la guerre', *Alternative libertaire*, Paris, December 2012, p. 223.
399 Guillaume Davranche, *Trop jeune*, op. cit., pp. 287-289; 448.
400 Ibid, pp. 343-5.
401 *Le Mouvement anarchiste*, October 1912, No. 6-7, p. 146, January-February 1913.
402 Guillaume Davranche, *Trop jeune*, op. cit., p. 426.
403 Pierre Martin, 'Erreur et peur', *Le Libertaire*, 19 July 1913. Guillaume Davranche, *Trop jeune*, op. cit., p. 370. See also: http://www.alternativelibertaire.org/spip.php?article5348
404 Pierre Monatte, *Souvenirs sur La Vie Ouvrière*, 1959.
405 Guillaume Davranche, *Trop jeune*, op. cit., p. 416.
406 Alfred Rosmer, *Le mouvement ouvrier pendant la première guerre mondiale*, Paris: Librairie du travail, 1936, Vol. 1, p. 533.
407 Ibid. p. 535.
408 Guillaume Davranche, *Trop jeune*, op. cit., p. 288 ; Jean Maitron, *Le mouvement anarchiste*, Vol. 1, op. cit., p. 372.
409 Errico Malatesta, (Vernon Richards, Ed.), *Malatesta: Life and Ideas*, London: Freedom Press, 1965, pp. 216-9.
410 Quoted in Giampietro Berti, *Errico Malatesta e il movimento anarchico*, op. cit., p. 540.
411 Ibid, p. 546.
412 This was an era in which telecommunications were limited and the telegraph was in government hands.
413 *Volontà*, 20 June 1914.
414 Fabbri, 1986, pp. 19, 23.
415 Editorial, front page, *Les Temps nouveaux*, 8 August 1914.
416 Jean Grave, *Le mouvement libertaire sous la 3e République*, Paris: Les Oeuvres représentatives, 1930, pp. 239-40.
417 Our emphasis, Marx & Engels, *Collected Works*, Vol. 44, Moscow & London: Progress Publishers & Lawrence & Wishart, 1989, pp. 3-4, See also http://www.marxists.org/archive/marx/works/1870/letters/70_07_20.htm; published by James Guillaume.
418 Carl Schorske, *German Social-Democracy*, op. cit., 1955, pp. 288-290.
419 The SPD had around a million members, and attracted four million voters. Its apparatus was served by 90 daily newspapers, 62 printing offices, 267 editors, 89 office managers, 273 business officials, 140 administrators, 2,640 technicians and 7,589 paid news agents. A. Ramos Olivera, *A People's History of Germany*, London: Victor Gollancz, 1942, p. 73. Another estimate suggests 4,000 paid functionaries and 11,000 salaried employees.
420 Wayne Thorpe, *"The Workers Themselves"*, op. cit., p. 57.
421 Pierre Monatte, 'Pourquoi je démissionne du Comité confédéral', *L'Émancipatrice*, December 1914, http://cras31.info/IMG/pdf/larevolutionproletarienne-n046.pdf
422 March 1915, *International Socialist Review*.
423 Fears of just such an eventuality were expressed by the government in 1911, when troops were mobilised against a strike in the port of Liverpool: Sam Davies and Ron Noon, 'The rank-and-file in the 1911 Liverpool General Transport Strike', *Labour History Review*, Vol. 79, 1, April 2014, p. 59.

424 Anton Pannekoek wrote in *Vorbote,* in May-June, 1917: 'conceptions of socialism and state industries have been hopelessly confused in the minds of our Social-Democracy…' See A.W. Zurbrugg, *Not Our War:* London: Merlin Press, 2014, pp. 185-7.
425 From Otto Rühle, *From the Bourgeois to the Proletarian Revolution,* London: Socialist Reproductions, pp. 25-6; 28-9.
426 *The Miner's Next Step,* Tonypandy: Unofficial Reform Committee, 1912.
427 Douglas Kellner, Ed, *Karl Korsch: Revolutionary Theory,* Austin: University of Texas Press, 1977, p. 128.
428 Gerald Arlettaz, 'La Suisse une terre d'accueil en question. L'importance de la première Guerre mondiale', *L'émigration politique en Europe aux XIXe et XXe siècles. Actes du colloque de Rome,* Rome: École Française de Rome, 1991, pp. 139-159. (*Publications de l'École française de Rome,* 146).
429 Helge Döhring, *Syndikalismus in Deutschland, 1914-1918,* op. cit., p. 22.
430 Ibid., pp. 38-39, 60.
431 Dieter Nelles & Hartmut Rübner, 'Avantgarde einer egalitären Bewegung', *Moving the Social,* No. 51, (2014), p. 185.
432 Helge Döhring, *Syndikalismus in Deutschland, 1914-1918,* op. cit., pp. 73ff.
433 Ibid., p. 133.
434 Hans Manfred Bock, in Marcel van der Linden & Wayne Thorpe, Eds., *Revolutionary Syndicalism,* op.cit., p. 62.
435 Alexandre Skirda, *Facing the Enemy: A History of Anarchist Organisation from Proudhon to May 1968,* Edinburgh & Oakland: AK Press, 2002, p. 107.
436 Pierre Besnard, Pierre, *La Confédération Générale du Travail,* first published in Sébastien Faure, Ed: *l'Encyclopédie anarchiste,* Paris: 1925-1934; available on http://monde-nouveau.net/spip.php?article241; and http://www.fondation-besnard.org/IMG/pdf/Besnard_CGT_2.pdf.
437 *La Révolution prolétarienne,* No. 216, February 1936.
438 Alfred Rosmer, *Le mouvement ouvrier pendant la première guerre mondiale: de l'union sacrée a Zimmerwald,* Paris: Librairie du Travail, 1936, p. 179.
439 Véronique Rebetez, 'Des anarchistes contre la première guerre mondiale', *Cahiers d'histoire du mouvement ouvrier,* Vol. 23, 2007 (http://dx.doi.org/10.5169/seals-520237).
440 Jean Grave, *Le mouvement libertaire,* op. cit., p. 242.
441 Guillaume Davranche, *Trop jeune,* op. cit., pp. 514-6.
442 30 July and 3 September 1914.
443 G. Cerreto, *L'antimilitarismo anarchico in Italia nel primo ventennio del secolo,* n. p. Samizdat, 1996, p. 51.
444 Armando Borghi, *Mezzo secolo,* op. cit., p. 159
445 Willy Gianinazzi, 'Le syndicalisme révolutionnaire en Italie', op. cit., p. 53
446 Ibid, p. 162.
447 Adriana Dadà, *L'anarchismo in Italia,* op. cit., p. 264.
448 Santerelli, 'L'anarchisme en Italie', op. cit., p. 150.
449 Luigi Fabbri in *Plus Loin,* quoted by Hem Day. See: *Le Manifeste des seize,* from http://bibliolib.net/article.php3?id_article=229
450 G. Cerreto, *L'antimilitarismo anarchico in Italia,* op. cit., p. 62.
451 Adriana Dadà, *Class War, Reaction & the Italian Anarchists,* http://www.fdca.it/fdcaen/press/pamphlets/sla-3/1.htm
452 Carl Levy, *Gramsci and the Anarchists,* op. cit., pp. 87-9.
453 Giampietro Berti, *Errico Malatesta e il movimento anarchico,* op. cit., pp. 598-601; Levy, 1999, p. 92. Some estimates speak of hundreds being killed.
454 G. Cerreto, *L'antimilitarismo anarchico in Italia,* op. cit., p. 70-71.
455 IWW, Official Proceedings of the [November] 1916 Convention, p. 138.

456 1 June 1917, *The Blast*.
457 See chapter four: Eric Thomas Chester, *The Wobblies in their Heyday*, Amherst: Levellers Press, 2014.
458 Interview in Paul Avrich, *Anarchist Voices*, op. cit., p. 39.
459 Rudolf Rocker, *The London Years*, Nottingham: Five Leaves Publications, 2005, p. 143.
460 'A Letter on the Present War', *Freedom*, October 1914.
461 Wayne Thorpe, 'El Ferrol, Rio de Janeiro, Zimmerwald, and Beyond: Syndicalist Internationalism, 1914-1918', *Revue belge de philologie et d'histoire.* Vol. 84 fasc. 4, 2006, p. 1011. (Histoire médiévale, moderne et contemporaine, pp. 1005-1023.) Reports on the congress are in Joan Zambrana, *El anarquismo organizado en los orígenes de la CNT (Tierra y Libertad 1910-1919)*, 1915, pp. 773-780, 1106-08; http://www.cedall.org/Documentacio/IHL/Tierra%20y%20Libertad%201910-1919.pdf
462 Jason Garner, *Goals and Means,* Edinburgh: AK Press, 2016, pp. 72-73.
463 Joan Zambrana, *El anarquismo organizado*, op. cit. p. 1082.
464 Jean Maitron, *Le mouvement anarchiste*, Vol. 2, op. cit., pp. 12-13, 46.
465 Wayne Thorpe, 'El Ferrol, Rio de Janeiro, Zimmerwald, and Beyond: Syndicalist Internationalism', op. cit., p. 1017; *Guerra di classe*, 23 October 1915; M. Antonioli, *Armando Borghi e l'Unione Sindacale Italiana*, Manduria, 1990, p. 33.
466 Wayne Thorpe, 'El Ferrol, Rio de Janeiro, Zimmerwald, and Beyond: Syndicalist Internationalism', op. cit., p. 1020, *Guerra di classe*, 13 April 1918
467 Michaël Confino, 'Anarchisme et internationalisme : Autour du Manifeste des Seize', *Cahiers du monde russe et soviétique*, Vol. 22, No. 2-3, 1981, pp. 232-233.
468 George Woodcock & Ivan Avakumovi , *The Anarchist Prince: A Biographical Study of Peter Kropotkin*, op. cit., p. 289, 381. In October 1914, he had proclaimed in *Freedom*: 'the duty of everyone who cherishes the ideals of human progress…to do everything in one's power, … to crush down the invasion of the Germans into western Europe.'
469 Errico Malatesta, (Vernon Richards, Ed.), *Malatesta*, op. cit., Appendices 1 & 2.
470 Jean Maitron, *Le mouvement anarchiste*, Vol. 2, op. cit., p. 15.
471 Errico Malatesta, (Vernon Richards, Ed.), *Malatesta*, op. cit., pp. 243-7.

INDEX

A Batalha, 13
A Plebe, 13
A Voz do Trabalhado, 13
Action-directe, 48
Africa, North, 44, 134
Africa, South, 74, 124
Africa, South-West, 135fn
Albert, Charles, 34
Aldred, Guy, 44
Algeria, 127
Allemane, Jean, 52
Almereyda, Miguel, 127
Altink, 44
Amalgamated Society of Engineers, 170
American Federation of Labor, (AFL), 26, 48, 71-3, 162,
Amiens Charter, 33, 35, 41, 42, 52, 54, 88, 89, 100, 105, 129, 131
Amsterdam Anarchist Congress (1907), 44-64
Anarchist Communist Federation (France), 93-7, 98, 146-8, 163, 173
Anarchist Federation of Germany, 82, 83, 112, 136
Anarchist Socialist Federation (Italy), 31
Anarcho-Syndicalism, 13, 60
Andler, Charles, 145
Anti-Militarism, 33-34, 43, 62, 66, 85, 109, 123-4, 125-39, 146-50, 162-4, 172, 176, 180-81
Antonioli, Maurizio, 60-61
Arbeter Fraint, 44, 178
Argentina, 15, 20, 65, 69-70; *see also* FORA, UGT
Argentinean Regional Workers' Federation (CORA), 142

Armand, Émile, 19, 137
Atlanta Journal, 127
Austria, 44
Australia, 74, 90, 124
Avanti!, 104, 175

Baer, James, 65
Baginsky, Max, 45
Bakunin, M, 1, 3, 5, 11, 80, 91
Barenboim, Axel, 8
Bebel, August, 16, 75, 76, 129, 135, 137, 138-9, 161
Belelli, Ennio Enrico, 44
Belgium, 44, 45, 48, 90, 95, 165, 179
Berkman, Alexander, 177, 179
Bernardo, Antonio 143fn
Bernstein, Eduard, 80
Berry, David, 8
Bertoni, Luigi, 90-91, 99, 100, 103, 135, 173, 179
Besnard, Pierre, 172
Beylie, Henri, 44
Binazzi, Pasquale, 174
Bismarck, 75,
Bissolati, Leonida, 105, 109
Blanqui, Louis-Auguste, 51, 56fn
Boer War, 120
Bolivia, 22
Bolsheviks, 3
Bombings, vi, ix, 12, 29, 63, 160, 176
Bonnot gang, 93,
Borghi, Armando, 30, 31, 91, 104, 106, 109, 111, 122, 174, 176, 179
Boudet, A, 91
Bourderon, Albert, 179
Bourey, Pierre, 136
Bower, Fred, 125

Bowman, Guy, 143
Brazil, 14, 69, 113, 178
Briand, Aristide, 92, 98
Brille, 44
Britain and Ireland, 36, 44, 47, 104, 110, 112, 125-6, 142, 145, 166-7, 170
Brousse, Paul, 51
Broutchoux, Benoît, 44, 93, 148, 149, 173
Bruijn, J. L., 44
Bulgaria, viii, 44, 112, 158
Bullard, D.A., 45
Burevestnik, 45

Carrión, B. S., 127
Catalonia, 65, 165, 179
Catholic Church, 22, 65, 67, 106; unions, 21, 48, 77fn, 108, 115
Ceccarelli, Aristide, 44
Ce qu'il faut dire, 174
CGT (France), 33-43, 46. 48-54, 88-94, 97-102, 122, 127-35, 142, 143, 146-50, 161-4, 172-4, 179
CGT-SR (France), 172
Chapelier, Émile, 44
Charter of Amiens, *see* Amiens Charter
Cherkesov, Varlaam, 145, 180
Chile, 20, 123
China, 39fn,
Cipriani, Amilcare, 17
Clemenceau, Georges, 133
Clément, Léon, 44, 61
Cole, G. D. H., 100-101
Colombo, Eduardo, 22
Colonies, 37, 39, 66, 126
Combat Syndicaliste, 13
Combes, Henry, 146, 147, 179
Comité d'action internationale, 173
Confederación Nacional del Trabajo, (CNT), 21, 39fn, 64-8, 118, 142, 144, 161, 165, 168
Confederazione Generale del Lavoro, (CGL), 105-6, 115-16, 151-2, 175
Connolly, James, 119-21, 163, 164
Co-operatives, 65-6
Corio, Silvio Celestino, 44
Coriol, Louis, 44

Cornelissen, Christiaan, 17, 44, 47-8, 57, 60, 62, 141, 142, 143, 144, 180
Corridoni, Filippo, 107
Couture, J., 142
Cronaca Sovversiva, 13
Cuba, 23-26, 66, 165
Cuzzani, Ettore, 107
Czech Anarchist Federation, 44, 45-6, 112

Damiani, Luigi (Gigi), 113
D'Andrea, Virgilia, 30,
Davranche, Guillaume, 92-3
de Ambris, Alceste, 105, 142, 144, 152, 174
de Ambris, Amilcare, 107
de Marmande, René, 44
de Quintana, Luis Bulffi, 19
De Vrije Socialist, 45
Debs, Eugene Victor, 73, 74
Delcassé, Théophile, 128
Delesalle, Paul, 17, 39, 51
Delgado, Román, 26
Der Freie Arbeiter, 83, 160
Der Pioneer, 84
Der Syndikalist, 13, 183
Desplanques, Charles, 94
Die Aktion, 82
Die Einigkeit, 85, 141, 160
Die Freie Arbeiterwelt, 44
Die Freie Generation, 44
Die Internationale, 13
Dielo Trouda-Probuzhdenie, 13
Döhring, Helge, 171
Donna Libertaria, 111
Dumoulin, Georges, 149, 150
Dunois, Amédée, 44, 58, 60, 61, 90,

Ecuador, 69
Eight-hour day, vi, viii, 23, 69,
El Ferrol international congress, 178
Engels, Friedrich, 76, 135

Fabbri, Luigi, 22, 29, 31-2, 106, 108, 109-10, 152, 175-6; Amsterdam Congress: 44, 58,
Faure, Sébastien, 93, 173

Federação Anarquista do Rio de Janeiro, 6-7
Federación Regional Anarquista Catalana, 178
Federación Obrera Regional Argentina (FORA), 21-3, 69-70, 142, 144, 178
Fédération Communiste-Anarchiste de la Suisse Romande, 46
Fédération révolutionnaire communiste, 146; see also Anarchist Communist Federation
Ferrer, Francisco, 19, 26, 66-7, 69
FIOM (metalworkers), 106, 175
First International see International Workers' Association
First World War, 145-81
Flatt, 44
Fletcher, Benjamin Harrison, 72
Foster, William Z., 140-41
France, 33-43, 46 87-102, 138, 172-4; see also CGT
Frauböse, Paul, 44
Free (*Generalkommission*) unions (Germany), 4, 77, 79, 80-83, 86, 130-31, 160, 166, 168,
Freedom, 13, 15-16, 44, 104, 121, 124
Friedeberg, Raphael, 44, 59, 77, 145
Freie Vereinigung deutscher Gerwerkschaften (FvDG), 44, 77-86, 130, 141, 142, 170-71
Frigerio, Carlo, 44, 179
Fuss-Amoré, Henri, 44, 58, 61, 90, 180

Galleani, Luigi, 32, 46, 104, 176, 177
Gender, 8, 18-19, 21, 25, 29-30, 34-5, 65, 97, 111, 164
General strike, 35, 52, 58-60, 78-9, 83, 93-4, 101, 135, 137, 157
General Workers' Union (South Africa), 124
Generalkommission see Free unions
Germany, 2, 17, 38, 44, 54, 75-86, 100, 119, 131, 134-8, 142, 145, 159-62 *passim*, 165, 168, 170-71; see also Anarchist Federation, FvDG, Free unions, Social-Democrats
Germinal, 44

Ghezzi, Francesco, 14
Giolitti, Giovanni, 105
Giovannetti, Alibrando, 30
Girard, A, 46
Goldman, Emma, 3, 18-19, 30, 38, 45, 66-7, 177
Gompers, Samuel, 26
Gori, Pietro, 17, 21
Gorter, Herman, 119
Grave, Jean, 46, 74, 75, 93, 157, 158, 173, 180
Griffuelhes, Victor, 36, 37, 128-31 *passim*, 147
Groupement communiste libertaire (Belgium), 45
Grossmann, Rudolf see Pierre Ramus
Guerra di Classe, 174
Guesde, Jules, 42, 51,
Guillaume, James, 3, 46, 80, 91, 92, 100, 122, 145, 180

Hamburger, 44
Hardie, Keir, 17
Hargreaves, Leonard, 170
Haywood, Bill, 71
Hesp, 44
Hervé, Gustave, 93
Heyman, Maurice, 44
Hirsch, Steven, 7
Holwerka, J. H., 112
Hyslop, Jonathan, 126

Iglesias, Pablo, 139
Il Libertario, (Italy), 174
Imperialism, 23-24, 145, 159
Independent Labour Party, 16, 17
Indigenous peoples, 20, 24

Industrial Syndicalist Education League, 113, 142
Industrial Worker, (USA), 106, 108, 140-42
Industrial Workers of the World (IWW), 2, 4n, 72-4, 125, 131, 140, 176, 177

International Federation of Trade Unions (IFTU), 140-41, 161-4
International Secretariat of National Trade Union Centres (ISNTUC), 46, 128-31, 140-44, *see also* International Federation of Trade Unions
International Socialist League (South Africa), 124
International Workers' Association (First International), 1, 6, 11, 18, 27, 50, 57, 70, 79, 113
Irish Citizen's Army, 164
Italy, 12-13, 27-32, 46, 103-11, 151-3, 165, 174-7, *see also* CGL, USI, Socialists (Italian)

Jacobins, 5-6
Janssens, Henri J, 44
Janvion, Émile, 93, 127, 137
Japan, 48
Jaurès, Jean, 138, 139, 157
Jensen, Albert, 144
Jewish Anarchist Federation (London), 44
Jouhaux, Léon, 82, 88, 91, 93, 94, 146, 148, 172

Kampf, 112
Kater, Fritz, 82
Kautsky, Karl, 76, 81, 84
Keell, Thomas, 44, 104, 179
Kelly, Harry, 179
Khleb i Volia, 45, 46
Klein, 45
Koekoek, 45
Knotek, Ladislav, 44
Korsch, Karl, 80, 168
Korver, Nelly, 45
Kropotkin, Peter Alekseevich, 13, 17, 18, 34, 46, 100, 104, 112, 176, 178, 180, 181
L'Agitatore, 109
L'Endehors, 33
L'Humanité, 88, 157
L'Internazionale, 141
La Bataille, 179

La Battaile syndicaliste, 88, 89, 99, 148, 149
La Guerre Sociale, 89, 93, 149
La Guerra Sociale, 175
La Huelga General, 13
La Pace, 109
La Protesta, La (Argentina), 14, 21, 70
La Protesta, La (Peru), 123, 127
La Revue Anarchiste, 33
La Revue Libertaire, 33
La Vie Ouvrière, 61, 90, 91, 99, 141, 145, 149, 173
La Voix du Peuple, 39, 43, 50, 51, 99, 130, 133, 147
La Voz de la Mujer, 21
Labour congresses, 15-18
Labriola, Arturo, 109
Lagru, Dominique, 94
Landauer, Gustav, 17, 46, 76, 83, 85
Lange, Rudolf, 44
Larkin, James, 142
Latin America, 20-22, 69, 168-69
Le Bulletin de l'Internationale anarchiste, 63
Le Bulletin de l'Internationale Libertaire, 45
Le Bulletin du congrès anarchiste international, 112
Le Bulletin International du Mouvement Syndicaliste, 62, 144
Le Cri typographique, 33
Le Libertaire, 89, 92, 93, 94, 97, 147, 148, 149, 173
Le Meillour, Pierre, 173
Le Mouvement anarchiste, 94, 145
Le Père Peinard, 33
Le Pot-à-Colle, 33
Le Reveil/Risveglio, 14, 91, 173
Le Révolté/La Révolte, 33
Le Riflard, 33
Lecoin, Louis, 77, 147, 173
Legien, Karl, 79, 128, 129, 131, 161
Lepetit, Jules, 173
Les Temps nouveaux, 14, 34, 44, 46, 63, 79, 89, 93, 99, 100, 127, 136, 140, 142, 157, 158, 172, 173, 179

Lévano, Delfín, 123
Levy, Carl, 8, 103-04fn
Libya, 109, 123
Liebknecht, Karl, viii
Liebknecht, Wilhelm, 16, 75, 161
Lilyan, Evelyn, 44, 142
Linder, Solo, 44
Lípiz, Vicente, 26
Little, Frank, 177
Local Workers' Federation (FOL, La Paz, Bolivia), 22
Lodewijk, Johan. J., 45
Ludwig, 44
Luxemburg, Rosa, 4, 78-82 *passim*, 86, 168

McDonald, Ramsey, 139
MacDonald, Thomas Fauset, 124
Magón, Ricardo Flores, 74, 112, 177
Maitron, Jean, 39, 93
Malatesta, Errico, 3, 11-13, 16, 17, 24-5, 27-31, 91-2, 104, 109-11, 113-19, 122, 123, 151-2, 178, 179, 180-81; and Amsterdam Congress: 44, 46, 54-8, 60-63; anarchists' organisation, 92, 109-10; means and goals, 56; organisation, 47, 104; workplace organisation, 16, 54-56, 61, 114-19
Malato, Charles, 11, 180
Malyscha, Arthur, 136
Mann, Tom, 17, 121, 124, 145
Margoulis, H, 44
Marestan, Jean, 19
Martín Fierro, 21
Martin, Pierre, 94, 173
Masetti, Augusto, 109
Marx, Karl, 85, 179
McKinley, W (President), 18
Merrheim, Alphonse, 179
Mexico, vii, viii, ix, 69, 74, 112
Michel, Louise, 11, 17
Miéville, Ariane, 89
Migrants, Migration, 15, 20, 65, 103, 127
Millerand, Alexandre, 17, 76

Mines & Miners, vii, 84, 100, 126, 166-7, 176
Monatte, Pierre, 42-43, 89, 90, 92, 94, 99, 106, 108, 141, 143, 145, 149, 162-3, 172; Amsterdam congress, 44, 46, 48-56, 58
Montseny Mañé, Federica, 30
Morand, Jeanne, 97
Morocco, 66, 128, 129, 130, 134
Most, Johann, 82
Mother Earth, 47, 124
Mougnitch, Peter, 45
Mühsam, Erich, 46
Mussolini, 175

Nacht, Siegfried, 44, 58, 137
Narodnaya Volya, 64
National Labour Secretariat/ *Nationaal Arbeids Secretariaat, (NAS),* (Netherlands), 44, 47, 131, 142, 180
National Union of Railwaymen, 4, 120
Nechaev, 13
Nederlands Verbond van Vakverenigingen, (Netherlands Labour League, NVV), 47
Netherlands, 44, 45, 112, 130-31, 162
Nettlau, Max, 46, 145
Neues Leben, 82
New Zealand, 90, 124
Niel, Louis, 48
Nieuwenhuis, (Ferdinand) Domela, 17, 18, 45, 112, 122, 137, 179
No-Conscription League, (USA), 177
Norway, 144, 192 n189
Noske, Gustav, 137

Oerter, Sepp, 44
Oestreich, Rudolf, 137
Organización Obrera, 22
Orlovsky, 63
Onrubia, Salvadora Medina, 21
Ottoman Turkey, 109
Panama, 25
Pannekoek, Anton, 84, 119, 165
Paraguay, 69, 70fn
Paris Commune, 1, 5, 50, 134

Parti Ouvrier (POF), 51
Pataud, Emile, 87-8
Pelletier, Madeleine, 97
Pelloutier, Fernand, 17, 18, 106, 108
Péricat, Raymond 173
Peru, vii, viii, ix, 23-4, 69, 70, 123, 127
Pfemmert, Franz, 82
Pierrot, Marc, 46, 122, 180
Philippines, 66
Poincaré, Raymond, 146
Poland, 45, 46, 165, 179
Portugal, vii, viii, ix, 13, 62, 137, 158, 178
Pouget, Émile, 17, 18, 39-41, 51, 87-8
Prada, Manuel González, 23-4, 123
Prampolini, Camillo, 105
Prat, José, 68
Pratelle, Aristide, 142
Press, (libertarian), 13-15, 33, 113, 160
Puerto Rico, 25

Rabauw, Sergher, 44
Race and racism, 23, 25, 73, 124-7, 140
Radowitzky, Simón, 14, 69
Rail workers, 4, 21, 36, 38, 77, 85, 98, 99, 105, 106, 108, 120, 151, 152
Ramus, Pierre (Rudolf Grossmann), 44, 46, 82, 136-7
Reclus, Élisée, 16, 17
Reclus, Paul, 180
Renard, Victor, 41, 89
Resseler, Victor, 44
Revista Blanca, 13, 14
Revolutionär, 83, 136
Reyndorp (Rijnsdorp), Bernard, 45
Rieger, Ernst, 130
Rijnders, Gerhard, 45, 179
Rio de Janeiro peace congress, 178
Robin, Paul, 16, 19, 137
Rocker, Firmin, 178
Rocker, Rudolf, 12, 44, 63, 76, 83, 158
Rogdaev, Nicholas, 45, 63
Roller, Arnold, 78, 135-6
Rompete le file!, 109
Rosmer, Alfred, 100, 142, 144
Roussel, Nelly, 19, 35, 97

Rühle, Otto, 78, 166
Russia, 13, 45, 46, 62-4, 112

Sabotage, 36-7, 53
Sacco & Vanzetti, 14
Sacred union, *see*: union sacrée
Saint-Imier congress, 57
Samson, I. Izak, 45
Sánchez Saornil, Lucía, 30
Sauter, Karl, 136
Scarfo, Josefina América, 21
Schapiro, Alexander M., 13, 44, 63, 112, 142, 158, 179
Schauf, Paul, 136
Schermerhorn, Nicholas, 45
Schouteten, 44,
Schreiber, Otto, 44
Schreyer, Paul, 179
Schweber, Joseph, 45
Second International, 2, 16-17, 85, 113, 122, 130, 143, 145, 149, 159
Serbia, 45
Serge, Victor, 89-90, 93
Shatov, Vladimir (Bill), 179
Singer, P, 16
Socialistenbond, 17
Social-Democrats (German, SPD), 11, 46, 75-82, 98, 134, 135, 136, 159-60, 165-6
Socialist Party (Italy, PSI), 31, 104-6, 109, 175
Socialists (Argentina), 70
Socialists (French), 41, 49, 51-2, 89, 98, 134
Solidaridad Obrera, 13
Solidarity, 13
Sorel, Georges Eugène, 34, 80-81, 100
Soviet, 64
Sozialistische Bund, 83
Spain, 6, 15, 65-8, 137; *see also* CNT, UGT
Stad, 45
Studi Sociali, 14
Swedish Workers' Centre (SAC), 141
Switzerland, 44, 46, 91, 99, 103, 112, 135, 137, 168, 173, 176

INDEX 209

Syndicalism and Trade-Unionism, 53, 57-61, 64, 113-22; Syndicalist Congress London 1913, 142-4; *see also* General Strike, Sabotage
Syndicalist Defence League, 173
Syndicalist Information Bureau, 144
Syndicalisten, 141

Taylor system, 98-9
Tenorio, Juan, 26
Thonar, Georges, 44, 137
Thullier, Jean Louis, 173
¡*Tierra!*, 13, 25, 26
Tillet, Ben, 17
Titi, 30
Toller, Ernst, 85
Trades Union Congress (TUC), 4, 84
Tresa, Carlo, 176
Treves, Claudio Graziano, 105
Turner, John, 63

UGT (Argentina), 21, 22
UGT (Spain), 65, 67-8, 165
Umanità Nova, 13
Umberto I, (king of Italy), 29
union sacrée, 150, 180
Unione Italiana del Lavoro (UIL), 174
Unionen, 4, 168
United Kingdom (UK) *see* Britain
United States, 14, 25, 26, 47, 48, 112, 177-8
Uruguay, 20, 69, 137

USI (Italian syndicalists), 30, 107-11, 142, 174, 176, 178, 179

Vallet, Jean-Baptiste, 173
Van der Walt, Lucien, 7, 8
Van Rees, Jacob, 45
Velev, S., 44
Vernet, Madeleine, 19
Vita Operaria, 22,
Vohryzek, Karl, 44, 57, 60
Voice of Labour (London), 44,
Voice of Labour (South Africa), 124
Voluntà, 91, 113-14, 151
Vorwärts, 136

Wagner, 44
Walter, Karl, 44, 58
Wehner, Wilhelm, 171
Wetkov, Emilie, 45
Willems, Henri, 44
Wilquet, Jean, 44, 63
Wodnef, Sophie, 45
Wood, Leonard, 25

Yvetot, Georges, 35, 39, 91, 93, 127, 132-3, 137, 145-9

Zabrezhnev, Vladimir, 45
Zaïkowska, Sophia, 35
Zibelin, Albert, 44
Zielinska, Iza, 45, 58
Zimmerwald, 179

Forthcoming volumes in the *Anarchist Perspectives* series

Volume 2
Revolution and Syndicalism: From 1917 to 1930
Introduction; Revolutionary Syndicalisms, Revolution in Italy?; Revolution in Germany?; Reflections on Revolution and Fascism in Italy; France after 1917; Germany in the 1920s; North and South America; North Africa & Spain; International Organisation in the 1920s; Reflections on Revolution in Russia; The Platform; Reviewing the Platform; Transition and Socialism; 1927 and After; Appendix 1: 'Constructive Problems of the Social Revolution'; Appendix 2: 'The Two Octobers'.

****

Volume 3
Revolution in Spain, 1931-1939
Introduction; International Perspectives; The International Workers' Association; France and Germany; German Anarchists and Syndicalists in the 1930s; Palestine and the Jewish Question; Latin America; Spain 1931-1933; Spain 1933-1936; Spain in Revolution; 1936-39; May 1937 and after; International Criticism; IWA perspectives; Socialisation and Collectivisation; Communities; Gender and Mujeres Libres.

****

Volume 4
After the Second World War
Introduction; The Post-War Scene; France; The Algerian War; Spanish Exiles; Italy 1939-1960; Latin America after 1943; The 60s and after; Parecon and Collective Management; The Cuban revolution; Spain after the death of Franco; France: 1968 and after; Organisations; Ideas; Synthesis; Manifesto for a Libertarian Alternative; Concluding Thoughts; Notes on Persons; Bibliography.

Also available in Anarres Editions

ANARCHIST ENCOUNTERS: RUSSIA IN REVOLUTION
Emma Goldman, Gaston Leval,
Angel Pestaña and Jack Wilkens
Edited with an introduction by A.W. Zurbrugg

There was a general rejoicing when the regime of Tsar Nicholas II fell in February 1917; a new era of liberty dawned. But what would come next? This book presents sketches of encounters in the new Russia.
Emma Goldman relates her experiences of daily life, her meeting with Peter Kropotkin and tells the story of the life of Maria Spiridonova, a famous SR activist who escaped from a mental hospital where she had been locked up.
Gaston Leval and Angel Pestaña were members of a delegation from the Spanish CNT union and reported back on what they found, especially how trade unions functioned with policeman keeping order in union meetings.
Armando Borghi tells of a meeting with Victor Serge.
Jack Wilkens wrote a series of articles for the French journal Le Libertaire. They tell of how Soviets functioned, of how workers live, of working conditions for men and women and of rural life.
160 pages
ISBN. 978-0-85036-734-8 paperback

BAKUNIN: SELECTED TEXTS 1868-1875
Mikhail Bakunin
Edited and translated by A.W. Zurbrugg

This book brings together a selection of texts: letters, a lecture, newspaper articles, finished and unfinished works. The selection begins in 1868, the year Bakunin moved to Geneva and became a member of the local section of the IWA. Bakunin discusses the development of politics in and around the IWA.
Many of these texts appear here in English for the first time.
300 pages
ISBN 978-0-85036-722-5 paperback

www.merlinpress.co.uk

SOCIAL-DEMOCRACY AND ANARCHISM
in the International Workers' Association, 1864-1877
Rene Berthier

This book explores the conflicts that took place in the First International. Social and economic conditions varied greatly in Europe in the 1860s and 1870s. The strategies adopted by the various federations and sections of the International Workers' Association, or IWA, reflected this diversity.
Although Marx and Engels have been seen as the leaders of the International, there were many who rejected their leadership. In September 1872 an extraordinary congress took place in Saint-Imier (Switzerland) which rejected the decisions taken at The Hague congress by Marx and his friends. A year later six IWA federations met in a regular congress in Geneva and reasserted the principle that political organising should be subordinate to workplace – economic – organisation. The great aim of the IWA was for working people to liberate themselves.
The ongoing IWA disregarded edicts of expulsion issued by the New York based General Council, at the instigation of Marx and Engels. The latter discovered they were generals without an army, isolated and at odds with the bulk of the organised labour movement.
René Berthier reviews the historiography of this conflict. Much of the ongoing IWA were inspired by Bakunin. He argued for the priority of labour solidarity. But it was not an anarchist International that was created in 1872. Anarchism was born some five years later, when Bakunin was dead. Rather, the adoption of anarchism by the remnants of the IWA marked a breach with Bakuninism.

'highly recommended' *Chartist*.

'profoundly illuminating.' *Weekly Worker*.

'an excellent work, recommended to both anarchist activists and those interested in the rise of modern revolutionary anarchism. Berthier, a veteran French anarcho-syndicalist activist, has produced a work which successfully challenges both the standard narrative on the First International (written, as usual, by the winners) and those who seek to deny the actual history of anarchism and its roots in the European labour movement (and, somewhat surprisingly, that number includes Berthier himself).' *Anarchist Studies*.
223 pages
ISBN. 978-0-85036-719-5 paperback

www.merlinpress.co.uk